THE CENTER CANNOT HOLD

The Search for a Global Economy of Justice

Marvin Mahan Ellison

UNIVERSITY
PRESS OF
AMERICA

Copyright © 1983 by

University Press of America, Inc.

P.O. Box 19101, Washington, D.C. 20036

All rights reserved

Printed in the United States of America

ISBN (Perfect): 0-8191-2964-X
ISBN (Cloth): 0-8191-2963-1

To my mother
Esther Alexander Ellison

and
in memory of

my father
Marvin Mahan Ellison

and

my father-in-law
Harry Frederick Hollingshead

ACKNOWLEDGEMENTS

This book is a very slightly revised form of my doctoral dissertation which was submitted to the Faculty of Union Theological Seminary in New York in 1981. I have been tempted to delay publication in order to bring my analysis of the debates over global economic development "up to date," certainly because events, in this country and elsewhere, have not stood still in the past year and a half, but also because I have not stood still either personally or professionally. There have been more than a few occasions for me to reconsider aspects of my own perspective, as well as reasons to deepen my appreciation for - and at times my criticisms of - the insights of others whose contributions to the search for a global economy of justice far outweigh any of my own. The decision not to redraft or expand this study comes, in part, from my strong sense of the urgent need to call attention to the moral significance of the "development debate" and to sharpen the terms and issues of contention. I also am convinced that this project has an integrity of its own, sufficient to support the validity of my thesis, but I await the testimony of others on that score.

The "debts outstanding" which follow are still owed - and deeply felt - to those named and unnamed for their encouragement and support. Let me add words of appreciation for John Eagleson of Orbis Books for his interest and graciousness, and especially for Helen Hudson at University Press of America for her counsel and care with this project. Jane Tucker Watson managed to type this manuscript with dispatch and remain a friend throughout, and my thanks, too, to Staley Hitchcock, who "came to the rescue" by typing the concluding chapter.

For permission to quote from copyrighted material they have published, I am grateful to: Atheneum Publishers (Denis Goulet, The Cruel Choice); Basic Books (Sylvia Ann Hewlett, The Cruel Dilemmas of Development); Fortress Press (Jose Miguez Bonino, Doing Theology in a Revolutionary Situation); Mexican-American Cultural Center, San Antonio, Texas (Gustavo Gutierrez, Praxis of Liberation and Christian Faith); Orbis Books (Hugo Assmann, Theology for a Nomad Church; Jose Comblin, The Church and the National Security State; John Eagleson, ed., Christians and Socialism; Rosino Gibellini, ed., Frontiers of Theology in America; Denis Goulet, A New

Moral Order; Gustavo Gutierrez, A Theology of Libera-
tion; Sergio Torres and John Eagleson, eds., Theology
in the Americas; Sergio Torres and Virginia Fabella,
eds., The Emergent Gospel; and The Gospel of Peace and
Justice, presented by Joseph Gremillion); Overseas Development Council (Guy F. Erb and Valeriana Kallab, eds.,
Beyond Dependency, and Denis Goulet, The Uncertain
Promise); Penguin Books, Limited (Henry Bernstein, ed.,
Underdevelopment and Development); Simon and Schuster
(Michael Harrington, The Vast Majority); The Westminster
Press (Alistair Kee, ed., A Reader in Political Theol-
ogy); the World Council of Churches (Richard D. N. Dick-
inson, To Set at Liberty the Oppressed, and M. M. Thomas
and Paul Abrecht, eds., Christians in the Technical and
Social Revolutions of Our Time); and Yale University
Press (Albert O. Hirschman, The Strategy of Economic De-
velopment, copyright (c) 1958 by Yale University Press).

My indebtedness also extends to President G. Wayne
Glick of Bangor Theological Seminary for his generous
provision of funds to underwrite publication expenses.

Fay Hollingshead Ellison knows why words alone will
never express my appreciation to her.

                         Marvin Ellison
                         Bangor, Maine
                         October 1, 1982

. . . and Debts Outstanding

This project has put the grandson of an owner of coal mines in Harlan County, Kentucky, "on the road," so to speak. In undertaking the present study, I have moved away from concerns about economic justice which are situated, quite literally, closer "to home" for me, but ones over which I have long had less critical distance than needed. One personal as well as professional benefit I have gained from the inquiry at hand is that I have made headway toward connecting issues and problems which are not merely "out there" across the globe but very much related to dynamics still at work in Harlan County. As Hannah Arendt taught me to expect, each ending does mark a new beginning, and so completing this project encourages me, with a roadmap now better marked, to travel back toward my point of origin. The stories from that journeying, however, must wait to be told.

What needs to be said at this juncture is that I have not had to build my own road along the way, nor depend alone upon my rather poor sense of direction to gain my bearings. Denis Goulet first opened up the topic of global economic development for me, but after a critical re-reading of his writings, especially in light of the current social scientific debates, I found that his perspective could not take me in directions I needed to go. My better traveling companions have been the Latin American theologians of liberation. My studies with Gustavo Gutierrez at Union Theological Seminary in 1976 and 1977 and some more recent conversations with Jose Miguez Bonino have helped to confirm my perceptions about the radicality of the liberationist break from the dominant developmentalist paradigm and about the merits of their proposed "new way."

Roger Shinn and Will Kennedy served on my dissertation committee and offered me valuable advice, criticisms, and words of encouragement even at a time when one was officially on sabbatical leave and the other was new on the Seminary faculty and working hard himself to stay on course. Samuel Roberts helped me to start this project, and Lee Cormie flew in from Toronto to partake in the oral examination and bring closure to the process.

Three student colleagues in Christian Ethics, Marie Giblin, Gene Jones, and Rich Knox, read an earlier draft

vii

of the dissertation and engaged me in dialogue that brought home new insights and suggested some beneficial revisions. Mary D. Pellauer gave me cups of coffee, time and space to "de-brief" about the costs of writing a dissertation, and practical reminders that no single manuscript can encompass the work of a social ethicist. Sally Bentley and Gary Ritner crossed paths with me when I most needed to be with friends.

Herb Kellogg generously provided carpool service and office space, and Hazel Hertzberg sat in the front seat and nudged me to think about other questions. Nancy Griffing typed portions of the original draft but, more importantly, listened and helped me laugh at the end of long days. The congregation of the Palisades Presbyterian Church connected me to the world outside my study and kindly supported my work with their gifts, financial and otherwise. Virginia Carlson has been, in every good sense of the word, a neighbor to me, and Jim and Elaine Wyatt appeared when spirits failed.

Because of Staley Hitchcock's expertise and efficiency, this study has been typed in fine form. His patience exceeds even his talents.

At exactly the point at which I needed incentive to complete this project, the faculty of Bangor Theological Seminary welcomed me to join in their work. Students enrolled in Ethics 304 during the Spring of 1981 allowed my to "test out" my thesis in relation to the State of Maine.

Without two others, however, I would not have gotten through this project and beyond. Beverly Wildung Harrison has been my advisor, mentor, colleague, friend. She opened her door and shared her wisdom, her convictions, and her strengths for compassion in those constant ways that alone make education for justice possible. Fay Hollingshead Ellison has been my pastor, co-parent, friend, and center of gravity. Without her gentle steadfastness, her graceful integrity, and her loving tenacity not to "let go," I would not have moved the distances along which I was most reluctant to travel.

Marvin Ellison
April 24, 1981

CONTENTS

x

INTRODUCTION

IN SEARCH OF A GLOBAL ECONOMY OF JUSTICE

In The Radical Imperative John C. Bennett urged
those of us who identify ourselves--and sometimes earn
our professional keep--as religious ethicists to own up
to the fact that "a new debate is needed about economic
institutions, and on a much more fundamental level"
than his own generation had managed to sustain.[1] This
present study is a response to his recent call for a
"return to economic ethics."

I am in full agreement with Bennett's claim that
an economic debate is very much needed especially in
relation to issues of global economic development. I
am also aware that the contours of such a debate have
been steadily emerging since the close of the Second
World War. This debate over the global economy has involved and continues to engage social scientists, the
ecumenical church movement, and professional theologians and ethicists. It is a debate which has also
taken shape amidst and sometimes alongside various personal and institutional responses to the phenomenal
lack of well-being among the world's poor, those who
Michael Harrington, among others, has reminded us are
the "vast majority" of humankind.[2] For reasons to be
enumerated in the course of this study, it is my judgment that this debate is of great significance both for
those living in the affluent North of the globe and for
those in the poor South. Questions not yet resolved,
such as how this emerging debate is to proceed, with
which parties included, on what terms, and with what
likely outcome for either enhancing or diminishing the
life prospects of this vast majority, in particular,
are matters of normative ethical and theological importance that are literally global in scope.

Although our immediate concern is to identify some
limitations on the dimensions of this study and to outline the course that our inquiry will follow, it is
fair and even necessary to make at least one acknowledgement early on. The full radicality of Bennett's
invitation to return to economic ethics comes into
view only when recognition is also given to his recom-
mended test for judging the adequacy of addressing
issues of economic justice and for taking the study of
economics with sufficient seriousness. That test is
whether "a new generation of persons concerned about
Christian ethics" is willing and able "to press the

socialistic questions even though they do not accept ready-made socialistic answers."[3] I accept without reservations the validity of Bennett's test. In fact, to anticipate remarks and the direction of an argument I shall defer until the conclusion of this book, I have become convinced that we, religious ethicists included, will not be able to speak accurately about what is going on in the world, nor will we be able to arrive at effective action for economic justice until and unless we do "press the socialistic questions" and the socialist option to become better advocates for economic democracy.[4]

Because I judge this need to press the socialist option to be valid, what is no less urgent, in my estimation, is the adoption of a particular agenda and focus of our work by those of us who regard "true speech" and "effective action for justice" as human activities of fundamental religious import. We need to begin to admit publicly and explicitly what we now may know privately but share only among intimates, namely, that

> The future of Christianity does not
> lie in the defense of the bourgeois
> and capitalist style of life that
> dominates in the western world but
> in the midst of the various kinds of
> search for new civilizations, of new
> styles of life and new ways of living,
> being carried out by the most restless
> spirits in today's world, especially
> in the Third World, but also in the
> most sensitive minorities in the Old
> World, whether North American or
> European.[5]

It is in hopes of not deflecting attention away from this urgent agenda to effect socio-economic transformation toward more justice at home and abroad--and perhaps even of contributing to the many diverse efforts now underway to generate "new styles of life and new ways of living"--that this particular project is making its own public appearance.

I.   The Purpose of This Study

The purpose of this study is to analyze and evaluate the normative socio-ethical significance of a "great economic debate" currently in process between

developmentalists and liberationists over issues of
global economic development, particularly the development of the so-called Third World.[6] My thesis is that
we are now witnessing the emergence of an irreconcilable
conflict between parties to the debate, along with the
appearance of two quite incompatible sets of conceptual
frameworks and policy recommendations for shaping the
world political economy. I wish to argue, further,
that religious ethicists, among others, cannot successfully "hang free" in relation to this conflict. My
contention is that, from a normative Christian ethical
perspective, in which direction we turn from within the
debate is of the utmost significance because our lines
of vision either brighten or dim our moral perceptions
and, therefore, either help or hinder our capacities
for effective agency for justice in the world.

To say that the current debate over global economic development has generated a monumental, quite irreconcilable, and normatively significant conflict between
the various parties involved is a claim that requires
justification. This justification will be offered in
the course of this study. If the validity of this
claim is tentatively granted, however, the fact that a
conflict which is so much at work has not yet received
adequate attention, especially among Christian ethicists, is quite telling. One example of this lack of
recognition comes from Orbis Books, which has published
extensively in the area of Latin American liberation
theology and has almost single-handedly made liberationists' critiques of First World economic development
policy and theory available to the North American audience. Even this otherwise observant theological press
has apparently missed--or at least minimized--this
point about the irreconcilable nature of the economic
debate at hand. I say they have missed this point because at the same time that the Maryknoll Fathers have
issued Hugo Assmann's Theology for a Nomad Church and
Gustavo Gutierrez's A Theology of Liberation, both of
which offer profound critiques of economic developmentalism and the dominant "theology of development," they
have also published Robert J. Alexander's A New Development Strategy which discounts the merits and urgency
of any economics (or theology) of liberation.[7] What is
problematic here is not the publication of authors with
differing viewpoints on economic development, but
rather that even the publisher which has done so much
to introject liberation theology into the mainstream
has presented the developmentalist side but not made

available works on economic justice more consistent with
its theological publications. A primary reason for my
project at hand, therefore, is to avoid such an imbalance and to illuminate and draw out the significance of
the debate and the radical conflict over economics which
it expresses.

In order to accomplish this task, I wish also to
acknowledge my agreement with Philip Wogaman, who argues
that the current "great debate," the historical prece-
dent for which is the economic debate of the 1930's, is
best understood as a re-evaluation process "of worldwide
and historic magnitude on the question of how economic
life should be organized." Not only does it "call forth
consideration of profound philosophical differences and
long-run consequences" between socio-economic theories
and economic policy choices, but it also provides an opportunity to clarify the value questions "at stake in
economic questions . . . [namely], the well-being and
community relationships of the whole human family, each
of whose members is a person of incalculable worth."
Wogaman has also rightly insisted that this debate, as
presently evidenced, is unavoidably ideological in character.[8]

I find that Wogaman's characterization of this
great debate fits well with dynamics I perceive to be
at work between primary parties to the debate over global economics. I shall postpone further comment about
the internal dynamics of the present controversy, however, and move, instead, to address two preliminary but
foundational considerations. These considerations first
gave rise to and then have shaped this study in rather
unmistakable ways. In doing so, I shall also be identifying some of my own working assumptions as a Christian
social ethicist concerned with issues of global poverty
and inequalities. These assumptions are important for
clarification of the normative criteria which govern the
selectivity of sources and the structure of the argument
to follow.

II. The Need to Clarify Some Working Assumptions

One assumption I wish to clarify concerns the compelling reasons for a social ethicist to take up the
issue of global economic development in the first place.
These reasons, in my judgement, should not be taken for
granted. In the Conclusion of this study I shall return
to speak more specifically about a related methodologi-

cal concern, namely, how it is the case that the quality of our moral agency in the world is so dependent upon our capacity to understand adequately what is going on. For the moment, I want to consider the prior wisdom of not assuming that a normative ethical problem will be recognized as such, much less be responded to in any automatic or satisfactory fashion.

It seems to me important, especially in any highly conflictual situation such as the present world economic crisis, to remain sensitive to the fact, as Beverly W. Harrison contends, that

> . . . when everything is going on at once, . . . what we choose to notice about what is going on reveals much about who we are. The moralist's old claim that understanding itself is a moral act gains fresh credence once again. When everything is happening, the decision to understand or not is a moral act and it makes very good sense to put the question of responsibility in such a situation.9

There shall be opportunity forthcoming to note that even poverty on a global scale and the persistent and widening inequalities between rich and poor, both within and between nations, are by no means recognized "naturally" or universally as socio-ethical problems. Perhaps this realization should not be altogether surprising in a society in which no consensus exists about whether economic activities and institutional arrangements should be subject to moral scrutiny and, further, where no adequate political vehicle is in place for sustaining such a process of moral and political evaluation. The general absence of that ethical discourse, no less than the difficulty of successfully pressing moral claims on the economy, most certainly does have consequence, moral and otherwise. The consequences are quite real for those who suffer from poverty and social inequality, but most certainly also for those who do not "see"--or, perhaps, can literally afford not to see--the problem at hand.10

A second assumption to be clarified follows upon my need to acknowledge that it has been necessary to bypass or grant only peripheral attention to some issues and controversies which are not, to be sure, inconsequential to the "great economic debate" under immediate consideration but which it has proved necessary to keep out of the primary "field of vision" for the purposes of approximating some reasonable scale and proportion within these pages. Reasons for restricting a field of inquiry to only certain issues and dynamics within a more encompassing set of controversies are matters no less important than the identification of a normative socioethical problem as a problem.

I would be remiss, indeed, not to indicate, however briefly, that the debates over global economic development are more inclusive and more far-flung than this present study will envelop within its parameters. Discussions about the natural or environmental limits to social and economic growth, for example, are quite relevant to this debate, but I shall not incorporate those discussions in any direct way.[11] There is also not sufficient time or space to attend to more specific issues, such as world hunger, the arms race, the role of multinational corporations, or technology transfers between North and South, each of which enters into and complicates the "great economic debate" on world development. Although it is not possible to "prove" that an analysis of each or any of these issues would lead to or, in fact, open up further the dynamics of the ongoing debate I find between developmentalists and liberationists, it is, nonetheless, quite conceivable, as Philip Wogaman has also argued, that there is an unmistakable "bedrock" debate which provides the connecting ground among more specific issues. Attention to this larger debate may, therefore, provide useful insight for normative ethical inquiry into related matters. For the purposes of this study, I shall proceed on the working assumption that this is, in fact, the case.

Since my primary attention in this study will be given to the theoretical assumptions and divergences among parties to the economic development debate rather than to differences in policy formation around specific issues, I also wish to clarify my principle of selection among the possible sources at hand in the economic development "field of contenders." More to the point, I want to suggest a rationale for the exclusion of certain contestants to the debate from this inquiry. Limitations of time and place have by no means been the essential cause for my selecting out what might otherwise appear to be admissable parties from purview. What will be omitted from this inquiry are representatives of positions which fail to recognize global poverty as a socio-ethical problem and which so imbed economic activity within the natural order of things that questions about justice and injustice are not considered applicable. An explanation is, therefore, called for to account for what I concede may be their noticeable absence but which, I will argue, is, nonetheless, their quite justifiable dismissal from our examination.

III. First Assumption: Global Poverty is a Socio-Ethical Problem

Our first consideration, the identification of global poverty and inequalities as an ethical problem, governs selectivity of sources for this study in a quite fundamental way. Only those who believe that global poverty raises justice issues, who perceive that there is a problem at hand, have been used in this study of the dynamics of the economic development debate. In order to explicate the significance of this criterion of selectivity, let me begin by stating unequivocally that no assumption shapes my own interests and perceptions more fundamentally than my conviction that our principal obligation as moral agents is to act to rectify injustice and to engage ourselves in what Brian Wren speaks of as a continuous process of collaborative "education for justice." This education is experienced as a process which seeks "to increase people's knowledge of injustice and inequality, to widen their range of comparison, and to create a critical consciousness which turns grievance or guilt into hopeful and constructive action."[12] Similarly, the concern to transform injustice into justice may also be appropriately described, as Mary D. Pellauer has done, as an interest in "practical righteousness" or as the commitment to maximize concrete justice rather than to remain content with explicating formal requirements of justice considered in the abstract or merely with analyzing shades of distinction among various possible definitions.[13] This concern for concrete justice also moves us decidedly beyond preoccupation with minimal standards of justice, understood, for example, in terms of procedural fairness, due process, or treating "like cases alike." As moral agents we are moved on toward sustained responsiveness to actual human needs and social suffering. We are moved or, better yet, impassioned toward a shared commitment to challenge as effectively as possible social inequities as they arise within particular socio-historical contexts and as their expression and intensity are shaped and reshaped through shifting institutional dynamics.[14]

When we speak, therefore, of global poverty as a
socio-ethical problem, we do so not simply because of
the existence, even on such a large scale, of poverty
per se or because of the disastrous consequences poverty
has for human lives, not the least of which are ill
health, illiteracy, and chronic hunger. We can identify
poverty as a socio-ethical problem because this poverty
is distributed so unjustly in the present world economic
order. A few statistics, even in narrative form, begin
to illustrate proportions of this unfair distribution.
Between nations, we should recognize that

> The major capitalist powers have two
> thirds of the globe's income, but only
> 20 percent of its population; the
> underdeveloped nations, with more than
> 50 percent of the people, have less
> than 13 percent of the income. . . .
> It is [also] possible to indentify a
> 'Fourth World' of the very poor. Tak-
> ing those countries with less than
> $150 per capita GNP in the early sev-
> enties, they contained about 1.1 bil-
> lion people . . .--one quarter of
> mankind [sic]--which lives a daily
> agony.[15]

The social inequalities which exist within nations, however, are no less staggering, as Mexican economist
Pablo Gonzales Casanova concedes, for example, about his
own country, which, he notes, "with an income per capita
of $2,100, . . . might be mistaken for a developed na-
tion":

> . . . development has been more unbal-
> anced in Mexico than it has been in
> many other countries and . . . the im-
> balance is growing. For example, in
> 1958 the income of the richest 5 per-
> cent of families was 22 times greater
> than that of the poorest 10 percent;
> in 1970 it was 39 times greater. In
> 1977 the poorest 10 percent received
> 1 percent of the national income and
> the richest 5 percent received 25 per-
> cent. Among all families 32 percent
> received the minimum income needed to
> satisfy the most elementary necessi-
> ties, and 14.5 percent received less
> than the minimum. . . .[16]

With even this little evidence before us, we find
ample reason to suggest that present global arrangements violate our basic sense of justice as fairness.
As Michael Harrington has rightly argued,

> A system is fair, [John] Rawls says,
> if a person can accept it even though
> she or he does not know her or his
> place in it. . . . A world in which
> the poorest 30 percent of humanity
> has 3 percent of the income, while
> the top 20 percent has 66 percent,
> is purely and simply wrong. It is an
> offense to a minimal sense of fair-
> ness.17

What may also be argued is that socio-ethical awareness
of the injustice of global poverty is only heightened
by the modern historical consciousness that poverty is
not "natural" or an inevitable fate but socially conditioned, that is, susceptible to perpetuation or to reduction through historical human agency. Therefore,
even to admit, as we must, that there is not and may
never be any guarantee that poverty itself can be eradi-
cated once and for all, such an admission is not, in and
of itself, to be regarded as license for abdication of
moral responsibility. Rather, what I would suggest is
more significant ethically is the contemporary realiza-
tion--or, should we not say, suspicion--that insistence
upon natural causation for poverty in the world is more
often than not a reactionary gesture and, therefore, can
no longer serve as adequate justification for a "hands
off" response. Therefore, what Dorothee Soelle has reflected in general about the distinctive forms of human
suffering in our world is particularly suggestive for a
normative socio-ethical perspective on global poverty
and social inequality:

> . . . the natural cause means virtually
> nothing compared with the social situa-
> tion, on which the conquest even of nat-
> ural and irreversible suffering deci-
> sively depends. Then all suffering
> would be dependant [sic] on the situa-
> tion that people have created for one
> another and the share of purely natural
> suffering reduced to a minimum. That
> all suffering is social suffering, then,
> means that all suffering is to be worked

on. No suffering can be clothed and
transfigured any longer with the appearance of fate.[18]

   If global poverty confronts us, as I believe it
does, with a concrete situation of injustice and inequity, a situation of suffering which is social and,
therefore, "to be worked on," let there also be no doubt
that there is an unmistakable urgency in engaging in
this work. As Gustavo Gutierrez has detailed, a pending
consequence of this unjust division within our globe is
a further and perhaps irreversible split within humanity
itself:

> Should things continue as they are, we
> will soon be able to speak of two human
> groups, two kinds of people: 'Not only
> sociologists, economists, and political
> theorists, but also psychologists and
> biologists have pointed with alarm to
> the fact that the incessant widening of
> the distance between the developed and
> the underdeveloped countries is pro-
> ducing a marked separation of two groups;
> this implies the appearance, in a short
> time, of a true anthropological differ-
> entiation. . . .'[19]

Given this sobering reality, both theologians and economists alike have had compelling reasons to identify
and to seek promotion, at the very least, of minimal
but necessary requirements for social justice in the
present global situation. Sylvia Ann Hewlett's description of these requirements is now typical of those
"progressive" economists who do not suppress the issue
of social equity in relation to concerns about economic
growth:

> Social justice in underdeveloped na-
> tions must involve the elimination of
> the desperate forms of poverty in
> these countries. . . . Social justice
> . . must ensure that everyone has ac-
> cess to 'minimally acceptable life-
> sustaining and life-enhancing support
> systems involving food, shelter,
> health, work and culture'--in short,
> the essentials of a decent life.
> Social justice also implies a reduc-

tion in the gap between the rich and
the poor, a gap that is extremely
wide in many Third World nations and
exacerbates the suffering of the
poor.[20]

Richard Barnet and Ronald Müller have offered a quite
similar criterion for judging the fairness of development measures by suggesting that the most adequate "criterion for determining whether a social force is progressive is whether it is likely to benefit the bottom
60 percent of the population."[21] This criterion is also
fully compatible with a standard of justice for assessing world development which has emerged with noticeable
clarity during recent Roman Catholic and Protestant
church-based ecumenical discussions, a criterion which
theologian Jose Miguez Bonino has described. In the
process of outlining the primary work of the Christian
ethicist, Miguez Bonino directs our attention to

> . . . the search for ways of realizing
> concretely in the world the power and
> efficacy of solidary love. . . . Love
> operates in this alienated world by
> establishing justice. And justice is
> not measured by some impartial or
> legal regulations but by the redres-
> sing of the condition of the weak.[22]

However important these reflections may be, my own
sense is that the "great economic debate" to which I
wish to draw our attention does not actually move into
place with ease or in any straightforward manner if we
limit our concern only to these and similar attempts to
articulate appropriate moral norms for informing human
agency in the pursuit of global well-being. Rather, I
have found that what we might term the foundational or
bedrock controversy over global economic justice comes
into view only as attention shifts to proposed strategies for moving toward a more equitable world situation
and to those conflicting interpretations of why it is
that present economic arrangements are not only unfair
but continue to generate such disastrous divisions.

Let me be more precise. The fact of the matter is
that our understanding is not likely to be advanced until we recognize that the contemporary "great debate"
over economic policies and theoretical frameworks is
itself occasioned by the collapse of any recognizable

consensus about what would make a global "economy of justice" possible. A new debate is, in fact, being called forth precisely because there is no longer any prevailing consensus. As we shall observe throughout our study from the testimony of various parties to the debate, simply too much evidence has been accumulated and too many questions raised to be able to keep conventional sensibilities about the "rightness" or intrinsic validity of capitalist economics in place or unshaken any longer. What may be equally significant, however, as Robert Heilbroner has acknowledged, is that the dominant

> . . . sense of assurance and control
> has vanished, or is vanishing rapidly.
> We have become aware that rationality
> has its limits with regard to the en-
> gineering of social change, and that
> these limits are much narrower than we
> had thought; that many economic and
> social problems lie outside the scope
> of our accustomed instrumentalities of
> social change; that growth does not
> bring certain desired ends or arrest
> certain undesired trends.[23]

To understand what is going on presently, we need a brief description of this dominant consensus, which has either collapsed or is in the process of collapsing. To do so, I suggest that we must give prime importance especially to particular aspects of the economic "conventional wisdom" which were most taken for granted among liberal (capitalist) economists in the post-World War II era. Certainly included in that assumed wisdom was the expectation that expansion of the capitalist market system throughout the globe, along with the integration of newly independent nations into that network of trade and finance, would manage to develop these former colonies throughout the Third World into centers of modern agricultural and industrial growth. The progressive development of these modern economies would, moreover, guarantee the transcendence of a colonial division of labor which had structurally limited the role of the Southern peoples to that of "drawers of water and hewers of wood." Even if it was necessary to concede that economic progress could be advanced only at some social and human costs, this kind of economic tradeoff between generating growth economies and attending to social needs and human well-being was dismissed either as a "non-economic" concern or merely as a transitory problem. Therefore, it did not provide reason enough to doubt that poor nations could, indeed, "follow in the footsteps" of the industrialized nations and imitate their course of modernization although, granted, at a necessarily accelerated pace.

We shall examine the contours and assumptions of this modernization theory of economic development in Chapter I, but what is immediately relevant to our discussion is the centrality of two claims that liberal economists and developmentalists have advanced. The first of these claims is that economic growth would be the primary and most important engine for producing social justice, and the second is that socio-economic inequalities within underdeveloped nations were only temporary phenomena and, in fact, justifiable because they spurred on efforts to maximize economic growth. These assertions then grounded a "trickle down" theory of economic development which, at least in the advanced industrialized nations, operated to justify inequalities in the world economy. What is important to recognize is that this economic theory and model of development has consistently claimed that there was a beneficial function for the seemingly omnipresent "gaps," "snags," and "lags" within poor nations, a beneficial function that would increase the well-being of those least well-off in society.

Michael Harrington has suggested that what is especially devastating from the point of view of those concerned with social justice is that this dominant model of economic development has served, in fact, as a "brilliant, well-documented case against the pursuit of social justice," a case which has had "support of more than one hundred years of academic thought in the West." Equally disastrous is not only the fact that this model has remained intact for such a long time, but that it has also been so persuasive, even on the point that

> The intelligent reformer, it is argued,
> should avoid all questions of equity.
> What is important for a national econo-
> my is that there be growth that creates
> more and more resources to be divided
> up. If this demands tolerating some in-
> equality, the thesis continues, that is
> actually to the benefit of the least
> equal in the society, for even though

> their share of the wealth remains un-
> fair, their absolute consumption is
> steadily on the increase.[24]

What we need to understand is that because economic priorities are also moral priorities, it follows that if
the dominant consensus about economic arrangements has
broken down, the moral thesis that accompanied it also
no longer holds up. More specifically, the belief that
cannot be sustained with any ease these days is that
inequality in the world economy functions, directly or
indirectly, to produce equality. The moral claim that
cannot now be substantiated is that socio-economic inequality, as persists on such a vast scale throughout
our globe, is or can be morally defensible even "in the
long run."

Testimony about the shattering of this dominant
faith, that economic growth is socially and humanly
beneficial to most, if not all, nations, has been forthcoming recently from mainstream economists as well as
from neo-marxist critics. So, too, has there been widening public recognition that liberal economics is itself in disarray. Perhaps no testimony has been more
damaging, however, or, in their own words, "shocking"
than the following assessment arrived at from within
the liberal ranks, from economists Irma Adelman and
Cynthia Taft Morris. Much to their own--and their liberal colleagues'--dismay, they concluded from their 1973
cross-sectional survey of underdeveloped nations that
economic development, as presently conducted by means of
what Heilbroner has labelled "our accustomed instrumentalities," is "accompanied by an absolute as well as a
relative decline in the average income of the very
poor." Their documentation in support of this conclusion has also lent credence to their judgement and prognosis that

> The frightening implication of the
> present work is that hundreds of mil-
> lions of desperately poor people
> throughout the world have been hurt
> rather than helped by economic develop-
> ment. Unless their destinies become a
> major and explicit focus of development
> policy in the 1970's and 1980's, eco-
> nomic development may serve merely to
> promote social injustice.[25]

This very realization, that economic growth policies have not only failed to develop underdeveloped
countries but actually worsened social and economic conditions within these nations, has contributed greatly to
an emerging sense of a global economic crisis situation.
A mood of apprehension about effecting socio-economic
progress has come to replace any lingering optimism
that what the Third World needs is only to undergo a
"capitalist revolution" that will then automatically
result in the creation of autonomous economies of growth
in the South. As the report of the United Nations Independent Commission on International Development Issues has indicated from its recent findings, the truth
of the matter, given present global arrangements with
such significant differences in economic strength among
unequal nations, is that "in the world as in nations,
economic forces left entirely to themselves tend to produce growing inequality."[26] Moreover, the result of
this inequality is not the production of equality even
at a slow rate, but on the contrary, that

> Current trends point to a somber fu-
> ture for the world economy and inter-
> national relations. A painful out-
> look for the poorer countries with no
> end to poverty and hunger; continuing
> world stagnation combined with infla-
> tion; international monetary disorder;
> mounting debts and deficits; protec-
> tionism; major tensions between coun-
> tries competing for energy, food and
> raw materials; growing world popula-
> tion and more unemployment in North
> and South; increasing threats to the
> environment and the international com-
> mons through deforestation and desert-
> ification, overfishing and overgrazing,
> and pollution of air and water . . .
>
> For these trends to continue is
> dangerous enough but they can easily
> worsen. . . . The 1980s could witness
> even greater catastrophes than the
> 1930s.
>
> Such developments are not improb-
> able . . .[27]

As will become clear during the course of this

study, there is much more recognition of the fact that
we are entering (or have moved well into) a global economic crisis than there is any agreement about the nature of that crisis. Much less is there any unanimity
on reasons proffered to explain the origins of this
crisis or to account for the present dynamics of our
global socio-historical situation. And, to be sure,
there is little or no unanimity about the applicability
or efficacy of proposed remedies. We shall return in
the conclusion of this study to examine more closely
the nature and dynamics of this crisis, but for the moment, we can at least say with some certainty that Sylvia Ann Hewlett's advice to us does seem sound in this
situation. She has suggested that if we are, in fact,
to locate accurately where the substantive debate over
economic development has arisen and is now taking place,
we would do well to "scratch the surface" and take careful measures to identify differences among primary participants in this controversy. As she herself has observed recently, for example, in reviewing the current
debates over human rights, including economic rights,
among First World policymakers and social scientists,

> Public discussion on the issue of
> human rights in the Third World is
> floundering in a sea of platitudes
> and good intentions. . . . Fine-
> sounding, noble ideas, but scratch
> the surface and one finds little
> consensus as to what causes misery
> and brutality in today's undeveloped
> world, and an extremely confused
> sense of which policies, if any, are
> capable of ameliorating these condi-
> tions.[28]

In this inquiry we will be "scratching the surface"
between developmentalists (or modernists) and liberationists within the ranks of social scientists and within the ecumenical church movement. Our purpose is to
characterize these parties to the economic development
debates--and their differences--in order to disclose
and then join the substantive issues at hand. My own
sense is that this exercise then takes on its particular
significance, from the point of view of a Christian
social ethicist, as it enables us to gain distance toward judging the effectiveness or, better yet, the "justice potential" of different economic policies, as well
as the various "yields," we might say, of distinct the-

ories of economic development, especially in terms of
actualizing concrete social justice.

Before we proceed with this task, an additional
word can be added to provide further accounting for the
fact that we are "scratching the surface" only between
developmentalists and liberationists and not over a
wider field of contestants to these development debates.
We are limiting our inquiry to the debates between what
may be described, for lack of better terms, as the liberal and the radical contingencies or, to use spatial
designations, between the development center and the
liberation left. We shall now move to consider the wisdom of, in fact, not attending, at this time, to the
conservative social scientists, church people, and theologians-ethicists who may, nevertheless, be interested
in and influential on the development debates.

IV. Second Assumption: The Fundamental Socio-Ethical
     Debate is Between the "Development Center" and the
     "Liberation Left"

In accord with the first criterion of selection, I
am including in this study only those parties to the
economic development debate which recognize global poverty as a socio-ethical problem. This criterion alone
does not account for or generate the structure of the
argument which will follow. The other claim I wish and
need to make at this juncture is that the fundamental
socio-ethical debate is being waged now between a "development center" and a "liberation left." What cannot
be assumed a priori, however, is that restricting our
examination of the development debate to the clash between liberals and radicals will actually enable us to
do well what I understand to be the work of a Christian
social ethicist. In this instance, that is, in relation
to issues of economic justice, the work of the ethicist
would include the need to account for what is going on
in the world economy, to describe and assess significant
differences between theoretical perspectives on economic
policy issues, and to judge the adequacy of various proposals for action, including but not limited to those
from religious communities. In my judgement it is quite
tempting to proceed in this work as if the fundamental
debate arises as a matter of course between radicals and
conservative parties and that the liberal or reformist
position appears--most readily after the fact--to offer
a compromise or at least a more moderate standpoint from
which to mediate the claims on either side of the con-

troversy. Without elaborating on issues to be addressed
in the forthcoming study itself, I can at least suggest
reasons that this temptation or "recourse to the middle"
is misleading, especially in regard to the "great economic debate" on global development.

It is when we ask the question of who is actually
pressing the development debate that we begin to suspect
that this conventional right-left-and-back-to-center
movement along a supposed linear spectrum does not hold
firm. It becomes almost immediately apparent that conservative social scientists, for example, are not interested, in the first place, in drawing attention to the
collapse of the dominant consensus about the adequacy of
capitalist theory or institutional arrangements. On the
contrary, we may take Herman Kahn as an example of a
conservative who refuses even to enter into the development debate we have been interested in locating, namely,
the debate generated precisely in response to the question of why liberal economic policies since World War II
have failed to develop the underdeveloped world. Kahn's
World Economic Development study deftly bypasses any
call to assess the meaning of the counterproductive capitalist revolution in the Third World. Instead, his
analysis moves along steadily to the point at which he
can reassert the now specious claim that global inequalities make for progress toward global equality. Therefore, on the problem of the gap between the rich and the
poor, Kahn has stated:

> Unlike others who discuss the popular
> concept of the 'widening gap' between
> the rich and the poor, we focus on the
> positive aspects of the gap. The in-
> creasing disparity between average in-
> comes in the richest and poorest nations
> is usually seen as an unalloyed evil to
> be overcome as rapidly as possible
> through enlightened policies by the ad-
> vanced nations and international organi-
> zations. . . .
>
>   In contrast, we view this gap as
> a basic 'engine' of growth. It gen-
> erates or supports most of the basic
> processes by which the poor are becom-
> ing rich, or at least less poor.[29]

Moreover, Kahn would have us even less concerned about
the reality and human consequences of this gap between

rich and poor because he himself is reassured that "actually, the world is doing a lot better than most people realize."[30]

At the conservative positioning on a traditional political spectrum from right to left, analysts such as Kahn appear to live and work either above or outside of the present development debate. Global poverty itself is not presented or approached as a normative socio-ethical problem, as we have discussed the process of problematizing and identifying such issues, nor does Kahn, to continue with this one example, find matters of social justice and injustice at stake. Rather, he has found fault most especially with "the modern liberal view [which] holds that an international system which perpetuates inequalities among nations is morally unacceptable." He goes on to tip his own hand even further when he suggests how regrettable it is that affluence in today's world is "more a source of guilt than of pride" and especially when he claims that "such guilt is even less justified today than a hundred years ago."[31]

Although it is quite possible and, I would suggest, appropriate to agree with Kahn that guilt is not the most effective or morally satisfactory response to the realities of world poverty and injustice, what his response indicates is the reluctance among conservatives even to entertain questions of moral responsibility and accountability in relation to realities of economic inequities or to examine the possible connections between the production of wealth and poverty. So pervasive is this reluctance that Kahn's associates at the Hudson Institute, Max Singer and Paul Bracken, have argued the case not only that the gap between rich and poor benefits the poor but also that the affluent are morally entitled to their wealth, as they explain, because

> . . . it was earned by hard and creative work. It was not taken from anyone. In fact, the industrial development that created [North] (sic) American wealth played a leading part in the process that is making it possible for the whole world to become wealthy over the next century or so. . . . Not only does the gap between rich and poor nations not grow out of anything we need to be ashamed of, but that gap is an engine pulling the rest of the world from its poor past

to its rich future.[32]

What these conservatives would have us focus our attention upon is not the injustice of global inequities, much less the human and social costs arising from the maldistribution of social and economic resources and rewards, but rather upon their rather defensive call "to help the [North] (sic) American people understand the moral basis of our national wealth" and their concern to verify the so-called fact that the good fortune of the well-off is merited and unrelated to the misfortune of others.[33]

What is immediately problematic about this conservative response to the realities of global poverty and inequality is that Kahn and his associates do not aid us in the process of becoming more sensitive to global injustices, nor do they encourage us to become increasingly impassioned toward responding ever more effectively to these concerns. Because they fail to recognize that the persistence of poverty in the world and the widening gap between rich and poor are matters of normative socio-ethical significance, that is, matters which raise questions about the possibilities for maximizing concrete justice throughout our globe, they themselves have taken steps to move away from the "great economic debate" over global development. By attempting to disengage themselves from or at least to sidestep the debate now emerging between developmentalists and liberationists, they do not give any immediate signals that they wish to be included--or should be--within the scope of our inquiry. Let me now indicate two additional reasons, one on moral and the other on empirical grounds, for not chasing after them and for going ahead and excluding them from the scope of this study.

On moral grounds alone, it is possible to object to these and any other conservative appeals to dissociate issues of wealth and poverty from concerns about social injustice. What Robert McAfee Brown has said about reactionary theologies is no less true about reactionary social scientific theories and perspectives:

> Theologies that fail to hear the cries
> of the hurting, and fail in their responses to seek to alleviate the need
> for those cries, are no longer theologies worthy of attention.[34]

xxxii

The writings of Kahn and his associates, as we have noted, certainly qualify as "no longer . . . worthy of attention" because they unashamedly deny that fundamental ethical issues are at stake in relation to global poverty and injustices. What is equally significant--and, let me add, surprising and disconcerting--about their responses from the right is that they have consistently failed to communicate any moral outrage or passion about human suffering on such a global scale. This lack of expressed feeling is not insignificant from a normative socio-ethical perspective, for as Hannah Arendt observed in a somewhat different context, it is fair to say that in relation to certain human realities, not moral outrage but its "conspicuous absence is the clearest sign of dehumanization." Even the frequent explanation from social scientists that displays of feelings or evidences of passions interfere with objectivity and verifiable investigations and are, therefore, inappropriate, does not finally bear up under moral scrutiny, for as Arendt has gone on to argue,

> Absence of emotions neither causes nor
> promotes rationality. 'Detachment and
> equanimity' in view of 'unbearable
> tragedy' can indeed be 'terrifying,'
> namely, when they are not the result of
> control but an evident manifestation of
> incomprehension. In order to respond
> reasonably one must first of all be
> 'moved,' and the opposite of emotional
> is not 'rational,' whatever that may
> mean, but either the inability to be
> moved, usually a pathological phenom-
> enon, or sentimentality, which is a
> perversion of feeling.[35]

We shall not speculate on either the pathology or the sentimentality to which social scientists and theologians-ethicists on the right may be susceptible, but we can suggest empirical as well as moral grounds for not including conservatives in our present inquiry. Kahn and other conservatives demonstrate a firm reluctance to speak of development in other terms than economic growth. Gross national product per capita remains their most appropriate, if not the quintessential, criterion for judging the presence or absence of human and social well-being.[36] We shall discuss the socio-ethical significance of definitions and proposed criteria for judgment in Chapter I, but we may note at this juncture that an _economistic_ understanding of development is certainly deficient from a normative socio-ethical perspective. Consider the following comment made by Richard Barnet and Ronald Müller on this score:

> A mechanistic definition of development based on growth rates is obscene in a world in which most people go to sleep hungry. A development model like Brazil's in which the stock market booms and two-thirds of the population is condemned to an early death by poverty, hunger, and disease, is a caricature of progress. If a development model is to have any real meaning in a world in which most people are struggling just to stay alive, it must . . . provide solutions to the most critical, interrelated social problems of the late twentieth century: poverty, unemployment, and inequality. (A development strategy that does not cope with these problems must assume either escalating mass misery on a scale that cannot even be imagined or the mysterious disappearance of the world's poor.)[37]

Because Kahn and company refuse to let go of the questionable assumption that global inequalities function to produce greater equality and because they also equate development with rates of economic growth, we do have reason on empirical grounds to ask, along with Barnet and Müller, whether those on the right "must assume either escalating mass misery . . . or the mysterious disappearance of the world's poor." Kahn in his book, The Next 200 Years, published on the occasion of the United States' Bicentennial, opted for the "mysterious disappearance" of the poor, in that he made the following assertion:

> . . . Two hundred years ago almost everywhere human beings were comparatively few, poor and at the mercy of the forces of nature, and 200 years from now, we expect, almost everywhere they will be numerous, rich and in control of the forces of nature.[38]

In his more recent World Economic Development, Kahn has reiterated that claim and added, "We still believe in that prediction--barring (an essential caveat) bad luck or bad management."[39] His consistent assumption is that global poverty is a technical "problem" for which there are or will be technical solutions.

As I shall argue in the course of this study, however, the well-being of the world's poor, the "vast majority" of peoples on the globe, depends on more than either luck or management skills. Moreover, their welfare cannot be easily predicted or reduced to a technical issue. Rather, the future of this vast majority depends to a very great extent, I would argue, on what socio-economic policies and programs are adopted by and within communities of social concern throughout the world. Accordingly, the problem of global poverty and injustice is not merely a problem for definition or prediction, but fundamentally a problem arising out of and posed for normative ethical inquiry. And I agree fully with John Bennett that the stakes involved are quite significant:

> Two things are at stake: the survival of a large part of humanity, and the humanity of those who survive because they live in privileged and protected countries.[40]

Should we need additional reason to limit our investigation of the development debate to the liberal and radical parties to that controversy, we might also take seriously Hugo Assmann's claim that precisely because the split between rich and poor is the fundamental reality of the contemporary world, only those social scientific perspectives and theologies which take that split as their starting point can begin to do justice to what is going on throughout the globe or begin to perceive, however adequately or not, the true dynamics which shape human existence. Moreover, as Assmann explains,

> The starting-point is by no means a local Latin American phenomenon, and the task for [the social sciences and] theology is not one of local importance only. Of course it has to look at this particular situation; but it must do more than that: if the state of domination and depen-

xxxv

dence in which two-thirds of humanity
live, with an annual toll of thirty
million dead from starvation and mal-
nutrition, does not become a starting-
point for any [social science and]
Christian theology today, even in the
affluent and powerful countries, then
[social science and] theology cannot
begin to relate meaningfully to the
real situation. [Their] questions
will lack reality and not relate to
real men and women.[41]

For this very reason, that those on the right, such
as Kahn and his associates, attempt to remove or at
least obscure this fundamental division within the human
community from our moral vision and to de-escalate the
stakes involved in responding to this split, they do not
and cannot facilitate our ethical thinking or practice
in relation to this omnipresent global reality, What I
shall attempt to demonstrate in this study, however, is
that the dynamics and normative ethical significance of
the socio-economic development debate may be and, indeed, are rather fulsomely disclosed by a controversy
now being generated between developmentalists (or modernists) and liberationists, those two parties which do
begin their analysis with the starting point suggested
by Assmann.

A further and also quite important validation for
our setting up the debate at hand between a "development center" and a "liberation left" comes from Latin
American economist and theologian Enrique Dussel, who
has commented that there is now little doubt remaining,
throughout Latin America at least, that the fundamental
confrontation among social scientists and theologians
is one between liberals or progressives and neo-Marxists
or radicals.[42] Our study will now proceed to indicate
that this is the case and why the two views are so incompatible. In the process we shall not only characterize the foundational assumptions of each side of the
debate, but also make some judgements concerning the
normative socio-ethical significance of this debate for
effecting movement toward greater global economic justice.

V. The Outline of the Study

In Part One we shall sketch the dynamics of the de-

bate over global economic development as currently exemplified between developmentalists and liberationists.
Chapter I covers the debate in the social sciences;
Chapter II looks at the debate within the ecumenical
church movement. I have selected from a massive range
of available literature with a concern in these pages
not to be exhaustive in portraying the parties or the
issues of the controversy in either setting, but rather
to indicate the range of concerns and the differences at
work, especially in the foundational assumptions, between the two sides to the debate. In this attempt, as
well as throughout this inquiry, sources from Latin
America, among both social scientists and theologians-
ethicists, will be relied upon to provide our depiction
of the liberationist perspective on global economic justice issues. This reliance is partially dictated by a
need to limit the scope of this study, but a more positive reason is that the Latin Americans are among, if
not the most articulate spokespersons for a theory and
model of economic development which is well-grounded in
its critique of the dominant developmentalist perspective. Without claiming that Latin America's history and
present struggle for economic justice is necessarily
prototypical in all its particularities for the entire
Third World, we can, nonetheless, say accurately, along
with Barrington Moore, Jr., that our choice is not simply arbitrary, for

> . . . one can see that some of the
> most important things that have hap-
> pened . . . in other countries hap-
> pened also in [Latin America], but
> in a more intense form.[43]

Part Two considers responses to the development debate from a "center" perspective (Denis Goulet, Chapter III) among religious moral thinkers and from a
"left" perspective (selected Latin American liberation
theologians, Chapter IV). Differences between Goulet
and the Latin Americans are generated, in part, by their
diverging judgements regarding the relative justice of
the present world economic order.

The Conclusion to our study will take up three remaining tasks which will offer an occasion to provide
further elaboration on and justification for my thesis.
First, I wish to amplify and test the claim that the
ideological tensions within the development debate are
irreconcilable. Recent events suggest new twists and

permutations in the debate, both within the social sciences and in the ecclesiastical discussions, and these events supply additional confirmation of the validity of the thesis. Second, I have several constructive suggestions of my own concerning insights I perceive are necessary for any adequate socio-ethical analysis of economic development issues. These insights will be discussed with particular reference to the writings of Goulet and the Latin Americans discussed in Part Two. Third, I want to consider the importance of the theological stakes raised by this ongoing debate and issue a call to my professional colleagues both to continue to "break silences" and also to work to ground ever more securely our passions in the long struggle ahead to make possible a truly global "economy of justice."

NOTES

1. John C. Bennett, <u>The Radical Imperative: From Theology to Social Ethics</u> (Philadelphia: The Westminster Press, 1975, p. 6. Chapter 6, "A Return to Economic Ethics," is particularly suggestive for and germane to our present discussion of global economic issues.

2. Michael Harrington, <u>The Vast Majority: A Journey to the World's Poor</u> (New York: Simon and Schuster, 1977). Charles Lindler has also correctly located the "Third World" not at the edge of history or world events but at the center: "The voices of protest come from the world's majority, corporately considered. So the idea of fringe makes sense only in that these people are on the fringes of power." Glenn R. Bucher and Charles E. Lindler, "Liberation for Straight White Males," p. 114, in Glenn R. Bucher, ed., <u>Straight/White/Male</u> (Philadelphia: Fortress Press, 1976).

3. Bennett, p. 156.

4. By the "socialistic option," I understand what British socialist Tony Benn describes by his definition of economic democracy: "To secure for the workers by hand or by brain the full fruits of their industry and the most equitable distribution thereof on the basis of the common ownership of the means of production, distribution, and exchange, and the best obtainable means of popular administration and control of each industry and service." Benn's definition is found in Alexander Cockburn and James Ridgeway, "Talking to Tony Benn: Can European Socialists Teach Americans Anything?" <u>The Village Voice</u>, Vol. XXV, no. 50 (December 10-16, 1980), p. 28. The

term "economic democracy" is no less controversial, however, than the term "socialism" or "economic development," for that matter. Penny Lernoux has observed, for example, that in Latin America, "economic democracy" is used by executives in multinational corporations to speak euphemistically of their interest in bringing about a "capitalist revolution" in under-developed nations, a transformation and integration of eco-nomies in the South within the global capitalist economy. Cf. Penny Lernoux, Cry of the People: United State Involvement in the Rise of Fascism, Torture, and Murder and the Persecu-tion of the Catholic Church in Latin America (Garden City, New York: Doubleday and Company, Inc., 1980), esp. pp. 446f.

5. Jose Comblin, in Teofilo Cabestrero, ed., Faith: Conversa-tions with Contemporary Theologians, trans. Donald D. Walsh (Maryknoll: Orbis Books, 1980), p. 34.

6. For a discussion of the problematic nature of the language and definitions of terms used in the development debates, see be-low, Chapter 1, "Preliminary Definitions of a 'Contentious Concept,'" pp. 12-17.

7. Cf. the Complete Orbis Catalog 1980 (Maryknoll: Orbis Books, 1980), p. 1.

8. J. Philip Wogaman, The Great Economic Debate: An Ethical Analysis (Philadelphia: The Westminster Press, 1977), pp. vii and ix. Wogaman employs Julius Gould's definition of ideology, as follows: "'a pattern of beliefs and concepts (both factual and normative) which purport to explain complex social phenomenon with a view to directing and simplifying sociopolitical choices facing individuals and groups'" (p. 10). For Wogaman's own argument concerning the inability to avoid thinking ideologically about economic issues, see es-pecially his Chapter 2, "Can We Avoid Ideological Thinking?" pp. 14-33. Cf. Brian Wren, Education for Justice: Pedagogi-cal Principles (Maryknoll: Orbis Books, 1977), p. 103: Wren argues similarly that ideologies should be approached criti-cally as "working hypotheses which must be continually modi-fied through action and reflection," but which have indispens-able value, both descriptively and normatively, since they present us with conceptualizations as to "how a society ac-tually works, and what it could become. These are not tech-nical questions with a single clear-cut answer."

9. Beverly Wildung Harrison, "Sexism and the Contemporary Church: When Evasion Becomes Complicity," in Alice L. Hageman, ed., in collaboration with the Women's Caucus of the Harvard Divin-ity School, Sexist Religion and Women in the Church: No More Silence! (New York: The Association Press, 1974), p. 195.

Harrison's emphasis.

10. For theological-ethical reflection of the problem of apathy in response to social suffering, see Dorothee Soelle, Suffering, trans. Everett R. Kalin (Philadelphia: Fortress Press, 1975). Soelle concedes that while it may well be "natural for us to close our eyes when we see someone suffering" and that, therefore, "the lack of solidarity with the afflicted is . . . the most natural thing in the world," her constructive proposal is to correlate apathy with hopelessness and powerlessness, such that "indifference to the suffering of others stands in direct relation to the experience that no change [can or] is occurring, as people of the 'First World' are learning" (Suffering, pp. 170, 14, and 36). We shall return to her suggestion about this correlation in the conclusion as we consider the problem of arriving at effective responses to global injustices.

11. The literature on the limits-to-growth debate is massive, but Robert L. Stivers, The Sustainable Society: Ethics and Economic Growth (Philadelphia: The Westminster Press, 1976) provides a succinct and useful introduction from the perspective of a Christian ethicist. In entering the discussions regarding natural or environmental limits to economic development, Douglas Meeks offers the following sound advice: "Of course there are shortages and limits to plenty in nature. Oil, coal, pure water, arable land and food are limited (though their limits have always had everything to do with the unjust use of the creation by human beings). But I think we have to be wary of the arguments about physical limits and material scarcity. Do not these ideological argements used by the economic powers lead to strange solutions of allocation? Since 1973 this has become a standard ploy of the energy corporations. The shrewdness of our faith sould prompt us immediately to ask what kind of economics is being constructed on the assumption of such argements about scarcity." Meeks' point is well taken that "in almost all situations of human life scarcity has been caused by human injustice" (M. Douglas Meeks, "Toward a Trinitarian View of Economics: The Holy Spirit and Human Needs," Christianity and Crisis, Vol. 40, no. 18 (November 10, 1980), pp. 313 and 312.

12. Wren, p. 56.

13. Mary D. Pellauer, "The Religious Social Thought of Three U.S. Women Suffrage Leaders: Towards a Tradition of Feminist Theology" (Ph.D. dissertation, The University of Chicago, 1980), Chapter 6: "Conclusions." Pellauer cites Chaim Perelman's The Idea of Justice and the Problem of Argument

xl

as the source for the distinction between abstract (or formal) and concrete justice, but then makes her own argument--which I find convincing--that concern for justice, historically embodied, requires the social ethicist to provide an adequately critical description of the social order, reasons for the urgency of rectifying the perceived injustice at hand, and grounding in a religious vision of what is valuable, important, essential, and, I would add, possible in the movement toward justice.

14. For an excellent theological discussion of the indispensable role of compassion in the pursuit of social justice, see Matthew Fox, A Spirituality Named Compassion and the Healing of the Global Village, Humpty Dumpty and Us (Minneapolis: Winston Press, 1979).

15. Harrington, pp. 16-17.

16. Pablo Gonzalez Casanova, "The Economic Development of Mexico," Scientific American, Vol. 243, no. 3 (September 1980), pp. 192 and 202.

17. Harrington, p. 23.

18. Soelle, pp. 105-106.

19. Gustavo Gutierrez, A Theology of Liberation, trans. Sr. Caridad Inda and John Eagleson (Maryknoll: Orbis Books, 1973), p. 86.

20. Sylvia Ann Hewlett, The Cruel Dilemmas of Development: Twentieth-Century Brazil (New York: Basic Books, Inc., copyright (c) 1980), pp. 9-10. Used by permission of Basic Books, Inc.

21. Richard J. Barnet and Ronald E. Müller, Global Reach: The Power of the Multinational Corporations (New York: Simon and Schuster, 1974), p. 364.

22. Jose Miguez Bonino, Christians and Marxists: The Mutual Challenge to Revolution (Grand Rapids: William B. Eerdmans Publishing Company, 1976), pp. 110 and 112.

23. Robert L. Heilbroner, An Inquiry into the Human Prospect (New York: W. W. Norton and Company, 1975), p. 17. My emphasis.

24. Harrington, pp. 23-24.

25. Irma Adelman and Cynthia T. Morris, Economic Growth and Social Equity in Developing Countries (Stanford: Stanford University Press, 1973), pp. 189 and 192. My emphasis.

26. *North-South: A Programme for Survival; Report of the Indepen-dent Commission on International Development Issues*, under the Chairmanship [sic] of Willy Brandt (Cambridge: MIT Press, 1980), p. 32.

27. Ibid., pp. 46-47.

28. Hewlett, p. 3.

29. Herman Kahn, with the Hudson Institute, *World Economic Devel-opment: 1979 and Beyond* (New York: Morrow Quill Paperbacks, 1979), pp. 60-61. Lest Kahn and his associates at the Hudson Institute be singled out as "exceptional" in their views, there is a quite significant and influential "pool" on the right which shares Kahn's sentiments. For example, British economist P. T. Bauer has published extensively on Third World economic development from his post at the London School of Economics. Cf. P. T. Bauer, "Western Guilt and Third World Poverty," *Commentary*, Vol. 61, no. 1 (January 1976), pp. 31-38, and P. T. Bauer and B. G. Yamey, "Against the New Econom-ic Order," *Commentary*, Vol. 62, no. 4 (April 1977), pp. 25-31. For a North American discussion with different assump-tions, see Garrett Hardin, "Lifeboat Ethics: The Case Against Helping the Poor," *Psychology Today* (September 1974), pp. 38-70.

30. Ibid., p. 62.

31. Ibid., p. 61.

32. Max Singer and Paul Bracken, "Don't Blame the U.S.," *New York Times Magazine* (November 7, 1976), p. 120.

33. Ibid.

34. Robert McAfee Brown, *Creative Dislocation--The Movement of Grace* (Nashville: Abingdon Press, 1980), p. 129.

35. Hannah Arendt, "On Violence," in Hannah Arendt, *Crises of the Republic* (New York: Harcourt Brace Jovanovich, Inc., 1972), pp. 160 and 161.

36. Cf. Kahn, pp. 53ff.

37. Barnet and Müller, pp. 150-151. My emphasis.

38. Herman Kahn, William Brown, and Leon Martel, *The Next 200 Years: A Scenario for America and the World* (New York: Wil-liam Morrow and Company, 1976), p. 1.

39. Kahn et al., _World Economic Development_, p. 2.

40. Bennett, p. 164.

41. Hugo Assmann, _Theology for a Nomad Church_, trans. Paul Burns (Maryknoll: Orbis Books, 1976), p. 54. Assmann's emphasis.

42. Enrique Dussel, "The Political and Ecclesial Context of Liberation Theology in Latin America," in _The Emergent Gospel: Theology from the Underside of History_, ed. Sergio Torres and Virginia Fabella (Maryknoll: Orbis Books, 1978), p. 179.

43. Barrington Moore, Jr., _Injustice: The Social Bases of Obedience and Revolt_ (White Plains, New York: M.E. Sharpe, Inc., 1978), p. xv.

PART ONE:

THE GLOBAL ECONOMIC DEVELOPMENT DEBATE
IN THE SOCIAL SCIENCES
AND IN THE ECUMENICAL CHURCH MOVEMENT

1

CHAPTER I

THE DEVELOPMENT DEBATE
IN SELECTED SOCIAL SCIENTIFIC LITERATURE

A debate over global economic development has emerged over the course of the past thirty years or so which has engaged social scientists from a variety of disciplines. Economists and sociologists have come to converse with historians, anthropologists, and others, all of whom have found development issues too multi-faceted to be circumscribed neatly by any one field of inquiry. They have moved or been moved toward colla-borative study precisely because the concerns at hand span and sometimes stretch beyond the customary borders of their scholarly interests.

In this chapter we shall examine two models of socio-economic development (and underdevelopment) and their accompanying theoretical perspectives which have been carved out from these separate fields of interest and scholarly expertise. What we shall be reviewing in detail are significant differences in the foundational assumptions which undergird these distinct models, one, a liberal capitalist model of development, the other, a neo-marxian model which followed upon the dominant the-ory as a critique and alternative theoretical perspec-tive. As we shall discover, the development debate among social scientists has been ideological as well as multi-disciplinary.

Taking our advice from Sylvia Ann Hewlett to "scratch the surface," we shall first speak of the ten-sions which now underlie the reigning moral consensus about the desirability of global economic development and then identify the historical context in which this debate has arisen. After preliminary classification of terms used, we shall then proceed to characterize the two competing models of global development.

I. Tensions Underlying a Moral Consensus about Global Economic Development

The term "development" has come to denote, in the post-World War II period, the aspirations and efforts made throughout the globe to overcome conditions of poverty. More specifically, development refers to the actions and policies deliberately pursued on a national and international level to effect the progressive trans-

3

formation of a socio-economic order[1] to provide for the population's basic needs for life-sustenance, health, education, employment, and general welfare. There is a shared value judgement from which few would dissent that such movements toward development are both desirable and necessary for the majority of the world's population.

In the 1950's and early 1960's Robert Heilbroner spoke for many North Americans when he suggested that "both moral concern and national self-interest have plunged us, at first hesitantly, then with mounting commitment, into support for economic development" globally.[2] President Truman's Point Four set the tone early on by declaring the need for the industrialized nations, and particularly the United States, to "embark on a bold new programme for making the benefits of our scientific advances and industrial progress available for the improvement and growth of underdeveloped areas," for reasons not the least of which was that "their poverty is a handicap and a threat both to them and to more prosperous areas."[3] While not underestimating the enormity and difficulty of the tasks ahead, Heilbroner could speak quite non-rhetorically of this struggle for economic development as the "Great Ascent" of humankind, as "the first real act of world history" upon which depended "the character of the world . . . not only in the poor and struggling nations, but in the rich and privileged ones as well."[4]

By the late 1970's, however, there had been a significant shift in mood about issues of global development, so much so that Michael Harrington has queried whether "the government and the people of the United States are turning their backs on the wretched of the earth."[5] In An Inquiry into the Human Prospect, Heilbroner speaks forthrightly of his more recent reassessment of the "limits [of rationality] with regard to the engineering of social change" and of a prevailing "civilizational malaise" in capitalist and socialist countries alike which suggests to him a stance of more guarded pessimism in assuming the challenges of global development.[6]

A partial accounting for this shift in public sentiment is discernible in comments made by the president of the Overseas Development Council,[7] midpoint during the United Nations' Second Decade of Development. While reaffirming the hopes and more "reasonable" expectations in the post-Vietnam War era that programs designed to "challenge constructively" the social and economic problems of developing countries would succeed in furthering the evolution of a more just world order, James P. Grant interjected two cautionary notes. First, in recognition of the mounting confrontation between rich and poor nations over the structure and terms of the world economy, he acknowledged that "during the past two years, the views held in industrialized and developing countries on development and international relations have become increasingly polarized."[8] A mere divergence of perspectives on global development would not, in and of itself, be either surprising or alarming, but Grant is referring to more than the controversies generated over the past thirty years by scholars or to a lack of consensus among policy-makers in the development field. What he finds disconcerting is not a "gentlemanly" difference of opinion but rather an unmistakable antagonism between developed and underdeveloped nations, signified by the emergence of two opposing and even irreconcilable models of development which differ fundamentally in their interpretations of the nature and dynamics of development and underdevelopment, their operative assumptions, and their policy implications.

Before we examine these two models of development, a capitalist or developmentalist model and a neo-marxian or dependency model, we should also bear in mind Grant's second cautionary note, which discloses even more clearly the degree of intensity of his concern about the current state of the debates over development. Without specifying his sample of "some commentators," he cites those who "have stated that the recent actions and rhetoric of the developing nations herald a new 'cold war' that threatens to diminish the living standards and political influence of the industrialized world."[9] The occasion for this remark is the demands from the impoverished South for a new international economic order, for a restructuring of the "rules of the game" by which unequal partners are related in economic exchange. The efforts made to press these claims have been accompanied by a resurgence in the affluent North of a rather self-serving and somewhat conventional argument, namely, that the welfare of the poor nations depends, first and foremost, upon the prosperity and economic well-being of the rich nations. As Geoffrey Barraclough has noted, however, any sustained argument to justify giving priority attention to the industrialized West and its problems is "more likely to commend itself to Western governments

than to the great majority of the world's population."
Furthermore, at this point in history what seems to be
causing despair among citizens of the North is no longer
"the plight of the poor nations but the plight of the
wealthy nations, and above all else the dislocation of
the economic system which has made the wealthy nations
wealthy."[10]

Although a broad-based moral consensus about the
desirability of eradicating global poverty may persist,
such an agreement on general ends, in the words of one
analyst of international affairs, "does not take us far
in understanding the realities of the contemporary
world."[11] Statements of moral resolve, for example,
even those whose language transcends the limiting preoccupation with economic growth and which also incorporate commitments to social justice and cultural change
as components of development, continue to be issued with
such regularity from development planners and politicians, from academics and business executives, that only
upon careful examination do they indicate how varied and
multiform are the interpretations, the interests and assumptions, and the actual proposals concerning the process of development. Since issues of development have
far-reaching economic and political significance for
both rich and poor nations, the controversies surround-
ing the development debates are neither unexpected nor
necessarily resolvable with ease.

In this chapter our purpose is not to evaluate particular programs or specific governmental and non-gov-
ernmental policies for global development. Rather, we
shall consider the character and terms of the development debate in selected social scientific literature.[12]
Theories of development generated and refined over the
past two and three decades by sociologists and economists, as well as by anthropologists, historians, social
psychologists, and political scientists, have shaped
research, policy formation, and programs regarding development issues, and from this literature we may dis-
till the two models of development which underlie what
Grant identified earlier for us as an increasing polarization between rich and poor nations. Our first re-
quirement, however, is to sketch the historical context
of these debates and to clarify, in a preliminary fashion, some definitions of terms.

II.   The Historical Context of the Development Debates

Interest in social and economic development as a

6

global phenomenon coincides with the collapse of the colonial era, the subsequent emergence of politically independent nation-states in Latin America, Africa, and Asia, and the post-1945 expansion of "economies of affluence" in the advanced industrialized nations. The concept of development certainly predates this period of decolonialization,[13] but it has taken on a more specific meaning in the context of the reshuffling of international relations following the Second World War and the proliferation of international agencies to promote development, most notably the United Nations Commission for Trade and Development (UNCTAD) but also including the International Development Bank, the International Monetary Fund, and such national programs as the United States' Alliance for Progress, inaugurated in 1961.[14]

From the beginning economists and politicians in the affluent Western nations shared a self-confident prognosis about the possibility of planning for and consciously directing economic growth and social change. K. K. S. Dadzie has even spoken about the "euphoria of success" pervasive especially among economists in the United States who witnessed the rapid economic recovery of Western Europe and Japan after World War II and extrapolated from that set of experiences to sustain their "hopeful expectations that the rich nations would render substantial economic and technical assistance to help ease and expedite development of poor countries."[15] At the same time and not uncoincidentally, however, they displayed a competitive interest in the increasing rivalry of socio-economic systems between the Soviet Union and the North Atlantic countries, particularly the United States. While United States Secretary of Defense, Robert McNamara presented this typical rationale and prospectus for a foreign aid program:

> Roughly 100 countries today are caught
> up in the difficult transition to mod-
> ern societies. There is no uniform
> rate of progress among them, and they
> range from primitive mosaic societies--
> fractured by tribalism and held feebly
> together by the slenderest of politi-
> cal sinews--to relatively sophisticated
> countries, well on the road to agricul-
> tural sufficiency and industrial com-
> petence. This sweeping surge of devel-
> opment, particularly across the whole
> southern half of the globe, has no

7

parallel in history.

> It has turned traditionally limitless areas of the world into seething caldrons of change.

> On the whole it has not been a very peaceful process. . . . Given the certain connection between economic stagnation and the incidence of violence, the years that lie ahead for the nations in the southern half of the globe are pregnant with violence.

> This would be true even if no threat of Communist subversion existed--as it clearly does . . . .

> Whether Communists are involved or not, violence anywhere in a taut world transmits sharp signals through the complex ganglia of international relations; and the security of the United Nations is related to the security of nations half a globe away.[16]

As an argument presented for domestic consumption to justify increased foreign aid, McNamara's assessment of this "taut world" situation indicates how the effort to overcome economic stagnation in poor countries was inextricably bound up with the perceived need to ward off the "threat of Communist subversion" and to regulate international relations so as not to jeopardize the internal security of the United States.[17] It is within this specific political context that research and policy formation with regard to development have been conducted in this country during the past three decades.[18]

North Atlantic economists and other social scientists were most willing and at times eager to speak of their policies and programs for development as necessary and even sufficient means to effect a transition in Third World nations from a condition of chronic poverty to a situation of economic growth, a transition which would also mark their entrance into a global network of nation-states with truly modern status. As we shall elaborate later in this chapter, Walt Rostow and other developmentalists could issue their proposals for effecting that transition under the label of a "non-Communist mani-

8

festo," and the United States was called upon to bring a "capitalist revolution," above all, to its neighbors in Latin America by providing for an influx of capital, technology, and development expertise.

It is from the perspective of those in Latin America who were recipients of this foreign aid that Peruvian economist Theotonio Dos Santos has described the 1950's and early 1960's as an initial period of optimism.[19] Ambitious plans for development were sponsored nationally, with the assistance of international agencies, to increase capital accumulation and to introduce technology and economic planning for accelerated industrial production and consumption. At this point in history the continent was characteristically described as approaching its turning-point from a course of development "towards the outside" to industrialization and "development towards the interior."

Developmentalists spoke accurately when they noted that since the nineteenth century, Latin American economies had become increasingly vulnerable in fluctuating world markets to unfavorable terms of trade for the export of their primary products and the import of manufactured goods. Their standard explanation for this state of affairs went as follows: Typically, in each Latin American country, as in other parts of the Third World, an export-based, usually monoculture economy had developed alongside a feudal agrarian economy and society whose population had not been integrated into the chain of national production and who continued to be bound by traditional customs and a static worldview. The hoped-for solution for creating independent, self-sustaining national economies was to be found in rapid industrialization with the aid of foreign capital and the opening up of local markets. During and immediately after the two World Wars, a process of import substitution had created light industries to provide inaccessible foreign goods, and this process was to be expanded to decrease reliance on foreign trade, as well as to incorporate the rural population into the labor force as producers and consumers.

During the United Nations' two Decades of Development, national policy in Latin America and most foreign trade and aid agreements were formulated in terms of these expectations for increased industrialization and for the "transfer of centres of decision-making towards the interior of underdeveloped economies, . . . replac-

9

ing a development 'induced' by uncontrollable foreign trade situations by national development as conceived by those in power within the country."[20] In addition, it was assumed that the growth of an independent national economy would be accompanied by a concomitant process of political democratization as control by traditional elites would be challenged by a strengthened middle class.

In his evaluation of Latin America's experience on this "path of Development" and of the performance of various developmentalist governments, Dos Santos concludes that "ten years of optimism were followed by ten years of pessimism, of economic stagnation and of failed development policies."[21] Contrary to initial expectations, Latin America has suffered a reduction of commercial independence during the past three decades. As Dos Santos has explained, "The combination of import substitution and the deterioration of currencies has provoked greater dependence on foreign trade."[22] Balance-of-payments deficits have increased dramatically with the decline in prices for raw materials and increase for manufactured products, and control of local industries has passed progressively to foreign interests. The rural population has been steadily marginalized from or, at best, only episodically integrated into patterns of production and consumption, and the political process has been dominated by military regimes, often in conjunction with industrial oligarchies. As one Chilean commented at the close of the 1960's, "If this is what one decade of development does for us, spare us from another."[23]

Explanations offered for the failure of development programs and policies vary significantly, as we shall see, but few dispute the rather cautious assessment that the developmental efforts of the recent past have been "valiant but somewhat disappointing."[24] In a less understated fashion, economic historian Phyllis Deane has summarized the current situation by saying,

> After more than two decades of development planning and internationally financed programs for progress, not a single one of these plans has produced an independent, viable economy. Their prospects for the future remain overshadowed by mounting burdens of debt and dependency.[25]

10

Even more disconcerting is the growing realization that if, as Gunnar Myrdal argues, "greater equality in under-developed countries is almost a condition for more rapid growth," progress toward development is doubtful or at least unlikely under present conditions "because in all underdeveloped countries economic inequality seems instead to be increasing . . . and social inequality . . . has usually not been decreasing."[26]

The failure of development policies suggests partial reasons for the increasing polarization between rich and poor nations, to which we referred earlier, but the antagonism is more explicable from the point of view of those who have followed the path toward development Dos Santos has outlined and have found that poverty and misery in their countries have not only not been checked but have, in fact, increased to the point of undermining present organized efforts. The late economist Samuel Parmar speaks of the "emergence of serious contradictions" in the economies of the South, which he illustrates from his own country's experience:

> National and per capita incomes have
> increased . . . but there has been an
> increase in the extent and intensity
> of poverty. . . . Although India has
> been commended for the success of its
> 'green revolution,' there neverthe-
> less is a shortage of foodgrains (de-
> spite a doubling of foodgrain produc-
> tion between 1951 and 1971), and
> prices of agricultural produce are
> rising sharply. . . . India's indus-
> trial progress is impressive, but it
> is accompanied by increases in indus-
> trial unrest, unemployment and under-
> employment. . . . The value of annual
> exports is now over two and a half
> times the 1961 level . . . But bal-
> ance-of-payments deficits continue,
> and debt-servicing will soon consume
> one third of export earnings. . . .
> 70 per cent of the population remains
> illiterate, and more persons are in
> that category today than were twenty
> years ago.[27]

If what Parmar designates as the "standard cures" pre-scribed by developed countries for the "ills" of underdevelopment, namely, "more growth, more aid, more trade," have "not only failed but also generated the contradictions that aggravate the disease,"[28] the question to be addressed is why this failure, and then what can be done to remedy the situation. It is precisely these questions which underlie the current debates over development in social scientific literature.

III. Preliminary Definitions of a "Contentious Concept"

While it is true that attention to issues of global development has gained momentum in a specific historical context, the general acceptance of development terminology into everyday language has, nevertheless, not guaranteed that differences in conceptualization have been transcended. In fact, a common characteristic of the writings and discussions of development is the almost obligatory clarification of terms used and weight attached to what Henry Bernstein aptly calls "that most contentious concept 'development.'" In his introduction to a collection of essays in the sociology of development, Bernstein appropriately suggests that

> To pursue the meaning of development therefore is not to initiate an exercise in semantics but is a necessary first step in thinking clearly about the range of situations, problems and possibilities subsumed in the uses of the term. Modes of definition embody particular assumptions and concerns and give rise to particular methods and uses.[29]

In the next sections, with an analysis of the two predominant models of development, we shall be able to account for substantive differences among usages of a shared vocabulary, but our immediate purpose is to indicate the range, as well as a common denominator, of meanings ascribed to the concept "development."

At the most basic level, there is a uniform designation of development as a particular kind of social change process. Development is "no longer conceived as spontaneously generated and in this sense (ultimately) guaranteed, but as a conscious goal pursued,"[30] through coordinated efforts to initiate and sustain change in a direction deemed desirable. The meaning of the term which first gained ascendency is that of development as

12

a process of the accumulation of wealth. In a purely
economic sense, development is understood to be synonymous with economic growth. This definition, by which
degrees of development among nations are measured quantitatively by comparative statistics of gross national
product and per capita income, remains a standard criterion often referred to but no longer considered a sufficient means of classification by itself. Two reasons
may be cited for the reluctance to define development in
this narrowly economic sense. First, the failure of development programs to establish independent and self-
sustaining economies in those poor nations which are,
nonetheless, undergoing industrialization, has brought
forward the quite sobering realization that "growth
without development is a frequent experience in the past
and present of the now underdeveloped countries."[31]
Second, the experience in advanced industrialized societies that an increase of wealth has not automatically
provided for development in the sense of well-being
among the general population has suggested a further
limitation to any purely economic interpretation. Presently, the value of this definition "lies in serving as
a yardstick to measure more intregral notions" although
"this [purely economic] focus continues to exist in a
more or less subtle form in the capitalistic view of
development."[32]

A more generally accepted definition of development
incorporates economic, political, social, and cultural
components as integral to development, understood as a
total social process. Benjamin Higgins indicates the
willingness now typical among economists to adopt this
more inclusive definition while he manages to retain
an emphasis upon economic factors:

> By the same token we shall mean by
> 'economic development' a discernable
> rise in total and per capita income .
> . . widely diffused among occupational
> groups and among regions and continu-
> ing for at least two generations. . .
> . The process will be accompanied by
> structural change, narrowing gaps in
> productivity among sectors and re-
> gions, and improved education and
> health.[33]

Other economists, such as the Brazilian Helio Jaguaribe,
are more ready to concede that any adequate definition

13

of development must necessarily include traditionally
"non-economic" as well as economic factors in its analysis and that "only for methodological convenience or
in a partial sense can one speak of economic, political,
cultural, and social development."[34] Jaguaribe, among
others, argues for an interpretive framework in which
the interaction of component factors may be studied to
ascertain how the advancement or retardation in one area
affects development as a total movement of social transformation.

This more comprehensive definition of development
as "economic growth plus social change" has encouraged
some theorists to insist upon analyzing the specific
social context in which development occurs (or fails to
occur), as well as the political dynamics which shape
the process. Robert Heilbroner's assessment that "economic development is not primarily an economic but a
political and social process,"[35] speaks to the need for
an interdisciplinary approach which has been frequently
requested but seldom arrived at because of the lines of
segregation separating distinct disciplines of inquiry.
We shall return to this problem in the following section, but suffice it to say that an understanding of
development as a total and complex social process requires consolidation of both external and internal factors which shape a national economy. Such a perspective
also prevents, or at least makes more difficult, any
inclination to ignore conditions "other than those rig-
idly defined as economic--by treating them as residual
as the term 'non-economic' implies, or by holding them
'constant'. . . ."[36]

A third definition of development is not discretely
separable from the previous, more comprehensive view,
but rather reinforces and extends its focus. The Cocoyoc Declaration, issued by participants of a United
Nations conference in the fall of 1974,[37] is representative of this third definition which explicitly identifies a concern for human values and locates that concern
in continuity with a humanistic tradition. The Cocoyoc
Declaration includes the following definition in its
statement:

> Our first concern is to redefine the
> whole purpose of development. This
> should not be to develop things but
> to develop man [sic]. . . . We are
> still in a stage where the most im-

14

portant concern of development is
the level of satisfaction of basic
needs for the poorest sections of
the population in society. The
primary purpose of economic growth
should be to ensure the improvement of conditions for these groups.
A growth process that benefits only
the wealthiest minority and maintains or even increases the disparities between and within countries
is not development. . . . We therefore reject the idea of 'growth
first, justice in the distribution
of benefits later.'[38]

Development is, therefore, to be understood as a process
best judged by qualitative as well as quantitative
changes, and while priority attention is to be directed
toward the satisfaction of basic human needs, other
goals and values, such as "freedom of expression and
impression," the "deep social need to participate in
shaping the basis of one's own existence," and the right
to find "self-realization in work,"[39] are judged to be
necessary components of development understood in this
normative sense.

This humanistic perspective is reflected in ecclesiastical documents concerning development issues, but
it is also apparent in writings from non-Christian
sources as well.[40] As we shall consider in Chapter II,
however, even those who share an interest in heighten-
ing ethical dimensions of development do not speak uni-
vocally, nor do they necessarily interpret the dynamics
of global development similarly. As Samuel Parmar
notes, while the acceptance of social justice as an objective in economic development may well be "the most
hopeful feature of the present world situation,"[41] the
necessary move from what he calls moral sentiment to
effective political strategy is the decisive juncture
at which significant differences begin to appear among
those who are attracted to this humanistic understanding
of development.

These three definitions of development are not exhaustive of the meanings or nuances attributed to the
concept, but they do indicate some uniformities among
the given range of expression. What may not be as apparent from this sample, however, is the recurrence of

fundamental problems which arise even at the definitional level and which are compounded when the correlative term "underdevelopment" is added.

A clue to such difficulties is the very fluidity of the development vocabulary. Michael Harrington is not alone in observing that "there has been a good deal of euphemism, much of it politically motivated, with regard to how one speaks about the poor countries."[42] Shifts in parlance have gone from designating these nations as "underdeveloped" to identifying them either as "developing" or, more recently, as "less developed countries" (LCD's).[43] Such terms are relative and imprecise, at best, but characteristically, underdeveloped nations are defined negatively in relation to those countries which are considered "developed" or "modern" in terms of advanced industrialization and the appearance of a mass-consumption society. One economist has attempted to remove any unfavorable connotations from the term "underdeveloped" by explaining its derivation as a policy consideration, in that

> . . . a country becomes classified as
> underdeveloped if it so declares it-
> self by applying for foreign aid and
> if the donor countries confirm its
> status by providing assistance.[44]

However, such policy decisions are also, by nature, political. Accordingly, if from the perspective of the United States and Western Europe, Latin America, Africa, and Asia have been designated as underdeveloped regions, the fact is that inequalities of international power relations have allowed the North Atlantic countries to name global realities for others and to determine the terms of their relationships. Development terminology must, therefore, always be interpreted within the dynamics of the specific historical context in which it is formulated and employed.

As we suggested earlier, definitions are not necessarily innocuous or politically neutral. We should also add that clarification of controverted terms is not always readily available. For example, although social scientists, especially North Americans, have become increasingly engaged in the study of economic development issues, the most recently revised edition of the International Encyclopedia of the Social Sciences includes no entry under the term "underdevelopment." Rather, the reader is referred to a listing under the category of

16

"modernization," which begins with the following statement:

> Modernization is the current term
> for an old process--the process of
> social change whereby less developed
> societies acquire characteristics
> common to more developed societies.[45]

Theories of modernity, in which the historical experiences of select Western nations are taken for granted as models of general applicability for the so-called less-developed countries today, offer a reconceptualization of the process of global social change which has more commonly been referred to as development. This perspective includes or, better yet, subsumes economic development as a component of modernization, presented as a mode of change "general in validity and global in scope"[46] to describe and interpret social reality in rich and poor nations alike. Because all nations, with varying degrees of success, are said to be engaged in this universal evolution toward modernity, some social scientists claim that this theoretical framework transcends certain problematic aspects of a general theory of development which retains a pejorative judgment against those societies labelled underdeveloped. That claim has not gone uncontested.

As we proceed to examine two conflicting theories and models of global development, we shall need to question whether ethnocentric biases and what has been called the "time-centric illusion" have been avoided by the assumption that there are "different routes, but only one destination" for all the nation-states of the world. Moreover, the failure of some countries to "modernize" at least raises the possibility that the deficiency lies as much with the theories offered to account for our contemporary world situation as with any actual deviation from the supposedly "attested" paths of development.

IV. The Emergence of Two Contradictory Models of Socio-Economic Development

The failure of development planning and programs over the past several decades to establish independent, viable economies in underdeveloped nations has been a sobering experience for economists and social scientists for whom the term "development" has, in the words of

17

Dale L. Johnson, "always implied a process of economic and social change for the better."[47] The prescriptions from conventional liberal economic theories of growth about the desirability of "more growth, more aid, more trade" have not cured the ailments of economic stagnation but have, on the contrary, produced two disastrous effects in lower income countries. As a World Bank report has concluded, economic growth measured in terms of increased national production has, in fact, "'actually worsened the distribution of income in underdeveloped countries'" and has been accompanied by a decline in political participation on the part of the majority of the population, as well.[48]

For these reasons it is now rather commonplace among development theorists from North America to concede the necessity of prescinding from overgeneralizations about the process of development and, as Albert O. Hirschman suggests, to investigate the dynamics of growth "in the small," that is, for one country or for a particular region within a national economy.[49] Reluctance to propose any general theory of development has come to replace an earlier, almost eager willingness to sketch all-encompassing theoretical frameworks, such as Walt Rostow's Stages of Economic Growth, which was presented in 1960 as "both a theory about economic growth and a more general, if still highly partial, theory about modern history as a whole."[50]

There is an additional consensus emerging, although by no means unanimously held, that liberal economic theories of growth which were devised in advanced industrialized nations are not strictly applicable to those countries which are now in the process of developing. After his work as an economic consultant in Colombia in the late 1950's, Hirschman wrote, and later revised, his Strategy of Economic Development, in which he makes the following argument:

> . . . the growth models were primarily
> designed to illuminate a condition
> which had been thought to be threaten-
> ing the advanced industrial countries--
> secular stagnation--but which during
> the postwar period has been one of the
> few worries from which we have been
> entirely free. Being thus relatively
> underutilized the newly perfected
> models were employed in a setting quite

> different from the one for which
> they were designed. . . . But if
> one thinks that . . . the model
> [is] a meaningful description of
> the development process, a point
> may be reached at which the model
> becomes a hindrance rather than a
> help in the understanding of the
> reality of underdeveloped countries.[51]

Although Hirschman's judgment about the vulnerability of industrialized nations to stagnation is fallible, his estimation of the usefulness of economic growth theory is, if anything, understated compared to Gunnar Myrdal's claim that much "conventional wisdom" from affluent countries about growth and development simply "becomes wrong" when "uncritically applied" to the problems of underdeveloped countries.[52]

In recent reassessments of economic development theories and policies, the assumption that the process of development, once initiated, will proceed smoothly along an evolutionary course has also been questioned. The realization that development programs have often not only failed to attain their goals but sometimes have aggravated pre-existing conditions has refocused the contemporary discussion upon the need "to account adequately for the sudden spurts or the unexpected relapses into stagnation that developing countries have often exhibited."[53]

At present there are two models or theories of development and underdevelopment which have assumed this task. Moreover, these two models offer significantly different, even contradictory interpretations of the nature and dynamics of the process of development. Although there are variations and particular intricacies, some of which we will investigate, within each model, there are basic uniformities in the operative assumptions and policy implications in each of these theoretical perspectives to be able to differentiate significant differences between them. Our purpose is to identify and make some preliminary assessment of the divergent lines of argument followed in the current debates over development in selected social scientific literature.

V. The Modernization Theory of Socio-Economic Development

The first model of socio-economic development, which continues to be influential particularly in the United States and Western Europe in the shaping of aid policies and governmental programs, as well as for research on development and underdevelopment, made its initial impact and may be still classified as the "lag theory." Underdevelopment, described variously as a state of backwardness, stagnation, and traditionalism, is measured in terms of the absence or "lack" of those characteristics associated with modern societies and, above all, in terms of industrialization and urbanization. These traditional societies are said to "lag behind" the advanced industrialized nations quantitatively in the amount of industrial productivity, accumulated capital, educational resources, health services, technology, and other indices of development incorporated by various theorists to establish comparisons among social and economic systems. Accordingly, development toward modernization is viewed as that "set of interdependent processes through which a 'traditional' social structure is transformed into a 'modern' social structure."[54] As we shall see, the compatability of this model with sociological theories of modernization is no less clear than its affinity with what Richard DuBoff identifies as "the prevailing Western myth of progress,"[55] that is, with a confident expectation of a continuous, cumulative, and linear progression toward improved conditions of individual and collective welfare.

An analogy may help to explicate this model of development. DuBoff has suggested that, by the logic of this interpretation, the process of development and the relationships among nations may be compared to a race of cross-country runners.[56] All the runners begin the race at approximately the same starting point and follow a predetermined course, but some are better runners and will become the leaders while others fall behind. Although not all the runners move at the same pace or demonstrate comparable agility, the assumption remains that everyone will be able to complete the course and eventually cross the finish line. Those who lag behind are, therefore, not disqualified from the race, but rather must increase their efforts and avoid unnecessary detours in order to "catch up" with the leaders. Judgments made about participants at various junctures along the development "course" remain relative and subject to reevaluation as progress is demonstrated.

The theory of development which undergirds this

model operates with several foundational assumptions. First, development is understood as the steady and sometimes not so steady advancement towards certain designated goals and, more specifically, towards the socioeconomic conditions which pertain to the most advanced societies. The terminal state in the transition from traditional to modern society is characterized variously as industrial society, mass society, high-consumption society, and so forth. Furthermore, inasmuch as the same goal exists for all societies, the implication follows that there is also a similar path of development along which all nations must travel even though no single history of development experience is replicable in any exact sense.

A second assumption is that the advancement of nations now considered developed is attributable to their own efforts to maximize capacities and "talents" for growth and integrated development and, correspondingly, that the underdevelopment of other countries results from the failure to utilize national resources or the incapacity or unwillingess to make the necessary effort, for whatever reasons. The development of some countries is, therefore, not causally related to or determinative of the underdevelopment of others. Some recognition is given to the fact that there may well be a conditional relationship between the two situations, especially in terms of what is called a "demonstration effect." A. O. Hirschman's characterization is quite representative of this point of view:

> Once economic progress in the pioneer countries is a visible reality, the strength of the desire to imitate, to follow suit, to catch up obviously becomes an important determinant of what will happen among the nonpioneers.[57]

The theorists who follow this modernization model also emphasize the internal dynamics of national development. They speak of their task as one of identifying and analyzing those factors which either accelerate or impede social change toward modernization. In the process of explaining why "slow" developers have lagged behind, developmentalists seek to locate the institutional obstacles which arise because of anachronistic social structures and attitudes within nations and their populations, and they then try to suggest either strategies appropriate to eliminate these obsta-

21

cles or, alternately, the means to create the positive social and cultural conditions conducive to development.

The obstacles which block the movement toward modernization are spoken of as "traditional" or feudal residues and structures which inhibit change in terms of economic, political, cultural, and psychological dynamics. Although a country may exhibit a progressive modern sector with urban centers and factories, as well as an emerging middle class of Western-educated entrepreneurs, an underdeveloped nation is characteristically a "dual society." The duality emerges because of the juxtaposition of this modern sector alongside an agrarian, stagnant, and traditional sector, and it is this traditional sector from which resistance to change is said to arise in response to any incursions from the outside. According to the typology employed to differentiate between the characteristics of this dual society, the traditional or archaic society is described as preserving social and cultural institutions from the colonial past and governed by kinship relationships with "rigid stratification of ascribed social statuses" and adherence to "norms and values which exalt or at least accept the status quo."[58] Such a society, to be sure, undergoes a certain, albeit slow process of modification, but significantly, such changes are "not internally generated but are imposed upon it by the modern society."[59] It is precisely this modern society which is oriented toward innovation and characterized by "secondary" social relations "determined by impersonal actions motivated by rational and utilitarian ends," by "functionally oriented institutions, in which status is attained through personal effort" and expressed by such quantitative indices as income and education. Moreover, a modern society is governed by norms and values "oriented toward change, progress, innovation, and economic rationality (e.g., maximum benefits at minimum costs)."[60] Therefore, according to this conceptual model, development is defined as the process by which a society engages in a transition from the archaic type to the modern type of society.

Because of the complex interaction of elements within a dual society, social scientists who speak of development as a process of modernization are willing to be critical of the limitations of a single factor, narrowly economistic interpretation of development. David Lerner, Everett Hagen, David McClelland, and Albert O. Hirschman are representatives of this model of

22

development who emphasize the significance of non-economic as well as economic barriers to growth.

Therefore, it is not surprising that they share a third assumption, that the addition or combination of factors heretofore absent or underutilized in a dual society will make mobilization of resources possible throughout a country for development planning. Whether a particular theorist singles out one process or "missing ingredient" over against another most often depends upon the expertise and interests of the person and the discipline from which he or she approaches issues of development, but conditions frequently cited include a required amount of accumulated savings (Hirschman), orchestrated political decision-making and implementation on behalf of development planning (Hirschman), the desirability of an openness to modern ideas and methods (Hirschman, Lerner, Hagen, McClelland), and even the presence of such personality traits as "psychic mobility" among members of a developing society (Lerner, Hagen, McClelland). Also, the judgment of these modernists remains in place that while these "missing ingredients" may be generated from within a society, more often they need to be injected from outside by means of foreign aid, technical assistance, communication systems, and so on.

A final assumption underlying this modernization model of development is that political and social forces within a society must rally together to support a coherent development policy and sustain the momentum of change in the difficult process of transition. The role of modernizing elites or of those persons whom David Lerner identifies as the "transitionals," "the innovators," and "the-men-on-the-move [sic],"[61] becomes critical to the movement toward modernization, for as Henry Bernstein explains of this model of development,

> Whether the 'will to be modern'. . .
> is held to be ubiquitous or not, it
> is generally regarded as finding its
> most strategic expression in the role
> of the modernizing elites. It is
> these groups--political, bureaucratic,
> intellectual (and often military)--
> which are charged with the articula-
> tion of development goals and super-
> vision of development strategies for
> their countries, and with the task

> of 'nation-building,' i.e. of cre-
> ating viable national societies
> from their socially and culturally
> diverse populations.[62]

In addition to the appearance of this leadership, an "ideology of development" must also be devised in order to unite and coordinate the interests and efforts of groups in the tasks of development.

Although social scientists from diverse disciplines have contributed to the analysis of development in terms of this model, economist Walt Rostow's schema for the stages of economic growth, which we have already mentioned briefly, was a formulation which received widespread attention in the early 1960's.[63] His schema has been subsequently refined by other theorists of modernization. In what he calls his "Non-Communist Manifesto," that is, his proposal for a "capitalist revolution" in the Third World, Rostow identifies underdevelopment as the "original state" for all nations prior to industrial development. He then sketches five stages through which each and every society must pass in the process of its maturation: the traditional society, the preconditions for take-off, the take-off, the drive to maturity, and the "age of high mass-consumption."[64] During the process of development, understood as the progressive evolution from one type of society to a higher type, a nation gradually discards its traditional characteristics as a feudal society and assumes the features of an urban, industrialized and modern society.

Sociologist David Lerner is no less candid than Rostow in his use of the Western European nation-states and the United States, in particular, as the model of the modern society to be emulated by the underdeveloped countries. This basic model of modernity, Lerner argues in The Passing of Traditional Society, "reappears in virtually all modernizing societies on all continents of the world, regardless of variations in race, color, creed . . . ," and, furthermore, signifies the transformation of the individual members of a traditional society into "the cash customer, the radio listener, the voter."[65]

Development, for Lerner, is a process of acculturation which proceeds by the diffusion of institutions, values, and attitudes from the advanced to the developing nations. Such diffusion has been accelerated by the

24

networks of global communications systems which transmit what Lerner designates as "pictures of the future":

> Every nation that regards itself as
> more developed now transmits pictures of itself to those less developed societies that figure in its
> own policy planning. . . . Every nation that is less developed, but regards itself as developing, receives
> the pictures . . . and decides, as a matter of high priority for its own
> policy planning, which of them constitutes the preferred picture of
> its own future. This decision is
> the crucial turn in the direction
> of modernization; whatever its particular configuration, it spells
> the passing of traditional society
> and defines the policy planning of
> social change.[66]

As Lerner views the world, traditional societies have historically been able to respond effectively to demands for institutional change which are produced <u>internally</u> and which allow for a protracted period of adaptation, but he argues that "they are typically incapable of rapid institutional changes to meet <u>externally</u> induced demands."[67] Because of the disruptive effects of introducing modern images and institutions into traditional social structures, Lerner concludes that an imbalance "between the will and the way to modernize" emerges as the "key problem of induced and accelerated social change."[68] The desire to modernize leads only to frustration and failure unless accompanied by sufficient institutional support and "psychic mobility" among people to assume the tasks of becoming a modern nation.

According to Lerner, the perpetuation of underdevelopment results from the <u>internal</u> resistance to change and the inability of persons to adopt modern ideas and methods.

> Modernization operates . . . through
> a transformation of institutions that
> can only be accomplished by the transformation of individuals--the painfully complex process which W. H. Auden

epitomized as 'a change of heart.'[69]

The persistence of "traditional folkways," no longer suitable for life in urban, industrialized society, prevents members of underdeveloped nations from realizing self-sustaining growth and from adequately balancing supply with accelerating demand. What Lerner diagnoses as the means for accomplishing the transition to modernity is a characterological transformation of individuals who are to become "upwardly mobile" and oriented toward change. As he concludes,

> The incorporation of an adaptive capacity of this magnitude can occur only in societies that diffuse widely among their peoples the lifeways and institutions of mobility, empathy, and participation. Mobility is the initial mechanism: people must be ready, willing, and able to move from where they are and what they are.[70]

Moreover, it is precisely the inadequate diffusion of these character traits, most notably psychic mobility, which Lerner takes to account for the failure of most development programs.[71]

In a variation of, rather than a deviation from Lerner's analysis, Everett Hagen and David McClelland emphasize psychological dynamics which they grant are ultimately determinative of the possibility either to enhance or impede the entire complex process of development. McClelland identifies his primary research interest as that of human motivation, specifically in relation to economic growth. While acknowledging the significance of external factors for rapid economic expansion, such as natural resources, favorable opportunities and terms of trade, and political stability, he suggests that certain internal factors, "the values and motives men [sic] have that lead them to exploit opportunities," may not only be correlated with economic development but also operate as causative factors, most especially the "need for Achievement."[72] According to his research findings, high levels of "n Achievement," as McClelland abbreviates this "desire to do well . . . to attain an inner feeling of personal accomplishments,"[73] are to be found among members of a rapidly developing economy; correspondingly, "slow economic

26

development" may be attributed to "a lack of n Achievement in its elite."[74]

In his On the Theory of Social Change Everett Hagen also speaks of the primacy of psychological barriers to development and of the differences in character formation between members of traditional and modern societies. Differentiating between creative and authoritarian personality types, Hagen characterizes the member of traditional societies as "uncreative because he sees the world as an arbitrary place, not subject to analysis and control."[75] The inability or unwillingness to engage in technological innovation, which he considers the sine qua non of economic development, is understandable, he suggests, given the reluctance to challenge the boundaries of traditional ways of life which are "custom-bound, hierarchical, ascriptive, and unproductive."[76]

In contradistinction to McClelland, Hagen also argues that the "demeaning and humiliating" patterns of relationships which are incompatible with technological and economic progress are explicable as an inheritance from the experience of colonialism and are not sui generis to a particular society or culture.[77] What remains true for both McClelland and Hagen, however, is a distinct tendency toward psychological determinism in their theoretical analyses of the process of development and underdevelopment. As Andre Gunder Frank advises, the limitations of a narrowly psychological approach to social change are in evidence, for

> As long as [human] activities are considered to be a function of values or personality, little attention need be directed to the immediate surrounding social environment. . . .[78]

Furthermore, "the present economic, social, and political structure does not matter at all: There is no need to change the contemporary status quo."[79]

As an economist, Albert O. Hirschman intends to offer an analysis of economic development and set of policy recommendations which will serve as a corrective to this tendency among some North Atlantic social scientists to psychologize the issues at hand or to reduce development efforts to dynamics internal to the self in society. For example, he is most adamant in his refu-

27

sal to neglect the external factors which condition the process of development or the institutional arrangements which obstruct economic growth. He speaks of development as a "chain or disequilibria" by which tensions and imbalances within the developing country are deliberately induced and maintained in order to sustain reciprocal sequences of growth and expansion within and among sectors of the society. He also outlines a strategy of economic development which attempts to mobilize existing resources and latent production forces within a developing country by means of what he calls "a series of pacing devices" or "inducement mechanisms."[80] His concern is also in the direction of analyzing international dynamics of the transmission of growth and addressing the need for underdeveloped countries to "be more closely integrated into the world economy."[81]

At the same time, however, Hirschman speaks of the compatibility of his own line of inquiry with the work of theorists of modernization who have turned their primary, if not exclusive attention "to the attitudes and value systems that may favor or inhibit the emergence of the required activities and personalities" for effecting economic development.[82] He, too, comes to locate the primary obstacles to development as internal to a society and, furthermore, he concludes that "our analysis . . . places the difficulties of development back where all difficulties of human action begin and belong: in the mind."[83]

In explaining why some countries have developed and others have not, Hirschman argues that "development depends on the ability and determination of a nation and its citizens to organize themselves for development."[84] Because of what he identifies as imperfections in their decision-making process, underdeveloped nations consistently fail to take advantage of potential opportunities for advancement. They demonstrate a lack of both determination and an accurate perception of the costs and the necessary means for effecting long-term progress. In his judgment, a "lack of confidence," inability to "move out of the depression doldrums," and an "absence of growth mentality" characterize the major stumbling blocks to be eliminated,[85] and Hirschman elaborates his own viewpoint in this manner:

> Our diagnosis is simply that countries
> fail to take advantage of their devel-
> opment potential because, for reasons

largely related to their image of
change, they find it difficult to
take the decisions needed for development in the required number
and at the required speed. . . .
Our approach leads us to doubt the
existence of a pent-up energy that
is held back by villainous obstacles. It rather views the obstacles as reflections of contradictory drives and of the resulting
confusion of the will. Everday
language expresses this interdependence between will and obstacles when a person who does not
act is said to be 'inventing all
kinds of difficulties and obstacles.' In such a situation obstacles hardly have a life of their
own, and removal of specific obstacles would be an unreliable method
of inducing action.[86]

In keeping with the analyses of Lerner, McClelland, and
Hagen, Hirschman proceeds to account for the failure of
development policies and programs in terms of the resistance which traditional or underdeveloped societies
may offer to change and their inability to surmount the
difficulties in the process of transition toward modernization.

Although not minimizing the problems of promoting
development planning in poor nations, Hirschman suggests
that there may even be advantages to being a "latecomer"
to the modern world, in the sense that their lagging behind is "bound to make their development into a less
spontaneous and more deliberate process than was the
case in the countries where the process first occurred."[87] A similar argument is made by other theorists of this modernization model of development who express the view that underdeveloped nations today are
in a position to take into consideration the mistakes
and even excesses of the process of economic growth in
the advanced industrialized countries and thereby avoid
some, if not most, of the social and human costs of
modernization. Quite similarly, the underdeveloped nations are also said to benefit from the availability of
resources and technology in the rich nations for their
own use in development planning.

Despite these reputed benefits, however, what
Hirschman insists upon is that development will not and
cannot succeed unless a further, quite basic problem is
solved. This problem is one that stems "from a basic
disbelief in, and distaste for, the <u>process</u> of economic
development and from the attempt to <u>jump</u> over it and
its difficulties."[88] The often disruptive and slow process of transition toward modernization is accompanied
by "disturbances," "lags," and even "breakdowns" which
modernization theorists argue are inevitable and yet,
most importantly, are ultimately of a transitory nature.
David Lerner agrees with Hirschman that the actual process of modernization may not be short-circuited without paying heavy penalties or ever successfully circum-
vented. Therefore, he offers the following explanation
to account for the persistent failure of some underdeveloped nations to overcome conditions of poverty and
to "catch up" with the advanced nations:

> . . . the modernizing lands are soci-
> eties-in-a-hurry. Emulating what the
> advanced Western societies have become
> today, they want to get there faster.
> Accordingly, <u>they</u> <u>force</u> <u>the</u> <u>tempo</u> <u>of</u>
> <u>Western</u> <u>development.</u> <u>Even</u> <u>more</u> <u>seri-</u>
> <u>ous,</u> <u>as</u> <u>a</u> <u>result</u> <u>of</u> <u>their</u> <u>hurried</u>
> <u>pace,</u> <u>they</u> <u>often</u> <u>disorder</u> <u>the</u> <u>sequence</u>
> <u>of</u> <u>Western</u> <u>development.</u>[89]

The underlying assumption of this argument is one which
is quite typical of the "lag model." An underdeveloped
country can and, indeed, <u>must</u> imitate a process of development toward modernization which the affluent Western nations have already followed out of their own original state as similarly underdeveloped countries. The
corollary to this proposition, one which has significant
socio-ethical as well as political implications, is
that underdevelopment is said to persist because of the
ways in which poor nations (choose to) deviate from this
sequence of development and refuse to follow the lead of
the powerful nations. As we turn now to examine an alternative model of socio-economic development, we find
that this assumption has by no means gone unchallenged,
nor, should we also note, has Lerner's statement of the
problem of underdevelopment remained unquestioned.

VI. <u>The Dependency Theory of Development and Its Criti-</u>
     <u>cisms of the Dominant Model</u>

30

A frequent criticism of the theories of modernization which we have been examining is their ethnocentric bias, most overt whenever modernization is equated with Westernization or more explicitly with Americanization.[90] In explicating what is meant by self-reliance in developing nations, Samuel Parmar speaks to the problems of imitating the experiences and policies of the North:

> Developing nations have much to learn
> from the experience of the developed--
> the most important lesson being that
> the latter have formulated theories
> and policies with reference to their
> own special conditions. But imitation
> will prove disastrous, as is already
> becoming evident, because it means
> misshaping one's own framework to make
> it conform to the realities and inter-
> ests of others.[91]

A second criticism is that theories of modernization are frequently subject to what may be called a "time-centric illusion," in promoting the false assumption that under-developed nations are closed, stagnant, and somehow fixed traditional societies which are just now, or at least only since the end of the Second World War, under-going a process of social change under the impact of external influences. Critics of modernization theories of development argue that to view the poor nations of the globe as representative of "some sort of eternal or perhaps slowly drifting type of social organization"[92] is to deny or, at best, distort the histories of these countries which have changed considerably, even in their most rural and isolated regions, under the impact of both colonialism and political independence.

The most significant objection to the modernists' "lag model" of development and to the theory of modern-ization follows upon this second criticism. Critics argue that underdevelopment is more adequately compre-hended not as a state-of-being but rather as an histor-ical process which must be understood in dynamic and relational terms. It is, furthermore, appropriate and necessary to recognize that there is a process of under-developing as well as a process of developing. Celso Furtado, for example, argues against even positing un-derdevelopment as a "necessary stage in the process of formation of the modern capitalistic economies," much less as an "original state" prior to economic growth and technological innovation. He contends that "to grasp the essence of the problem of contemporary underdeveloped economies this peculiarity must be taken into consideration," namely, that underdevelopment is a "discrete historical process through which economies that have already achieved a high level of development have not necessarily passed."[93]

From an analysis of the development of various regions in Brazil, Rudolfo Stavenhagen has reached a similar conclusion:

> . . . underdevelopment followed upon and did not precede development. The underdevelopment of these regions [Northeast Brazil] is largely the result of a previous period of development that was of short duration, followed by the development of new activities in other parts of the country. . . . We see, then, that in historical terms development and underdevelopment are connected in Latin America, and that frequently the development of one zone implies the underdevelopment of others.[94]

Theotonio Dos Santos takes this argument one step further in stating that underdevelopment is a process not only related to but, in fact, generated by the expansion of Western capitalism and the development of the advanced industrialized nations within the context of a global economic system.

> . . . underdevelopment, far from constituting a state of backwardness prior to capitalism, is rather a consequence and a particular form of capitalist development known as dependent capitalism.[95]

Over against the dominant liberal theory of modernization, then, a second model of development has emerged, a model which has Dos Santos and other Latin American political economists as its most articulate spokespersons. As a macro-level analysis of national and international dynamics of development, it offers a distinct alternative in terms of a "theory of dependency," which has quite different operative assumptions and policy

32

implications.

Critics of the dominant model of development deliberately intend to offer a corrective to the ahistorical
view of social change they find implicit in the preceding modernization model, which analyzes abstract and
formal relationships between ideal socio-economic types,
such as the traditional and modern society, or the movement between two stages in a process of transition, such
as the emergence of capitalism from feudalism. Theorists of dependency insist upon the adoption of an historical method for the study of development which allows
the history of the underdeveloped nations and particularly the history of colonialism to inform any analysis
of the contemporary world situation. Accordingly, they
argue that the appropriate starting point, in the words
of Henry Bernstein, is to "refrain from discussing modernization as such and ask what we mean by the 'modern
world' and what the historical processes were which
formed the modern world. . . ."[96]

Bernstein's own answer to that question is that
the modern world, first of all, is a novel situation
which has emerged over the course of the last three to
four hundred years as "an inclusive international structure of economic, political and cultural relationships."
Secondly, he takes note of the fact that these relationships were brought into existence primarily through the
expansion of Western Europe and the colonialization of
the globe.[97] In order to speak of a "modernization process," it is first necessary to recognize how the im-
position of a market economy altered the internal life
of the now underdeveloped nations and then to clarify
not only the present differences between the colonizers
and the colonized but also the historical relationships
which evolved between them. Even Hyla Myint, whom
Michael Harrington identifies as an analyst "from a
mainstream economic perspective,"[98] concurs with dependency theorists at least on this point:

> A popular idea of the underdeveloped
> country is of a closed society stag-
> nating in traditional isolation, like
> Tibet before the Chinese annexation.
> Paradoxically enough, such a society
> in complete isolation would have few
> of the typical problems of the pre-
> sent-day underdeveloped countries.
> . . . In contrast, the typical prob-

33

lems of the present-day underdeveloped countries arise, not because
these countries are in the traditional state of isolation, but because they have been 'opened up' to
outside forces, in the form of foreign trade, investment and colonial
rule.[99]

What theorists of modernization anticipate as a progressive integration of so-called "backward nations" into a
network of global relationships was, in fact, accomplished in the process of colonialism. Dependency theorists quickly add that contemporary structures of inequality between nations is our present-day inheritance
from that imperial history which, ironically enough,
cannot be "viewed merely as an experience which has had
an impact on the minds of men [sic] in the underdeveloped world."[100]

If, from the perspective of the dominant "lag model" of development, international relationships may be
described in terms of a race of cross-country runners,
Richard DuBoff suggests that, from a dependency perspective, this "network of global relationships" may better
be compared to the relations between member teams of a
professional football league, especially when the "in-
terconnection and the very subtle but real link between
the processes of impoverishment and enrichment" are
taken into account.[101] DuBoff describes his football
league analogy in this way:

Some of these teams obviously will be
and are more successful than the
others. They will attract bigger
crowds of spectators, they will get
bigger gate receipts, therefore they
can supply better training facilities,
better farm clubs, better television
contracts perhaps. They will therefore be able to attract and buy the
best players and the process goes on.
. . . They will go on becoming more
successful, they will win more than
their share of games with the other
teams in the league, they will attract
bigger crowds, bigger profits, plow
the profits back into expansion and
the cycle goes on and on. The success-

ful will therefore continue to increase their capacity to exploit their
advantages, obviously at the expense
of the less successful.[102]

What this analogy allows for is the possibility of envisioning a single world historical process in which
the underdevelopment of some nations occurs simultaneously along with the development of others. Although
he acknowledges that "a logical conclusion" of this process would be a situation of total monopolization by
those in the superordinant position, DuBoff completes
his elaboration of the football analogy in speaking of
the self-imposed regulative mechanisms by which the
existence of the "league" is perpetuated. Even from
the perspective of those in privileged positions within
the system, arrival at the point of total monopolization
is considered an undesirable condition to be reached,

> . . . because if that were the case,
> there would no longer be a sufficient
> number of teams in the league and we
> couldn't play any more games, could
> we?[103]

Accordingly, for the developed nations to concede their
interdependence with the underdeveloped nations and,
furthermore, to promote, at least to some extent, the
latter's economic development is not to be unexpected
in a situation in which compliance with the "rules of
the game" does not significantly jeopardize their position of dominance.

Theorists of dependency describe the present global economic system in terms of a metropolis-satellite
structure. What they seek to explain is how economic
growth results in the accumulation of wealth for the
developed countries at the center while at the same
time such growth produces what Andre Gunder Frank calls
"the development of underdevelopment" in countries at
the periphery. Of particular importance is the different historical experiences and possibilities available
to "first-comers" and "late-comers." For example, although the emergence of a capitalist economy in metropolitan countries was accompanied by severe dislocations
in the process of industrialization and urbanization,
their development of a market economy was self-genera-
ted and internally coherent. Even today, the expansion
of one sector of the economy continues to have a "multi-

35

plier effect" on other parts, and internal changes produce integrated growth. With the internationalization of a capitalist economic system in the process of colonization, however, the introduction of a market economy has had a disintegrative effect in the satellite countries. Michael Harrington describes the process as follows:

> Growth in the periphery was stimulated by the penetration of alien capital into a stagnant economy. Only part of the society was drawn into the web of monetary relations—the part that was brought to life to serve some of the specific needs of the metropolitan power. If the peasant in this sector did acquire some buying power in the process, he did not spend it on the home market, which did not exist. He had to import. . . . Given the limited domestic market on the periphery, there was no basis for a vigorous internal industrialization. . . . When investment did take place, it was complementary to that of foreign capital, not competitive with it.[104]

Because economic growth on the periphery is not determined by internal needs but rather stimulated and directed from the outside by "the foreign capital that called it into a new life," the economic structures of these nations lack "the reciprocal interactions that are necessary if there is to be self-sustained growth." Moreover, the internal workings of underdeveloped economies become comprehensible only in terms of their external relationships with the metropolitan centers.[105]

Harrington's analysis confirms the conclusions reached by Dos Santos in accounting for the persistent failure of Latin American countries to establish self-sustaining, independent economies.[106] The vulnerability of their export-based, usually monoculture economies to unfavorable terms of trade and to foreign capital which has increased its control of whatever domestic production exists, has maintained their status as dependent and unequal partners in their relationships with the advanced industrialized nations. Even when economic growth does occur within an underdeveloped country, the

36

fact remains that "the mass of profit it generates does not become integrated into the local economy" and, therefore, "despite an improvement in living standards, there [is] no structural modification in the economic system" to allow for what Dos Santos has called "development towards the interior."[107]

The present division of the globe into an affluent North pole and a poor South pole is, therefore, to be seen as the outcome of an historical process which began in the sixteenth century with the emergence of European capitalism and which was accelerated in the nineteenth century with the creation of a world market system through colonial expansion. The modern world, more importantly, "was not, and is not, the result of the inexorable workings of some inhuman necessity--geographic, geological, genetic, or what have you--but of economic and social structures."[108] If the original advantage of Western Europe and subsequently the United States was comprised of their social and technological revolutions and commercial development, they have been able to perpetuate their ascendency among nations by exploiting opportunities first and by sustaining their "initiatory power." Richard DuBoff defines this power not only in terms of the power of technological innovation, of creating demands and setting prices for goods, or of organizing the utilization of equipment and other labor force skills, but also in terms of the power of those "who perpetuate their own lead by having in their hands the power to change the rules of the game."[109] This power created and today maintains a system of international relations in which those nations which are now underdeveloped may attempt to "catch up" with the leaders but in the process remain dependent upon those who established the political and economic conditions for trade and foreign investment.

In analyzing the historical process of underdevelopment in Latin America, Dos Santos prefers to speak of dependence as a "conditioning situation," in that the economic development of some countries has been and continues to be conditioned by the expansion of others. More explicitly, he explains Latin America's conditioning situation in this manner:

> A relationship of interdependence between two or more economies or between such economies and the world trading system becomes a dependent relation-

> ship when some countries can expand
> through self-impulsion while others,
> being in a dependent position, can
> only expand as a reflection of the
> expansion of the dominant countries.
> . . . The basic situation of depen-
> dence causes these countries to be
> both backward and exploited. . . .[110]

Although there are distinct differences in the historical experiences of individual Latin American countries
and certain complexities in present patterns of development, an outline of a theory of dependency has been
advanced in the context of historical investigations of
the "development of underdevelopment" throughout the
continent.[111] The operative assumptions of this model
of development and underdevelopment contrast dramatically with those of the preceding theory of modernization.

First, development and underdevelopment are understood to be interdependent processes, and a theoretical
approach is called for which integrates "into one single historical account the capitalist expansion of the
developed countries and the consequences of that expansion in the countries which are today adversely affected
by it."[112] Similarly, any analysis which is based upon
the "dual society" thesis is considered questionable.
The alleged dualism within underdeveloped nations between an archaic or traditional sector and a modern sector actually misrepresents the historical development
of these sectors as component parts of a unified society, for "what the dualism notion sorely misses is any
concept of the whole."[113]

A second assumption is that this "concept of the
whole," as well as ongoing analysis of the relationship
of the parts to the whole, is indispensable for an adequate theory of social change and economic development.
For example, contrary to the contention of modernization
theorists that underdevelopment is explicable in terms
of the resistance to change originating from archaic
social structures and traditional "folkways," dependency
theorists insist that underdevelopment must rather be
analyzed in terms of the structural dynamics of the
world economy as these dynamics are worked out both nationally and internationally. Andre Gunder Frank speaks
most directly to this point:

> The social system which is today the

> determinant of underdevelopment cer-
> tainly is not the family, tribe, com-
> munity, a part of a dual society, or
> even . . . any underdeveloped country
> or countries taken by themselves. . .
> . It should be traced to the function-
> ing and structure of the international
> system. . . .[114]

Moreover, the task which Frank defines for the social
scientist is not limited to specifying actual differences which exist within a society but to account for
the structural relationships which created these differences and then to consider the systemic changes necessary for eliminating them.

Because of the significance attached to social relationships and to patterns of interaction among national and international interests, dependency theorists also argue that exercises in "comparative statistics" are
of limited value. It is commonplace that lists of characteristics are accumulated by modernization theorists
to indicate the relative status of developed and underdeveloped nations, and comparisons are frequently made
in terms of industrial productivity, degree of literacy
among the population, amount of labor engaged in agri-
culture over against industry, levels of capital savings, and so on. With this data in hand, development
planners may, for example, speak of the need for increasing the amount of foreign capital available to expand industrial production within an underdeveloped
country, and such capital is considered a "missing ingredient" preventing mobilization of resources. Michael
Harrington counters this strategic approach by refuting
the modernists' thesis that one or another "obstacle" or
"missing ingredient" explains the phenomenon of underdevelopment. His argument is as follows:

> It is not the presence or absence of
> foreign investment that is decisive,
> but the way in which the society is
> organized. The same amount of money,
> even an identical plant, can have a
> completely different effect in two
> different national systems. . . .

> Industrialization, some believe, is
> the sign of a developed economy. But
> then Hong Kong is more industrialized

than the United States. . . . Only,
Hong Kong specializes in the low-
wage production of products that
are no longer profitable for the
better-paid labor force and high
technology of the United States.
So it is not industrialization per
se, but the type of industrialization and the nature of the economy
in which it occurs, that are critical.[115]

Without a concept of the whole and an analysis of the
dynamics of its parts, theorists of modernization mis-
cast the "problem" of underdevelopment and misconceive
the reasons that the presence or absence of identical
factors may have contradictory consequences in different
societies. Dependency theorists are quite adamant, for
example, that Hong Kong is by no stretch of the liberal
capitalist's imagination to be seen as a truly developed, modern industrial "miracle" of development policies. Furthermore, they argue that a modernization approach also and not by chance engenders a "piecemeal
approach" to social changes and allows only for "a process of making innovations and changes totally unrelated to the social structure and way of life" of the
countries affected.[116]

Two additional objections are raised to the modernists' "diffusionist" method of social change. First,
dependency theorists argue that the transmission of resources and "development aid" has not been and is not
now unidirectional from the developed to the underdeveloped nations. On the contrary, a process of decapitali-
zation transfers wealth from poor nations to the rich,
in terms of the "profits" lost to foreign interests who
manufacture goods in low-wage, high productivity sectors
of the underdeveloped countries and in terms of the de-
teriorating terms of trade between nations. One esti-
mate calculates that Latin America, for example, provided
the advanced industrialized nations with $26.3 billion
in such "development aid" between 1951 and 1966.[117] Secondly, dependency theorists contend that the receipt
of foreign aid and investment is not always even advantageous to an underdeveloped country. From his own historical studies of Chile and Brazil, Andre Gunder Frank
has reached this conclusion:

. . . the satellites experience their

greatest economic development and especially their most classically capitalist industrial development if and
when their ties to their metropolis
are weakest. This hypothesis is almost diametrically opposed to the generally accepted thesis that development in the underdeveloped countries
follows from the greatest degree of
contact with and diffusion from the
metropolitan developed countries.[118]

What Frank observes is the detrimental effects to underdeveloped nations of their incorporation into the present world economic system which, as it is now struc-
tured, places their development under alien imperatives.

A third operative assumption of this dissenting
model of development is that the reality of dependence
can be understood only if the conflicting interests of
social classes are examined. Samuel Parmar has noted
the aceptic quality of those theoretical perspectives
which assume that societies as a unit have uniform interests and goals and which ignore that different groups
within a nation may have different aspirations and investments in development. A problem of mystification presents itself even in the use of terminology, as he explains:

The broad classification under which
a country is labeld 'poor' obscures
the existence in the same country of
a small affluent group that controls
the means of production and the levers
of economic and political power.[119]

As an important caveat, however, Dos Santos adds that
the preoccupation of some dependency theorists with the
relationships between metropolitan and satellite should
not thereby obscure the fact that "'external' domination, in a pure sense, is in principle, impracticable.
Domination is practicable only when it finds support
among those local groups which profit by it."[120] Therefore, contrary to the theorists of modernization who
look so readily to the "elites" of underdeveloped countries to mobilize national efforts to eradicate conditions of poverty and inequality, dependency theorists
recognize that persons from the upper classes in their
societies often identify their interests, politically
and culturally, with perpetuating the status quo and
with defending the advantages of "development" towards

41

the outside."

If, as defined earlier, dependence may be described as a conditioning situation which discloses limitations as well as possibilities for social change, Dos Santos has gone on to propose that there are two options which are available to those who confront such a situation: "they may either choose among the various alternatives internal to that situation or they may seek to change the conditioning situation itself."[121] Certainly, one test of the adequacy of any theory of development and underdevelopment is its ability to elucidate problems and to generate effective strategies for surmounting these problems. Theorists of dependency argue that the advantages of their perspective, over against that of theorists of modernization, is attributable to their use of an historical method of analysis, and to their concern for inquiry into the relational dynamics of the socio-economic whole. What they recongize is of equal, if not greater, importance is that the study of dependence

> . . . is informed by questions more relevant to the pressing needs of the present situation than those on which modernization theory is predicted, which is to say questions that do not disassociate the common concern with poverty, illiteracy and unemployment from the structural analysis of power and exploitation in their various forms.[122]

We shall return to consider the importance of strategy considerations as a component of socio-ethical analysis in the concluding chapter, but one final observation may be included at this point.

In the debates over development in the social scientific literature, this second model of development with its theory of dependency is identified as a neomarxist perspective and has been dismissed by its severest critics as "ideologically bound" and, therefore, unscientific. A question to be asked, although not answered, is whether the acceptability of this theoretical perspective has been limited precisely because of its association with a Marxist social scientific tradition or, even more to the point, because of its interest in "structural analysis of power and exploitation in

42

their various forms."

That question is also pertinent to the ecclesiastical discussions and pronouncements on development in recent years, which have also been informed by these social scientific theories. In the next chapter, we shall survey selected statements from national and international church bodies, particularly from the World Council of Churches and the Roman Catholic Church. The presumption that the churches, above all other institutions, have maintained the "moral point of view" throughout the debates on development will need examination in light of the fact that ecclesiastical documents disclose internal controversies of their own which have sharpened the development debate at several points.

NOTES

1. The customary units of measurement for such transformation are nation states, but I. Wallerstein argues that "this is not to suggest that nation-states are the only, or even the most important, operating entities" in the contemporary world. Multinational corporations, for example, "have a major, if not determinative, say in the global set of decisions. But when men [sic] say they are for 'development,' they are thinking of national units. . . ." (I. Wallerstein, "The State and Social Transformation: Will and Possibility," in Henry Bernstein, ed., Underdevelopment and Development: The Third World Today (Baltimore: Penguin Books, 1973), p. 277.

2. Robert Heilbroner, The Great Ascent (New York: Harper & Row, 1963), p. 19.

3. Quoted in Alan B. Mountjoy, ed., Developing and Underdeveloped Countries (New York: John Wiley and Sons, 1971), p. 9.

4. Heilbroner, pp. 17, 18.

5. Michael Harrington, The Vast Majority: A Journey to the World's Poor (New York: Simon & Schuster, 1977), p. 13.

6. Robert Heilbroner, An Inquiry into the Human Prospect (New York: W. W. Norton and Company, 1974), pp. 17, 21.

7. The Overseas Development Council is a Washington-based nonprofit research and educational organization established in

1969 to promote interest in and understanding of the social and economic problems of the developing countries. Denis Goulet was a visiting fellow at ODC from 1974 to 1976 and a senior fellow until 1979. He has since joined the faculty at the University of Notre Dame as Professor of Justice.

8. James P. Grant, "Introduction," in Guy F. Erb and Valeriana Kallab, eds., Beyond Dependency: The Developing World Speaks Out (Washington: Overseas Development Council, 1975), p. ix.

9. Ibid., p. x. My emphasis.

10. Geoffrey Barraclough, "The Great World Crisis," New York Review of Books, Vol. XXI (January 23, 1975).

11. Henry Bernstein, "Introduction: Development and the Social Sciences," in Bernstein, ed., op. cit., copyright (c) Henry Bernstein 1973, p. 14. By permission of Penguin Books, Ltd.

12. The principle of selection used is to follow Denis Goulet's suggestions, from his written work and from a private conversation, as to representative social scientific theories of development and their identifiable advocates. The selection is not exhaustive but rather indicative of the range and kinds of theoretical perspectives.

13. For a history of the concept of "development," see Robert A. Nisbet, Social Change and History: Aspects of the Western Theory of Development (New York, 1968).

14. For a description of these organizations, their nature and evolving functions in the global economy, see North-South: A Programme for Survival; Report of the Independent Commission on International Development Issues, under the chair of Willy Brandt (Cambridge: The MIT Press, 1980), pp. 36ff.

15. K. K. S. Dadzie, "Economic Development," Scientific American, Vol. 243, No. 3 (September, 1980), p. 59. Since 1978 Dadzie, a Ghanaian citizen, has served at the United Nations as Director General for Development and International Economic Cooperation.

16. Quoted in Harry Magdoff, The Age of Imperialism (New York: Monthly Review Press, 1969), pp. 116-117.

17. The United States' pursuit of economic development for the Third World, and especially for its hemispheric neighbors to the South, has gained or lost momentum in relation to the "temperature" of the Cold War and perceptions about the East-West conflict. Dadzie (footnote 15, above) has noted this

historical coincidence and commented that "with the thawing
of the Cold War, as symbolized by the detente between the
U.S. and the U.S.S.R., the U.S. substantially reduced its
outlays for economic assistance. Other countries followed
suit. . . . By the end of the 1970's the flow of economic
assistance had dwindled to half of the promise of .7 percent
of G.N.P. made at the beginning of that decade" (Dadzie,
"Economic Development," p. 64).

18. For a general survey of theories of development and underdevelopment in the post-World War II period, see Benjamin Higgins, Economic Development, rev. ed. (New York: W. W. Norton and Company, 1968), especially Part IV, "Theories of Underdevelopment," Ch. 11-16, pp. 209-360.

19. The following account of development efforts in Latin America
during this period is dependent upon an analysis by Theotonio
Dos Santos, "The Crisis of Development Theory and the Problem
of Dependence in Latin America," in Bernstein, ed., op. cit.,
pp. 57-80, but especially pp. 63-71.

20. Dos Santos, p. 64.

21. Ibid., p. 67.

22. Ibid. Lee Cormie has explained the flaw of the developmentalist strategy with regard to import substitution as follows: "Policies of import substitution initially relied on
the fact that internal markets already existed for the goods
that were to be produced; indeed, internal demand for them
was one of the major causes of balance of payments deficits.
But who could afford to buy imported goods during the preceding years? Only a small segment of wealthy people and a
middle sector of managers and professionals who served them.
New Cadillacs were indeed common on the streets of Buenos
Aires, Rio de Janeiro, and Mexico City after World War II,
but they did not reflect the buying capacity of most Latin
Americans. So industrial production was largely oriented
toward goods that middle and upper classes could afford. After an initial spurt, which did draw a small number of people
into this progressive sector and promote an increase in consumption, the rate of industrial expansion slowed down. The
masses remained peripheral to the new consumption markets.
And the balance of payments problems remained, since local
industrialists were forced to turn to the dominant nations
for the capital goooods and technology necessary for large
scale production" (Lee Cormie, "The Sociology of National Development and Salvation History," unpublished manuscript,
January, 1979, p. 24). A revised version of this essay will

45

appear in Gregory Baum, ed., Sociology and Human Destiny (Seabury Press, 1980), pp. 56-85.

23. The Chilean is Joel Gajardo, quoted in Gary MacEoin, Revolution Next Door: Latin America in the 1970's (New York: Holt, Rinehart and Winston, 1971), p. 1.

24. Alan B. Mountjoy, "Introduction," in Mountjoy, ed., op. cit., p. 9.

25. Quoted in Richard DuBoff, "What is Authentic Development?" (mimeographed, 1974), p. 6.

26. Gunnar Myrdal, The Challenge of World Poverty (New York: Pantheon Books, 1970), pp. 54, 60.

27. Samuel Parmar, "Self-Reliant Development in an 'Interdependent' World," in Erb and Kallab, eds., op. cit., pp. 8-9.

28. Ibid., p. 10.

29. Henry Bernstein, "Introduction," p. 14.

30. Ibid., p. 20.

31. James D. Crockcroft et. al., Dependence and Underdevelopment: Latin America's Political Economy (Garden City: Anchor Books, 1972), p. xv. My emphasis.

32. Gustavo Gutierrez, A Theology of Liberation (Maryknoll: Orbis Books, 1972), p. 24.

33. Higgins, p. 33.

34. Helio Jaguaribe, Economic and Political Development (Cambridge: Harvard University Press, 1968), p. 4.

35. Heilbroner, The Great Ascent, p. 24.

36. Bernstein, "Introduction," p. 18.

37. Participants at the conference included Samir Amin, Wassily Leontief, Rodolfo Stavenhagen, Mahbab ul Haq, and Barbara Ward (chairperson). Addressing problems of "overdevelopment" in affluent nations as well as issues of underdevelopment, the consultation spoke of the necessity of recognizing the "outer limits" of the planet's natural resources and its environmental integrity in conjunction with planning strategies for meeting the "inner limits" of fundamental human

needs.

38. "The Cocoyoc Declaration," in Erb and Kallab, p. 173.

39. Ibid.

40. Gustavo Gutierrez argues that "It would be a mistake to think that this point of view, which is concerned with human values, is the exclusive preserve of scholars of a Christian inspiration. Converging viewpoints are found in Marxist-inspired positions" (A Theology of Liberation, p. 25). For example, cf. Cockcroft et. al., op. cit., p. xvi and passim. This humanistic definition is also common to Gustavo Gutierrez, Denis Goulet, Richard D. N. Dickinson, and most others involved in the ecumenical church movement's debate over economic development.

41. Parmar, p. 27.

42. Harrington, p. 16.

43. The use of the phrase, "the Third World," is no less controversial. For example, Hannah Arendt argues that "the Third World is not a reality but an ideology," in that underdeveloped nations have little in common except "a contrast that exists with another world" and can, therefore, be spoken of as a unit only be perpetuating the prejudicial "imperialist leveling out of all differences" among formerly colonized countries (Crises of the Republic, pp. 123, 209-211). Pierre Jalee also questions the validity of this expression but for another reason. He finds it a mystification to speak of a group of nations as representing a "third way" alongside the only two economic systems which presently divide the globe, namely, capitalism and socialism. Cf. Pierre Jalee, "Third World? Which Third World?" in Revolution, Vol. 1, no. 7 (1963), pp. 3-9.

44. Higgins, p. 9. My emphasis.

45. Daniel Lerner, "Modernization," in David L. Sills, ed., International Encyclopedia of the Social Sciences, Vol. 10 (New York, 1968), p. 386.

46. Ibid., p. 387.

47. Cockcroft et. al., p. 272.

48. Quoted in DuBoff, p. 1.

49. Albert O. Hirschman, The Strategy of Economic Development (New York: W. W. Norton and Co., 1978), p. ix.

50. Walt W. Rostow, The Stages of Economic Growth: A Non-Communist Manifesto (New York: Cambridge University Press, 1960), p. 1.

51. Hirschman, pp. 31-32.

52. Gunnar Myrdal, Economic Theory and Under-developed Regions (London: Gerald Duckworth and Co., 1957), p. 99.

53. Hirschman, p. 40.

54. Robert I. Rhodes, "Introduction," in Robert I. Rhodes, ed., Imperialism and Underdevelopment: A Reader (New York: Monthly Review Press, 1970), p. xi.

55. DuBoff, p. 2.

56. Ibid.

57. Hirschman, p. 8.

58. Rodolfo Stavenhagen, "Seven Erroneous Theses About Latin America," in Irving Louis Horowitz et. al., eds., Latin American Radicalism (New York: Random House, 1969), p. 102.

59. Ibid., p. 103.

60. Ibid.

61. Daniel Lerner, The Passing of Traditional Society (Glencoe, IL: The Free Press, 1958), pp. 75, 406, and passim.

62. Henry Bernstein, "Modernization Theory and the Sociological Study of Development," in Journal of Development Studies, Vol. 7, no. 2 (January 1971), p. 145.

63. Gustavo Gutierrez speaks of the "special circumstances and carefully planned methods of distribution" by which Rostow's publication came to the attention of the underdeveloped nations. Cf. Gutierrez, op. cit., p. 38, footnote 8.

64. Rostow, p. 4.

65. Lerner, The Passing of Traditional Society, pp. 46, 50.

66. Lerner, "Modernization," pp. 387-388.

67. Ibid., p. 390. My emphasis.

68. Ibid.

69. Ibid., p. 388.

70. Ibid., p. 392.

71. Ibid.

72. David C. McClelland, "The Achievement Motive in Economic Growth," in Bert F. Hoselitz and Wilbert E. Moore, eds., Industrialization and Society (Mouton: UNESCO, 1966), pp. 74, 76.

73. Ibid., p. 76.

74. Ibid., p. 92.

75. Everett E. Hagen, On the Theory of Social Change (MIT: Center for International Studies, 1962), p. 192.

76. Ibid., p. 56.

77. Ibid., pp. 18-19.

78. Andre Gunder Frank, Latin America: Underdevelopment or Revolution (New York: Monthly Review Press, 1969), p. 70.

79. Ibid., p. 74.

80. Hirschman, p. 6.

81. Ibid., p. 200.

82. Ibid., p. 4.

83. Ibid., p. 11.

84. Ibid., p. 8.

85. Ibid., pp. 26, 136.

86. Ibid., pp. 25-26. Hirschman's emphasis.

87. Ibid., p. 8. On the "benefits" of colonialism for currently underdeveloped countries, cf. Robert Heilbroner, The Great Ascent, pp. 80-81.

88. Ibid., p. 210. My emphasis.

89. Daniel Lerner, "Comparative Analysis of Processes of Modern-
    ization," in Horace Miner, ed., The City in Modern Africa
    (London, 1967), p. 24, quoted in Bernstein, "Modernization
    Theory," pp. 151-152. My emphasis.

90. Henry Bernstein remarks that an attempt, even though an un-
    successful one, to avoid the ethnocentrism implicit in those
    perspectives which specify set historical patterns of modern-
    ization is David McClelland's concept of "n Achievement,"
    which only universalizes "certain traits at the level of per-
    sonality mechanisms," namely, those characteristics of the
    "prototypical" Western capitalist (Bernstein, "Modernization
    Theory," p. 148).

91. Parmar, p. 8.

92. Rodolfo Stavenhagen, "Changing Functions of the Community in
    Underdeveloped Countries," in Henry Bernstein, ed., op. cit.,
    p. 84.

93. Celso Furtado, "Elements of a Theory of Underdevelopment--
    the Underdeveloped Structures," in Henry Bernstein, ed., op.
    cit., pp. 41, 34. Cf. Andre Gunder Frank, op. cit., p. 4:
    "The now developed countries were never underdeveloped,
    though they may have been undeveloped."

94. Stavenhagen, "Seven Erroneous Theses," p. 106. My emphasis.

95. Dos Santos, p. 76.

96. Bernstein, "Modernization Theory," p. 153.

97. Ibid.

98. Harrington, p. 136.

99. Hyla Myint, "The Expansion of Exports and the Growth of Popu-
    lation," in Mountjoy, ed., op. cit., p. 58.

100. Rhodes, "Introduction," p. xi.

101. DuBoff, p. 6.

102. Ibid., p. 3.

103. Ibid.

104. Harrington, pp. 134-135.

105. Ibid., p. 137.

106. Supra., pp. 8-10.

107. Furtado, pp. 35, 37.

108. Harrington, p. 102.

109. DuBoff, p. 8.

110. Dos Santos, p. 76.

111. For example, cf. Andre Gunder Frank, Capitalism and Underdevelopment in Latin America: Historical Studies of Chile and Brazil, rev. ed. (New York: Monthly Review Press, 1969).

112. Dos Santos, p. 73.

113. Harrington, p. 135.

114. Frank, Latin America: Underdevelopment or Revolution, pp. 34-35.

115. Harrington, p. 132.

116. DuBoff, p. 6.

117. Harrington, p. 140 and passim. Cf. Stavenhagen, p. 108, and Frank, p. 49.

118. Frank, pp. 9-10.

119. Parmar, p. 13.

120. Dos Santos, p. 78.

121. Ibid., p. 77.

122. Bernstein, "Modernization Theory," p. 154.

CHAPTER II

THE DEVELOPMENT DEBATE WITHIN
THE ECUMENICAL CHURCH MOVEMENT

Debates over global economic development are by no
means the private property of social scientists exclusively. Since the Second World War the ecumenical
church movement, both Roman Catholic and Protestant
based, has become increasingly involved in and, some
would say, preoccupied by issues of global development.
We shall return in our final chapter to consider more
specifically some criticisms of this "preoccupation" and
also some very recent shifts and permutations in the
ecumemical debate. At this point, however, we may simply note that this ecumenical involvement did not origi-
nate "from the top down" or even "at the top," but rather it has been generated from and sustained by countless
local and regional responses by church peoples around
the globe. Moreover, their attention has been directed
toward a variety of concerns about human well-being and
particularly toward shaping and reshaping those socio-
economic and political conditions which produce or perpetuate suffering and injustice.

Because of these various involvements and their impact on the churches' self-perceptions and understanding
of Christian mission in the world (and of the theological and ethical grounding for that mission), we can also
safely say that the development debates have not only
come to but also have arisen out of the ecumenical movement during the past thirty years. In this chapter we
shall attempt to identify significant contours of that
debate and locate differences among various parties to
the controversy over economic justice worldwide.

As we begin, we might take cognizance of C. I.
Itty's observation, that "today there is far greater
divergence of views than ever before regarding the analysis, interpretation, goals, and processes of development."[1] Samuel Parmar has perhaps spoken even more to
the point by acknowledging that the differences which
now exist within the ecumenical movement are "not of
degree, but of fundamentals."[2] For the purposes of
this chapter, we shall work toward assessing the specific claim that we are making, that a debate over global
economic development has gained momentum within the
churches and, further, that this church-based debate

unmistakably parallels the concurrent debate within the social sciences between modernization theorists and their ideological counterparts, the dependency theorists.

We shall begin by identifying, briefly, the course of the emergence of global economic and social development as an ecumenical concern. It is fair to say that one of the most significant accomplishments following from the ecumenical attention to these issues has been that economic development has been irrevocably, we hope, linked with social justice concerns. In the second and third sections of the chapter, we shall attempt to characterize this ecclesiastical debate between developmentalists and liberationists by, first, examining the course of discussions within the World Council of Churches since the early 1960's. Our purpose is to illustrate both the emergence of the issue of global development on the Council's agenda and the subsequent appearance of ideological tensions within the Protestant church context.

Because of the consensual nature of the official reports of the World Council assemblies, however, these documents in and of themselves do not highlight or even readily disclose the radicality of the division between parties to this debate. Only as we turn, in the final section, to examine recent discussions within Roman Catholicism shall we be able to identify with greater specificity the shape and dynamic character of the debate now in process. Third World liberation Christians, particularly from Latin America, have directly challenged the teaching magisterium's position on global development and offered an alternative theological perspective which, as Gutierrez has argued, differs from the dominant, albeit progressive, theology of development "not only in its way of analyzing reality, based on more radical and all-embracing options, but also in its way of theologizing."[3]

I. Economic Development as an Ecumenical Concern

Two preliminary observations may be offered about the churches' engagement in development issues. First, what Rene Laurentin has said about the historical sequence which characterizes the involvement of his own church in questions of international economic justice is equally applicable to that of the Protestant churches:

The development movement did not orig-
inate in the Catholic church and it has
not spread centripetally as a result of
her preaching. She perceived it in the
world at large. She joined it.[4]

Furthermore,

. . . it was not in the charters and
instructions of the authorities or the
official organizations, nor in the
top-level decisions that the movement
started. All that they did was to take
on, guarantee, organize, and amplify
something that already existed as peti-
tions, research, and nascent realities.
They clarify and give scope to the
movement, but they are not its source.[5]

Along with Laurentin, we may concede that it is quite
accurate to state that the historical struggles undertaken throughout the globe to overcome conditions of
poverty and social injustice and to establish more
egalitarian communities in which all persons may attain
both "bread and dignity" is not, strictly speaking, a
church movement either in origin or in scope. It is,
nonetheless, also important to recognize the extent to
which the ecumenical movement has become increasingly
concerned with the problems of development and with
economic justice within and among nations since the mid-
1940's.

A reading of ecumenical documents during this period demonstrates how a moral consensus has steadily
emerged that this global striving toward development is
a "sign of the times" which calls for Christian involvement and unambivalent commitment. Moreover, the significance of a second fact should also not be underestimated, that Christians throughout the world and particularly in the Third World have come to identify this
quest for development as a primary locus for understanding and living out their faith in relation to what is
perceived to be an unmistakable, if not the central,
cultural dynamic of our time, namely, the aspirations
for and efforts aimed at human emancipation.

A second observation follows upon the first. Ecumenical interest in issues of economic and social development may not be so novel, but sustained involve-

ment is of relatively recent origin. Not until the United Nations' first Decade of Development was well under way did statements of concern about the problems of global poverty and underdevelopment begin to appear with any regularity either in the papal social teachings of the Roman Catholic Church or in the official reports of the World Council of Churches. As early as 1961, however, these issues were being placed on the church's agenda in rather unambiguous fashion. For example, Pope John XXIII included the following assessment of the contemporary world situation in his encyclical letter, Mater et Magistra:

> Perhaps the most pressing question of our day concerns the relationship between economically advanced commonwealths and those that are in the process of development.[6]

Delegates at the World Council of Churches assembly at New Delhi during that same year expressed a similar conviction and called for a "world strategy of development" to respond to the needs of both developed and underdeveloped nations facing the prospect of what they recognized would be unprecedented "rapid technological and social change" in the decades ahead.[7]

During the twenty years since those statements were issued, the ecumenical movement has become, in the words of C. I. Itty, quite "seriously exercised"[8] about the problems of economic development and also progressively more sensitive both to the injustices of the present world economy and to the complexities of the social change processes required to overcome the divisions between rich and poor. As we shall consider later on in this chapter, two ecclesiastical events, in particular, mark a turning point within the ecumenical movement for the placement of development concerns at the very center of the churches' efforts to define and implement their mission in the world: the 1966 World Church and Society Conference at Geneva and the 1967 publication of the papal encyclical Populorum Progressio. Because of their straightforward challenge to the churches to engage more effectively in concrete struggles for development, these events signal the point at which "the process of thought and action on the part of the churches in the field of development . . . gathered unprecedented momentum."[9]

Indicative of that momentum is the joining together of Protestants and Catholics in a truly ecumenical effort to promote interest in development issues and to sponsor conferences, programs, and projects on a range of related topics. In 1968, under the auspices of the Pontifical Commission for Justice and Peace and the World Council of Churches, a commission on Society, Development, and Peace, commonly referred to as SODEPAX, was established to facilitate these ecumenical ties and to elaborate the basis for a mutual "theology of development." As Alistair Kee has suggested,

> . . . reflection on this issue [global development] became the basis of a new kind of ecumenical theology. It was not, as so often in the past, a discussion about matters internal to the churches. It was an ecumenical response to an issue raised for the churches. And since the word 'ecumenical' originally referred to the whole inhabited world, then theology of development was doubly ecumenical, since it was a concern of all the churches with a matter affecting the whole world.[10]

In reviewing what he describes as this remarkably "ecumenical journey" in relation to issues of economic development, Robert McAfee Brown does not discount the significance of the increased collaboration of Protestants and Catholics in recent years, but he argues that what may be of even more importance is that over the course of the last two decades the churches have moved in a particular direction on that journey. Brown contends that the churches have moved steadily "onward and leftward."[11] Among the supporting evidence which can be gathered to justify that judgment, two rather noticeable shifts in ecumenical thinking about the goals and process of development may be mentioned at this point.

First, there has been a consistent tendency away from viewing development as a strictly economic phenomenon measurable in terms of increase in per capita income or similar quantitative factors and toward an understanding that economic growth is an essential but not exclusive indicator of social progress. It is true that "during the first Development Decade the churches by and large shared the view, prevalent among governments, UN agencies and secular organizations, which equated development with economic growth."[12] Alternative views began to surface, however, as soon as the churches were confronted with the historical evidence that even in those underdeveloped countries which had experienced significant rates of economic growth, the benefits of such growth had failed to "trickle down" automatically to improve the standard of living of the poorest members of their societies and, in fact, social inequities had increased rather than diminished as economic growth occurred. One such alternative view, for example, is found in Populorum Progressio, in which Paul VI deliberately speaks of development less in economic terms and more in terms of a comprehensive process of humanization whose goal is the "integral human development" of both persons and communities. In this process the maximization of human dignity and freedom for full participation in the life of a given society is regarded as no less important than the provision of material necessities for all persons. Therefore, the encyclical reaches this conclusion:

> Development cannot be limited to mere economic growth. In order to be authentic, it must be complete: integral, that is, it has to promote the good of every man [sic] and of the whole man [sic].[13]

The human good, understood as self-fulfillment in community with others, requires "the transition from less human conditions to those which are more human," namely, "the passage from misery towards the possession of necessities, victory over social scourges," but also "the growth of knowledge" and "the acquisition of culture." Paul also argues that authentic development is accompanied, above all, by "the acknowledgement by man [sic] of supreme values, and of God their source and finality."[14]

At the Uppsala assembly of the World Council of Churches in 1968, a similarly comprehensive view of development was presented to counter the narrowly economistic definitions prevalent in much of the contemporary social scientific literature. In the section of the report which addresses the problems of "world economic and social development," the delegates identified that "the central issue in development is the criteria of the human." Furthermore, they went on to explain:

> We reject a definition of development
> which makes man [sic] the object of
> the operation of mechanical forces,
> but view it as a process with potential
> for promoting social and economic jus-
> tice and world community and as an en-
> counter between human beings.[15]

To speak of human development in this way, as a
field-encompassing concept which incorporates all aspects of human life and social change, has seemed unnecessarily vague, however, for those who have insisted
upon the need to specify more sharply that the "'fundamental objective of development service of the churches
. . . is their participation in the war against poverty'" and that "'the cutting edge of the development
struggle [is] to eliminate mass poverty. . . .'"[16]
Charles Elliott has described a persistent problem which
reappears during ecumenical discussions, the tendency
to "spiritualize" or at least overgeneralize the concept
of development to the point of minimizing and even eliminating the quest for economic development as central to
the churches' concern. Elliott's assessment of this
situation follows, along with his own proposal for an alternative use of the development language:

> A linguistic analysis of recent ecu-
> menical pronouncements on development
> would, we suspect, show that the word
> is used in ecumenical circles to cover
> everything from spiritual conversion
> to the establishment of a more just in-
> ternational economic structure. Clearly
> such a large term of reference robs the
> word of any precise meaning and there-
> fore renders it almost useless. We
> therefore propose that development
> should be understood in a purely tech-
> nical sense as a process of the trans-
> formation of economic and social struc-
> tures of an individual country accompa-
> nied by quantitative and qualitative im-
> provements in general welfare and the
> generation of forces within the society
> and the sustaining of those improvements.[17]

Elliott's more restricted usage of the term development has not been readily adopted within the World
Council of Churces, but in response to the need for a

more coherent terminology, there has been a fairly wide
acceptance of a view first presented by Samuel Parmar
at an ecumenical consultation on development held at
Montreaux, Switzerland in 1970. Parmar defines development as a process of the self-development of peoples
with three component and inter-related goals, economic
growth, self-reliance, and social justice. Because the
movement toward development in Third World countries is
"a struggle for a better economic deal no doubt, but
more fundamentally for human dignity,"[18] the overarching goal of the development process is not economic
growth per se but, more appropriately, the increase of
social justice. The need for increased national wealth
receives due emphasis but is made subordinate to the
equally urgent claims for more equitable political and
economic relationships within developing countries and
between developed and underdeveloped nations. As Parmar explains,

> . . . self-development does not mean
> only a high rate of growth. It also
> implies a more equitable distribution
> of resources and economic power, and
> new relationships between social groups,
> so that development of one does not de-
> pend upon or lead to deprivation of the
> other. . . . Social justice reflected in
> greater equality of opportunity, a more
> egalitarian social order, a diffusion of
> economic and political power from the
> few to the many, is the most important
> element of self-development. . . . So-
> cial justice incorporates equality and
> human dignity.[19]

Accordingly, given this renewed emphasis upon social
justice as the fundamental goal of economic development,
throughout recent ecumenical literature an argument begins to appear more and more frequently that the most
adequate criterion for judging whether or not development is authentic and truly humanizing is to consider
whether the most marginalized members of society not
only receive the benefits of economic growth but, more
importantly, become empowered as participants in the
political decision-making process to determine social
and economic priorities in relation to their own exis-
tential needs. A consensus has been forming within the
ecumenical movement, therefore, that at most economic
growth but not true development can take place whenever

the poor are prevented from becoming active agents in their own process of self-development and the subjects of this movement toward social and economic transformation.

A second shift in ecumenical thinking indicates a similarly progressive revision in the approach taken to problems of economic development and, furthermore, complements the identification of social justice as the primary goal of a people's self-development. Marie Augusta Neal, among others, has noted that the churches have moved "from an old focus on the alleviation of the results of poverty to a new focus on the elimination of its causes."[20] This shift has come about, in part, from a gradual recognition that traditional approaches of the churches to the problems of poverty and underdevelopment, with their emphasis on the supply of emergency and relief services and the promotion of self-help programs on the local level, have failed to alter the underlying structural dynamics and power inequalities within and among nations which perpetuate conditions of poverty and oppression. Samuel Parmar has, again, been most articulate about this past inadequacy:

> . . . our involvement has been too piecemeal. Generally we focused on some of the unfortunate consequences of the social process (such as hunger, disease, illiteracy, etc.) rather than dealing with the process itself [which produces those consequences]. Such a first step is important, indeed essential; but it is not sufficient. Often it has meant 'service' within a given frame of political and economic life without raising any questions about the frame.[21]

If structural factors, including economic, political, and cultural dynamics, are root causes of underdevelopment, then the possibility of attaining social justice as fundamental equality between persons and groups is dependent upon radically altering those social and economic relationships which maintain disparities in power and prevent just distribution of goods and services. A necessary politicization of economic policy, therefore, follows upon this shift away from viewing the "problem" of underdevelopment as poverty per se toward an understanding that unjust distribution of wealth and misery and inequalities among persons and groups is the more fundamental issue to be addressed. This is the conclusion reached, for example by delegates at the 1975 assembly of the World Council of Churches in Nairobi:

> Poverty, we are learning, is caused
> primarily by unjust structures that
> leave resources and the power to make
> decisions about the utilization of
> resources in the hands of a few with-
> in nations and among nations, and that
> therefore one of the main tasks of the
> Church when it expresses its solidari-
> ty with the poor is to oppose these
> structures at all levels. . . . This
> makes it necessary to examine criti-
> cally the economic and social goals,
> the patterns of resource ownership
> and decision-making processes in the
> local and national situations, as also
> at the international context to reject
> all patterns that oppress the poor and
> to work for those which release the
> creative powers of people to satisfy
> their needs and decide their destiny.[22]

The most outspoken critics of the project or "service" approach to problems of underdevelopment have been those Christians involved in "theology of liberation" movements in Asia, Africa, and particularly Latin America who advocate the appropriation of a structuralist approach in which underdevelopment is to be seen not as a temporary or even long-term situation of backwardness or as a stage of development prior to industrialization and modernization, but as the historical product of the economic, political, and cultural dependence of some countries upon others and the exploitation of that unequal relationship to the detriment of the weaker partners. C. I. Itty summarizes the criticisms of these liberation Christians as follows:

> They have found convincing evidence from
> economic analysis that the poverty, in-
> equality and injustice prevalent in [the
> Third World] are the direct consequence
> of domination by foreign imperialism and
> of oppression by internal oligarchies.
> They see in the project approach of the
> churches similar pre-suppositions and
> consequences to those in the UN's ap-

proach and the 'Alliance for Progress'
of the US government: at best intended to alleviate the symptoms of poverty in certain local areas and at worst
aimed at enriching the already rich, in
both cases these preserve the status
quo and prevent the urgently needed revolutionary structural change. By no
means [is] such thinking confined to
Latin America. A great many thinkers
in the rest of the Third World as well
as in the rich countries, including the
socialist countries, share similar convictions.[23]

Jose Miguez Bonino similarly differentiates this approach from others which have influenced ecumenical
thought and practice in regard to problems of poverty
and underdevelopment and identifies the fundamental
difference in terms of divergent underlying perceptions
of world realities. What is the distinctive point of
departure for a liberation perspective, he argues, is
the view taken that

Development and underdevelopment are
not two independent realities, nor two
stages in a continuum but two mutually
related processes: Latin American underdevelopment is the dark side of
Northern development; Northern development is built on Third World underdevelopment.[24]

Furthermore, in characterizing the dividing line for
liberationists, he emphasizes that

The basic categories for understanding
our history are not development and
underdevelopment but domination and
dependence. _This_ _is_ _the_ _crux_ _of_ _the_
matter.[25]

According to this liberation perspective, authentic
development, judged both in terms of the economic well-
being of the poorest members of a society and in terms
of the capacitation of the marginalized as active participants in decision-making processes, becomes historically possible only when the patterns of dependence and
domination have been successfully challenged. What is

required by this challenge is a political confrontation
with those who resist changes in the status quo toward
greater egalitarianism and also a persistent struggle
to construct a new kind of society which minimizes political and economic exploitation. In Latin America and
elsewhere, this struggle has taken form as a movement
toward establishing a socialist alternative to the capitalist system which, in its global expansion, has created and perpetuated the dependence of poor nations on
the rich and thereby prevented their autonomous and
self-reliant development.

In an exercise of cultural autonomy in redefining
their situation on their own terms, liberation Christians also contend that the term development or "developmentalism" has necessarily acquired pejorative connotations for those who insist that only the radical
transformation of the existing political and economic
framework and not merely reforms or adjustments within
the social order will allow for true development to take
place. Gustavo Gutierrez argues the case for the necessity of a liberation perspective in this manner:

>Development must attack the root causes
>of the problems and among them the deep-
>est is economic, social, political and
>cultural dependence of some countries
>upon others--an expression of the domina-
>tion of some social classes over others.
>Attempts to bring about changes within
>the existing order have proven futile.
>. . . Only a radical break from the sta-
>tus quo, that is, a profound transforma-
>tion of the private property system, ac-
>cess to power of the exploited class,
>and a social revolution that would break
>this dependence would allow for the
>change to a new society, a socialist
>society--or at least allow that such a
>society might be possible.
>
>In this light, to speak about the pro-
>cess of liberation begins to appear
>more appropriate and richer in human
>content. Liberation in fact expresses
>the inescapable moment of radical change
>which is foreign to the ordinary use of
>the term development. Only in the con-
>text of such a process can a policy of

development be effectively implemented, have any real meaning, and avoid misleading formulations.[26]

Gutierrez' argument, however, that a liberation perspective is more adequate, "more appropriate and richer" for discerning the fundamental issues at stake in global development than that offered by prevailing liberal theories of economic development and modernization, has by no means received universal acceptance within the ecumenical movement. We shall turn now to see why that is the case, first, by examining the emergence of ideological tensions within the World Council of Churches, and then by reviewing a similar debate and split within Roman Catholicism.

II. The Surfacing of Ideological Tensions Within the World Council of Churches

At the Nairobi assembly of the World Council of Churches in 1975, delegates issued the following declaration of sentiment as they gave their report on global economic development:

> Since the Uppsala Assembly [in 1968], churches in all parts of the world have taken many initiatives to participate in the development process. . . . And yet today, more than ever before, we find it difficult to articulate our understanding of the development concept and consequently to decide on the patterns of particpation in the development process. . . . We find ourselves caught in a pensive mood, raising many questions and finding few answers.[27]

This "pensive mood," coupled with the noticeable absence of any Christian triumphalism with respect to issues of world poverty and underdevelopment, certainly differentiates the tenor of more recent discussions of the World Council from those dating at the beginning of the 1960's.

Throughout the report of the 1961 World Council assembly at New Delhi, for example, there is a consistently unambivalent optimism about the possibilities of mounting world cooperation for economic development. While the delegates did not deny that many were fearful of the prospect of "rapid technological and social change" throughout the world, which they identified as the characteristic dynamic of "this revolutionary age [which] confronts Christians and churches, indeed all people and nations, with urgent opportunities and challenges to serve,"[28] they were, nonetheless, confident about an underlying harmony of interests between developed and underdeveloped nations and about the mutual benefits to be gained on all sides from two distinct revolutionary processes currently underway. On the one hand, the advanced industrialized nations were experiencing a technological revolution which was fraught with certain dangers but, more importantly, had the potential of providing means to satisfy the material needs of all humanity through the application of modern scientific knowledge. The developing nations, on the other hand, were undergoing rapid transformation of their social, political, and economic institutions under the impact of modernization and industrialization and were experiencing a social revolution of "rising expectations" about the prospects of significantly higher rates of economic growth and the eradication of widespread poverty in their countries. Of primary concern to those who attended the New Delhi Assembly was the question of how Third World countries, with their status of newly independent nation-states, would be able to achieve, peacefully and in a relatively brief span of time, the level of economic growth and industrialization that the "Western" nations had accomplished over the course of several centuries. What elicited particular enthusiasm at this Assembly was the call for a world strategy of development by which the transfer of capital and technology from the rich nations would enable the poor nations to attain self-sustaining growth economies and, thereby, enter on more equal footing into the network of modern nations in an increasingly interdependent global community. The task for the churches was to exercise moral leadership in promoting education for citizenship in this newly emerging world civilization and "to champion the cause of making the riches of developed countries available to those poor in resources."[29]

Along with its equation of development as a positive, evolutionary process of social change toward modernization with the affluent nations as the model for the Third World, the New Delhi report also identifies governments and international agencies as the primary agents of change and calls upon them to advocate increased foreign aid to developing countries and even

66

more to promote their progressive integration in the world market. "In the long run," the report concludes, "trade, not aid, is the most effective instrument in furthering development."[30] According to this perspective, the problem of underdevelopment is to be solved by supplying missing resources, primarily modern technology, to those areas of the globe where economic growth has lagged behind. The proposed strategy for effecting change is so overwhelmingly resource-oriented rather than structure-oriented, however, that "unpalatable issues of unequal control of economic and political power, and unjust relationships emanating from it, were overlooked."[31] Instead, delegates at New Delhi were offering what may be described as a "technocratic" understanding of social change, which Julio de Santa Ana has characterized as synonymous with developmentalism:

> . . . this is a process which excludes the importance of the political aspect and the participation of the people, instead entrusting to a group of technicians the task of determining the future economic structure within any given stiuation, which in general is to the benefit of those who own the means of production. . . . It is the technicians who are charged with the responsibility for rationalization which must be applied in keeping with the demands of the modernization needed in the transition from 'traditional society' to 'modern and industrialized society,' characterized by secularization. The demands of the political sector carry little or no weight within such a system. This is what has characterized the action of the 'developmentalists' in Latin America: their failure to denounce the internal and external domination exercised by the power groups over Latin American peoples. . . . Development for 'developmentalists' means improving the system but not changing it.[32]

Although it is not difficult to demonstrate the compatability of the viewpoint represented by the New Delhi report with that of dominant social scientific theories of development as modernization, the question

67

remains why this perspective would be particularly attractive to participants in an ecumenical forum to discuss issues of global poverty. Members of the Commission on Church and Society in Latin America (ISAL) have offered one possible interpretation:

> The 'success' of developmentalism can be explained from many different points of view, among which stands out its proposal to bring about a social change toward modernization (opulent Western, consumer-oriented society), saying that this is a process from which violence has been removed. . . . Non-violence is an attractive option for Christians.[33]

Indeed, at New Helhi there were few voices from the Third World to question the prevailing assumption that development is a progressive, peaceful, and evolutionary process of gradual reforms and adjustments or to raise doubts about the "goodwill and generosity" of the affluent nations toward the developing countries. Instead, the report offers a vision of "development without tears" or social dislocations, speaks of "a matter of gratification that many of the more advanced nations have sought to aid the progress of the economically less developed countries," and finds no evidence to the contrary that nations are joining together to "collaborate for the creation of wealth for their common welfare."[34] Moreover, as Arend van Leeuwen contends, this prognosis of peaceful and orderly social change, susceptible to rationally controlled planning "from above" and carefully orchestrated engineering, fits quite neatly with what he identifies as the pervasive "ecumenical ethos" of the World Council of Churches, namely,

> . . . the long and deeply ingrained Anglo-Saxon tradition of thinking in terms of harmony, equilibrium, balance, integration and cooperation, responsible rationality, and evolutionary change . . . the backbone of the ecumenical movement to the present day. . . .[35]

A second and no less compelling reason for the attractiveness of the development-as-modernization perspective is that "developmentalism . . . proposes a sort of change that will 'allow things to continue the

way they are.'"[36] As Richard Dickinson has pointed out,
the World Council's deliberations were influenced, to a
great extent, during this period by a capitalist approach to economic issues which assumed that the path
to development for the poor nations was necessarily the
same as that of the wealthy North Atlantic nations and
that the dynamics of an international "free market,"
once adjusted to incorporate the developing countries
more fully as partners in trade and industrial expansion, would operate on its own accord to generate prosperity for all parties.[37] That the New Delhi participants managed to keep safely within a neo-liberal ideological framework is evident both by their willingness
to locate the problem of poverty in the "backwardness"
of underdeveloped nations and by their reluctance to
draw connections between the wealth and privilege of the
affluent North and the poverty and misery of the South.
The limitations of this perspective, particularly on
these two counts, were soon identified, however, at the
1966 World Church and Society Conference in Geneva.

The Geneva conference is significant not only for
its theme, "Christians in the Technical and Social Revolutions of Our Time," but also for the composition of
its participants. For the first time at such an ecumenical meeting, lay delegates outnumbered professional
theologians and members of the clergy, and perhaps more
importantly, there was more representative participation
by Christians from Asia, Africa, and Latin America.
Robert McAfee Brown has summarized the import of this
fact for subsequent ecumenical debates on global development in this way:

> . . . Third World Christians were fi-
> nally granted a major platform. They
> used it well. It soon became apparent
> that the 'cold war' mentality (sugges-
> ting that the struggle was east vs.
> west, Russia vs. the United States, com-
> munism vs. capitalism) was being re-
> placed by recognition that the real
> struggle was north vs. south, rich vs.
> poor, white vs. colored. The 'social
> revolutions of our time' would be be-
> tween northern rich white nations and
> southern poor colored nations. The
> former have a minority of the popula-
> tion but most of the wealth and power,
> and division of the world's resources

was no longer going to be accepted with equanimity by the impoverished majority.[38]

Furthermore, while New Delhi upheld a rather irenic view of development as a process of modernization dependent upon the goodwill and generosity of the affluent nations to "bring development to" the Third World, at Geneva the counterargument was made that development is better seen as a conflictual and revolutionary process which the poor undertake on their own behalf to effect a radical transformation of political and economic structures of oppression and injustice, internal and external, which "hinder the progress of the people and seem to reinforce their poverty." From this perspective, the fundamental challenge before the churches is political, to engage actively in this revolutionary struggle, since, as Julio de Santa Ana explains the rationality of a liberation perspective,

> . . . if change means change of the system, this demands political options and not merely technical recommendations. The latter are of course necessary, but their implementation depends on the exercise of power.[39]

Among the voices at Geneva which spoke pointedly about the necessity of altering political and economic dynamics between rich and poor nations, 'Boga Ige, a Nigerian lawyer, presented this challenge at a plenary session concerned with "the political and economic dynamics of new nations":

> There can be no peace in the world where two-thirds of mankind [sic] are patronizingly referred to as 'the poor,' 'the underdeveloped,' 'the third world,' and now 'the newly awakened peoples.' There can be no peace in the world where 75 nations have their economic (and therefore their political) future dictated by the narrow self-interest of Europe and America. There can be no peace where the Soviet Union and the United States arrogate to themselves the monopoly of directing the future of the world and of other na-

tions. And there can be no peace
as long as there is any colony in
the world, and as long as neo-
colonialism remains more vicious
than its parent--colonialism.[40]

The perception that the struggle against neo-colonialism
will be more difficult and more protracted than the
struggle for political independence follows upon the
realization gained during the first Decade of Development that economic power, in terms of wealth and technology, is concentrated in the hands of a minority of
nations who control both world trade and the distribution of capital for their own interests and who, thereby, structurally impede the possibility of emerging nations to design their own development according to their
internal needs. Ige acknowledged that "this minority
no longer holds visible, unfettered political power,"
but nonetheless, "the unseen powers of wealth and technology are more potent, more subtle, and more dangerous
than naked political power."[41]

The official report of the Geneva conference describes the plenary session at which Ige characterized
global realities in terms of the dynamics of neocolonialism as "one of the most controversial of the Conference."[42] There is no detailed record of the subsequent
debate nor precise indications of how perceptions were
altered by such presentations from Third World participants, but a recurring note that runs throughout the
final reports of the various working sections is that
"profound changes in the present structures of world
economic relations, including world trade and the transfer of capital" are needed if authentic development is
to occur in the emerging nation-states of the South.[43]
Furthermore, although delegates emphasized the desirability of more rapid economic growth to occur in lower-
income countries, they also carefully qualified their
endorsement of proposed plans to accelerate productivity and international trade by recommending a specific standard of judgment for any such changes: "Christians must insist that priority be given to the needs
of the poorest sections of society, and above all to
those of the developing world."[44] A final indication
that participants heard the challenge of Ige's remarks
is found in moments of self-critical awareness about the
moral responsibility to act, as this passage suggests:

All our fine phrases about 'human

71

solidarity,' 'one world,' etc. sound
hollow in the face of increasing international inequalitites. If contemporary economic and social policies are failing to arrest this tendency, they must be radically altered.
It is not enough to say that the world
cannot continue to live half developed
and half underdeveloped: this situation must not be allowed to continue.[45]

Throughout the conference reports a moral consensus is
reiterated that awareness of existing inequities must
be complemented by efforts to arrive at effective strategies to dissipate such disparities in wealth and power.

In addressing specific problems internal to developing countries, the delegates asserted that "no generally valid over-all prescription can be given for the
ways in which changes in the organization of political
and economic power . . . should occur."[46] They did not
exclude the possibility, however, that revolutionary
means may be necessary in some situations to transform
unjust power relationships. They acknowledged that even
though there is urgent need in Third World nations for
rapid changes, particularly "in the structure of property, income, investment, expenditure, education, and
political and administrative organizations,"[47] the fact
of the matter is that such changes are frequently resisted by elites "who rule at the expense of the welfare
of the majority." Therefore, the report offers this
generalization:

. . . in cases where such changes are
needed, the use by Christians of revolutionary methods--by which is meant
violent overthrow of an existing political order--cannot be excluded a priori.
For in such cases, it may well be that
the use of violent methods is the only
recourse of those who wish to avoid
prolongation of the vast covert violence which the existing order involves.[48]

Concerning the problems of reducing the vulnerabilities of poorer nations to the economic power of the advanced industrialized nations, the delegates also de-
clined to offer a resolution to the debate about whether

72

the involvements of the affluent nations in the Third
World are beneficial or whether their presence "ought to
be curtailed as much as possible" in order to allow developing nations "to give priority to self-reliance and
to increased cooperation among themselves."[49] While
there is a firm rejection of the use of "'Third World'
nations as instruments of Cold War politics," as, for
example, in Vietnam and Korea,[50] the report does not
then go on to present any alternative proposals for reordering the global political economy but instead offers
only guidelines for enabling international cooperation:

> One is that if, as is to be expected,
> the developed nations do continue to
> be substantially involved in the af-
> fairs of the developing nations, their
> involvement should be shaped as much
> as possible by concern for the promo-
> tion of the welfare of peoples in the
> 'Third World.' A second is that, in
> shaping policies . . ., the developed
> nations should consistently give care-
> ful attention to the views of people
> in these areas.[51]

There are additional recommendations in the report for
countering the dependence of underdeveloped nations,
which include increasing the quantity of aid and transfer of technology, improving the quality of development
assistance by replacing loans with grants and easing
the terms of debt repayment, establishing more equitable trade agreements, and promoting efforts through
the United Nations for the adoption of a World Economic
Plan.[52] The report also urges churches to "minister
more helpfully to their many members who are in advisory
and decision-making positions in economic affairs"[53] at
various levels in order to elicit their interest in and
support of more just economic development throughout the
world.

Although there are indications from the Geneva conference that the World Council was receptive to recast-
ing the problem of underdevelopment in terms of the dependency of the Third World upon the affluent North and
that concessions were made about the need for radical,
even revolutionary changes to take place within and
among nations, there is also countervailing evidence
from subsequent meetings and discussions that the Protestant churches have only modified but have not aban-

doned their original developmentalist position, much
less adopted a liberation perspective on issues of global economic justice. Even at Geneva, while the report
recognizes the need for organizing people's movements
for liberation and self-reliance at the grassroots level, the specific recommendations for strategy and for
the churches' own involvements give more emphasis to
persuading those in powerful positions to enlist in a
cooperative venture for promoting development on a global scale. As Samuel Parmar notes,

> . . . the focus was on canvassing the
> goodwill of decision-makers. It was
> hoped, rather optimistically, and
> certainly against the evidence of his-
> tory, that through well-reasoned argu-
> ments and responsible dialogue, deci-
> sion-makers (in both rich and poor coun-
> tries) . . . could be persuaded to use
> their power for structural change. In
> effect, they would voluntarily and
> without social dislocation, share power
> with the powerless. The 'enlightened
> self-interest' argument was relied upon
> to convince decision-makers that 'pover-
> ty anywhere is a threat to prosperity
> everywhere.'[54]

A similar strategic approach was also advocated at
the 1968 Beirut conference on "World Development: Challenge to the Churches," sponsored jointly by the Vatican
Commission of Peace and Justice and the World Council of
Churches. Participants self-consciously avoided what
they understood to be an unnecessary "politicizing" of
economic issues, as exemplified at Geneva, and instead
reverted to a full-fledged developmentalist position,
in that development issues were addressed in terms of
the need to accelerate modernization and industrialization in Third World countries and, above all, in terms
of the technical problems of stimulating higher rates
of economic growth. The political problem of confronting neocolonial exploitation was simply by-passed, if
not ignored, for the Beirut report argues that the major "obstacles to development are to be found within
the structures and attitudes of these countries themselves,"[55] that is, within the backwardness of underdeveloped countries and not within the dynamics of the
present world economic order. Furthermore, the report
reasserts the view that

In promoting economic and social development through their activities
and influence, the churches must rely
on qualified experts regarding specific programs.[56]

Even more to the point, churches were called upon to
limit themselves to taking on "the tasks of education
and information on a continuing basis" and to carrying
the banner high that "it is essential to avoid a division between the developed and developing world."[57]

At the 1968 Uppsala assembly of the World Council,
the ideological tensions which had first surfaced at the
Geneva and Beirut conferences between liberationists and
developmentalists reappeared but were, nonetheless, left
unresolved. In responding to the findings at Geneva,
the Uppsala report on "World Economic and Social Development" conceded, first of all, that the United Nations'
first Decade of Development had, in fact, been a "decade
of disillusionment." The historical evidence gathered
was too overwhelming to be able to deny that economic
inequality between rich and poor nations had successfully resisted substantial alterations in patterns of aid
and trade which could have benefitted the "two-third
world," and that a return to neo-isolationism was apparent in many advanced industrialized countries.[58]
Along with the liberationists, the report also acknowledged the need for revolutionary changes in developing
countries, most especially

. . . where ruling groups are oppressive
or indifferent to the aspirations of the
people, are often supported by foreign
interests, and seek to resist all changes
by the use of coercive or violent measures,

and spoke of the responsibility before the churches "to
participate creatively in the building of political institutions to implement the social changes that are
desperately needed."[59] In a final move leftward, the
delegates also admitted the inadequacies of earlier approaches to the problem of underdevelopment in which
the need for structural changes had been underestimated:

Both developed and developing nations
entered international cooperation
with wrong presuppositions. They as-

75

sumed that a mere transfer of capital and techniques would automatically generate self-sustained growth.
But effective world development requires radical changes in institutions
and structures at three levels: within
developing countries, within developed
countries, and in the international
economy. Precisely because such structural changes have not been promoted,
we find that as a community of nations
we are unable to do the good we would
and efforts for international cooperation tend to be paralyzed.[60]

Despite its own call for structural change, however, the Uppsala Assembly proposed reforms which remained essentially economical (e.g., increase of development aid from rich nations) and educational (e.g.,
programs to educate church members about the realities
of global poverty). Even more significantly, the delegates balked at moving beyond denunciation of existing
inequalities and injustices of the global scene toward
assuming a political, and therefore partisan, stance
by calling upon Christians to engage themselves in those
revolutionary changes of structures which they accepted
as necessary. As Beatriz Couch has observed from a liberationist's perspective, the World Council at this
point "had not yet cut its moorings from liberal idealism" or found itself willing to "advocate a political
rupture with the sources of oppression."[61] Although
somewhat critical of the dominant tradition of developmentalist thinking, the report specifically questioned
the validity of the claims made at Geneva that the rich
nations were, in fact, thwarting rather than making development possible in the Third World and that the present world economic order necessarily perpetuates the
dependency and poverty of underdeveloped countries. Instead of identifying politically with the poor countries
in challenging the external domination of their economies as well as their internal oppression by oligarchic
elites, the delegates advocated, as an alternative, a
supra-national and non-ideological approach to global
development. Once again, the welfare of the South was
linked politically and economically to the willingness
of the affluent North to promote "collective international action to improve conditions conducive to development," through such measures as the creation of "supra-national structures" to plan regional and world eco-

76

nomic patterns of production and trade, the establishment of an international taxation system to provide development funding, and the further regulation of multi-
lateral aid programs.[62] The Uppsala report, furthermore, reiterated the conclusion reached at both New Delhi and at Beirut that

> The most hopeful way of reducing eco-
> nomic injustice peacefully is to clari-
> fy the large areas of common interest
> of developed and developing nations in
> expanding their cooperation.[63]

As Trutz Rentdorff has suggested, the Uppsala Assembly chose to respond to the liberationists' critique
of neocolonial imperialism by signalling a "withdrawal
of the problem of revolution in favor of the problem of
development."[64] Although there was some recognition
that radical changes may be necessary internally to allow the poor nations to move toward autonomous development, what characterizes this report most accurately is
its pervasive reluctance to question the adequacy of
an ecumenical philosophy based on a presumed harmony of
interests and goals among classes and nations and a
similar unwillingness to find fault with an approach to
development based on world cooperation. With this frame
of reference unaltered in any significant way, the
churches continued to address their moral claims to the
advanced industrialized nations, to urge them to make
world development "a moral and political priority of our
times," and, in particular, to call upon them to "shed
all tendencies to exploit economically or to dominate
the poorer, and therefore weaker, economies of other
nations."[65]

In his review of ecumenical debates over global development, Arend van Leeuwen has argued that the fundamental weakness of this kind of development philosophy
is that

> . . . it deals with the economic
> issues of world development with-
> out the political context of in-
> ternational power relations. The
> result is a sympathetic Christian
> idealism, based on lofty moral
> principles and full of valuable
> recommendations, which derives its
> concrete significance from the ex-

> cellent advices of experts on inter-
> national economic policy-making.
> But it is a humanism which hardly
> touches the hard facts of a revolu-
> tionary world. . . .[66]

Delegates at the Fifth Assembly of the World Council of
Churches at Nairobi in 1975 indicated their concurrence
with this criticism by acknowledging that

> The struggle against oppression and
> injustice inevitably necessitates
> confrontations with power and the
> handling of power. Churches have,
> in the past, underestimated the di-
> mensions of these aspects even when
> they have marginally recognized
> them.[67]

Because they also acknowledged the structural roots of
injustice and called upon the churches to lend support
for grassroots movements for liberation in the Third
World, Robert McAfee Brown finds that the Nairobi participants were pushing the World Council "within hailing
distance of the concerns of liberation theology."[68]
This may well be the case, but the ultimate proof for a
shift to a liberation stance is not in what Hugo Assmann
describes a "a general, verbal drawing near to the theme
of liberation,"[69] but rather in the churches' abandoning
their traditional posture of ideological neutrality or
"political non-interference" and actively immersing in
the political process of liberation alongside the marginalized and dispossessed. A similar conclusion has
been reached by Gustavo Gutierrez, who adds that "It
is in deeds, not simply in affirmations, that we salvage
our understanding of the faith from all forms of idealism."[70]

III. The Debate Within the Roman Catholic Church: Is
      Development or Liberation the "New Name for
      Peace"?

The debate over global economic development within
the Roman Catholic Church has been even more visibly
divisive than the comparable Protestant-based debate,
in large measure because Catholics involved in Third
World liberation movements have so openly challenged
the authority of the teaching magisterium not only in
terms of the adequacy of papal social teaching regarding

development but also in terms of the hierarchy's understanding of the role of the church and the task of theology in the modern world. Because the development debate is, indeed, ecumenical, our expectation is fully warranted that many of the same substantive differences between developmentalists and liberationists appear among Catholics as they do among Protestants. We shall, therefore, examine these differences only briefly in order to attend more closely to the methodological disagreements at hand. After outlining the positions taken by John XXIII, Paul VI, and the Second Vatican Council, we shall then consider the critical responses offered on two separate occasions, at the 1968 Medellin conference of Latin American bishops (CELAM II) and at the 1972 Christians for Socialism conference at Santiago, Chile.

In his social encyclical, Mater et Magistra (1961), John XXIII viewed the differentials in wealth among nations with great alarm as a serious obstacle endangering the possibilities for world peace, but he assumed that the poor nations were only late-starters in the process of modernization and industrialization and would soon be developing their own economies at a faster rate. He located the underlying causes of poverty and hunger in the primitive state of Third World economies, and he encouraged the rich nations to transfer capital and technology in the form of "disinterested aid" to stimulate economic growth in underdeveloped regions. In particular, he stressed the importance of the church's role in promoting the common good and in arousing "a sense of responsibility in individuals and generally, especially among those more blessed with this world's goods."71 Also, because social and economic problems now existed on a global scale and were often beyond the competence of any one nation to resolve, John urged the formation of new forms of international cooperation, a theme he reiterated in his 1963 encyclical, Pacem in Terris, in which he carefully linked peace with justice rather than with the absence of disorder. Once again, he appealed to the economically privileged to aid the development of the poor countries, but he added a warning

> . . . that the wealthier states, in
> providing varied forms of assistance
> to the poorer, should respect the
> moral heritage and ethnic characteris-
> tics peculiar to each, and also that

79

they should avoid any intention of
political domination. If this is
done, 'a precious contribution will
be made toward the formation of a
world community, a community in
which each member, while conscious
of its own individual rights and
duties, will work in a relationship
of equality toward the attainment
of the universal common good.'[72]

One of the significant departures of Pacem in Terris is that, unlike previous papal encyclicals, this
one is addressed not only to the "faithful" within the
church but also to "all men [sic] of good will" who desire peace and justice throughout the world. An even
more significant gain, however, is that John acknowledged the legitimacy of Catholics' collaborating not
only with non-Catholics but also with socialists and
communists in the work of peace. By drawing a distinction between false philosophical teachings "regarding
the nature, origin and destiny of the universe and of
man [sic]" and social movements which are based on
those teachings but are, nonetheless, aimed at appropriate political and economic ends, John allowed the
possibility for Catholics to form political alliances
with those persons whom the church had previously condemned for their atheism. He added an important pro-
viso to this new freedom, however, by claiming the right
of the ecclesiastical authorities to decide when such
alliances were "opportune and useful":

For it must not be forgotten that the
Church has the right and the duty not
only to safeguard the principles of
ethics and religion, but also to intervene authoritatively with her children
in the temporal sphere when there is a
question of judging the application of
those principles to concrete cases.[73]

The conciliar document, Gaudium et Spes, published
in 1965 by the Second Vatican Council as the "Pastoral
Constitution of the Church in the Modern World," not
only issued its own call to the faithful to become active in the construction of a more just world, but also
emphasized the particular obligation before the church
to "scrutinize the signs of the times and . . . interpret them in the light of the gospel."[74] After survey-

ing various characteristics of the contemporary world,
the document speaks most affirmatively of the appearance of a newly gained consciousness about the human
capacity to transform the dehumanizing conditions within which persons live and of the universal quest for
maximizing human freedom and dignity. The Council also
acknowledged a significant shift in the church's own
understanding of its role as teacher and "living example" of Christian faith, by claiming that whatever indifference and even hostility the church had formerly
displayed toward "worldly affairs" had now given way to
a positive valuation of this search for freedom and social progress. Moreover, the Council reached the conclusion that in this modern historical context,

> . . . faith needs to prove its fruit-
> fulness by penetrating the believer's
> entire life, including its worldly
> dimensions, and by activating him [sic]
> toward justice and love, especially re-
> garding the needy. . . . The Church
> sincerely professes that all men [sic],
> believers and unbelievers alike, ought
> to work for the rightful betterment of
> this world in which all alike live.[75]

In declaring the church's "openness to the world"
and eagerness for dialogue on matters of political and
economic concern throughout the globe, the Second Vatican Council at the same time insisted that the church
itself, as a social institution, has no political, economic, or social mission _per se_ but rather a distinctively religious one, to evangelize by preaching the
truth of the gospel and to encourage, inspire, and in-
struct individuals to assume their moral responsibili-
ties as citizens within their various communities. The
argument was made that only by preserving its independence from the political community and not by acting in
the world directly but only through its individual members would the church be able to maintain its own autonomy and ability to speak on behalf of all humanity. The
Council elaborated on this theme by also declaring that

> . . . in virtue of her mission and na-
> ture, she [the church] is bound to no
> particular form of human culture, nor
> to any political, economic, or social
> system. Hence the Church by her very
> universality can be a very close bond

between diverse human communities
and nations, provided these trust
her and truly acknowledge her right
to true freedom in fulfilling her
mission.[76]

After delineating the scope of the church's mission
in the world, the Council then turned to address problems of special urgency, including that of underdevelopment in the Third World. The present trend toward
greater concentration of wealth and power in the hands
of a minority of nations and classes received special
condemnation, along with the perceived excesses of both
laissez-faire capitalism and state socialism. The simple equation of economic development with increased
industrial productivity and economic growth was also
called into question, because

> The fundamental purpose of this pro-
> ductivity must not be the mere multi-
> plication of products. It must not
> be profit or domination. Rather, it
> must be the service of man [sic],
> viewed in terms of his material needs
> and the demands of his intellectual,
> moral, spiritual, and religious life.
> And when we say man [sic], we mean
> every man [sic] whatsoever and every
> group of men [sic], of whatever race
> and from whatever part of the world.
> Consequently, economic activity is to
> be carried out according to its own
> methods and laws but within the limits
> of morality, so that God's plan for
> mankind [sic] can be realized.[77]

The document also stressed the obligation of the more
privileged to aid the poor and the role of the affluent
nations in eradicating immense economic inequalities,
but the Council took a significant stand in affirming
that the right of every person "to have a share of
earthly goods sufficient for oneself and one's family"
takes precedence over the right to own private property
and, furthermore, that "if a person is in extreme necessity, he has the right to take from the riches of
others what he himself needs."[78] However, in making
this claim, the Council did not intend to offer license
for social revolution but rather an additional incentive
to the affluent and powerful to initiate necessary so-

cial and economic reforms to promote authentic development.

Paul VI addressed many of the same concerns in Populorum Progressio which had preoccupied the Vatican Council and his papal predecessor, but by limiting the subject matter of his encyclical to global development, he was able to offer a more systematic treatment and also emphasize the continued importance of the issue. Paul also spoke of the aspirations of Third World peoples to overcome conditions of poverty and oppression as an unmistakable "sign of the times," indicative of what he understood to be a universal desire for the "fullness of authentic development," that is, "a development which is for each and all the transition from less human conditions to those which are more human." No less dissatisfied with narrowly economistic definitions, he identified development as the search for self-fulfillment and human dignity as well as for economic well-being, but he also claimed it as a fundamental human right taking precedence over both "those of property and free commerce." Furthermore, Paul insisted that unless the possibility of integral development for each person and all peoples was actualized, there could be no lasting peace in the world. Therefore, in a phrase made famous by this encyclical, Paul concluded that "development is the new name for peace."[79]

In surveying the contemporary world division between rich and poor nations and the obstacles to economic development within the Third World, Paul conceded that deep-seated changes were necessary to allow for a more equitable division and distribution of the benefits of economic prosperity now enjoyed by a privileged few. Within underdeveloped countries, for example, he argued that the "common good" may demand the expropriation of landed estates to make resources available to the general population, for "private property does not constitute for anyone an absolute and unconditioned right" and public authorities may intervene to alter existing property relationships in order to provide for the welfare of the poorer members of society. Paragraph 31 of the encyclical even allows the possibility of using "revolutionary means" to restore conditions of social justice in extreme circumstances.[80]

Paul's most vehement criticisms of modern economic arrangements, however, were aimed at the distortions in the capitalist world economy which perpetuate economic dependence among developing nations who "remain ever poor while the rich ones become still richer."[81] An international system of exchange has been constructed, the pope argued,

> . . . which considers profit as the key motive for economic progress, competition as the supreme law of economics, and private ownership of the means of production as an absolute right that has no limits and carries no corresponding social obligation. This unchecked liberalism leads to dictatorship . . . producing 'the international imperialism of money.' One cannot condemn such abuses too strongly by solemnly recalling once again that the economy is at the service of man [sic].[82]

To correct what he called the "imbalances" in world trade and to enable the developing countries to establish self-generating economies, Paul made a variety of proposals. The advanced industrialized countries were to contribute proportionate financial resources to Third World countries by sharing their "superfluous wealth"; train teachers, engineers, and technicians to place their expertise at "the disposal of less fortunate peoples"; devise means for more equitable pricing mechanisms for trade in order to create true equality of opportunity; and establish a common fund for world development.[83] Although the moral duty of human solidarity requires that the rich support the poor in such ways, Paul also made his argument in terms of enlightened self-interest:

> . . . the rich will be the first to benefit as a result. Otherwise their continued greed will certainly call down upon them the judgement of God and the wrath of the poor, with consequences no one can foretell.[84]

Paul's hope, however, was that peoples and nations would come to recognize their mutual interests in promoting development for all and, thereby, create a world community through dialogue and cooperation. "The work of development," he contended, "will draw nations together in the attainment of goals pursued with a common effort" if all involved are "inspired by brotherly love and. . .

world solidarity." The church's specific role was to infuse persons with those values through a ministry of evangelization and to offer "men [sic] what she possesses as her characteristic attribute: a global vision of man [sic] and of the human race."[85]

Without a doubt, Paul was more critical of the developmentalist model of global economic development than any of his predecessors, and in his 1971 apostolic letter, Octogesima Adveniens, he approached the problem of envisioning an alternative of the present world economic order:

> . . . as we have often said, the most important duty in the realm of justice is to allow each country to promote its own development, within the framework of a cooperation free from any spirit of domination, whether economic or political. The complexity of the problems raised is certainly great, in the present intertwining of mutual dependencies. Thus it is necessary to have the courage to undertake a revision of the relationships between nations, whether it is a question of the international division of production, the structure of exchanges, the control of profits, the monetary system—without forgetting the actions of human solidarity—to question the models of growth of the rich nations and change people's outlooks, so that they may realize the prior call of international duty, and to renew international organizations so that they may increase in effectiveness.[86]

Paul himself, however, offered no specific alternative to the neo-capitalist economic policies which he criticized so severely. Moreover, he ultimately abstracts the problem of underdevelopment from its political context and downplays the urgency of restructuring political and economic power relationships within Third World countries and the advanced industrialized nations, by speaking instead of effecting social change through "the development of moral consciousness, which will lead man [sic] to exercise a wider solidarity and to open himself freely to others and God." He also spirituali-

zes the notion of liberation in this context, for although he recognizes that

> today men [sic] yearn to free them-
> selves from need and dependence . .
> ., this liberation starts with the
> interior freedom that men [sic] must
> find again with regard to their goods
> and their powers.[87]

There are reasons to conclude, therefore, as
Christine Gudorf has concluded from her own study of
contemporary papal social teachings, that there are
significant limitations presented by papal social teaching on economic development. Gudorf has explained, for
example, that

> . . . Paul noted many aspects of 'de-
> velopment' policy which instead fos-
> tered dependency. He did speak of
> economic systems, institutions and
> models, and acknowledged that modern
> economics works to the disadvantage
> of the poor. But Paul offered no polit-
> ical or economic alternative to the
> capitalist economics he criticizes.
> The absence of any alternative, and the
> papal tradition of relying on evangeli-
> zation to gradually correct injustice,
> have not allowed Paul to abandon the
> dominant development model and begin
> afresh with the dependency model of
> liberation theologians.[88]

Additional evidence in support of this conclusion includes the fact that Paul continued to address his appeals primarily to the rich nations to engage them in
solving the problem of underdevelopment rather than
calling upon the poor and oppressed to organize and free
themselves from political and economic dependency and to
become the artisans of their own development. The problem with this papal strategy is described as follows by
Francois Perroux:

> Never in the course of the history of
> the West have we seen a class or a na-
> tion give up its own wellbeing for the
> benefit of a disadvantaged group. . . .
> Our societies are plutocracies that have

> to come to terms a little with the
> masses and with poor people, and
> they tend to shape technocratic and
> political power to their own inter-
> ests.
>
> This social structure is reflected
> in production methods, in consump-
> tion patterns, and in aid programs
> to developing countries.
>
> It would be culpable optimism to
> expect a conversion of classes and
> nations, say one night on the
> fourth of August.[89]

At the Medellin conference of Latin American bishops in 1968, the limitations of papal social teachings
regarding development and underdevelopment were beginning to be surfaced by those involved in grassroots political and ecclesiastical movements for social transformation throughout Latin America who had discovered
that economic, political, and cultural dependency was
the common condition of their countries and who were
searching for a theology and form of Christian ministry to address that situation. Rather than viewing engagement in movements for social justice as one "moral
duty" among others imposed upon the individual Christian's conscience, they had also discovered that political action aimed at liberation was the unique locus
for a new understanding and way of living the Christian
faith, and further, that

> Doing theology in today's Latin Ameri-
> can context implies living and think-
> ing our faith within and in opposition
> to oppression. That is to say, not
> from a general standpoint, but from the
> standpoint of a particular situation
> and by means of one option.[90]

At Medellin that situation was described as one of oppression, as a situation of internal and external neo-
colonialism, and the option called for was to join the
political struggle of the poor against such injustice
and for the construction of a new social order.

In A Theology of Liberation, Gustavo Gutierrez
briefly summarized some of the differences he perceived

between the perspective of the teaching magisterium and that of the Medellin participants:

> Vatican II speaks of the underdevelopment of peoples, of the developed countries and what they can and should do about this underdevelopment; Medellin tries to deal with the problem from the standpoint of the poor countries, characterizing them as subjected to a new kind of colonialism. Vatcan II talks about a Church in the world and describes the relationship in a way that tends to neutralize the conflicts; Medellin demonstrates that the world in which the Latin American Church ought to be present is in full revolution. Vatican II sketches a general outline for Church renewal; Medellin provides guidelines for a transformation of the Church in terms of its presence on a continent of misery and injustice.[91]

The further departure of great significance at Medellin was to redefine the church's mission "pastorally and theologically," as the documents emphasize, in relation to this process of liberation and to abandon any presumed political or ideological neutrality in favor of immersion into this revolutionary process.

Among the documents issued at the Medellin conference, the one on peace best characterizes the newly-found militancy among politically engaged Christians and details both their altered perceptions about Latin American realities and their search for new forms of the church's presence on the continent. As Hugo Assmann has explained,

> The historical incidence of the language of 'liberation' in the Latin American church is linked to growing awareness of our situation as oppressed peoples. It began to make its presence strongly felt from 1965 onwards, when theories of development were first disclosed in their true neo-capitalist light. Underlying liberation theology is the historical experience of the actual nature of under-development, as

a form of dependence. The notion of
'liberation' is correlative to that
of 'dependence.'[92]

The document on peace signals this shift in understanding by describing Latin American nations as dependent
rather than underdeveloped, as subject to external neo-
colonialism and, therefore,

> . . . dependent on a center of economic
> power around which they gravitate. The
> result is that our nations often are
> not masters of their goods or their own
> economic decisions.[93]

The consequence of this dependence is that "the countries which produce raw materials (particularly those
with one product) remain poor, while the industrialized
countries get richer and richer."[94] There is also the
phenomenon of "internal colonialism" within each country, the control of power and wealth by a small ruling
class which identifies its interests with those of the
metropolitan powers and pins "the label of 'subversive'
on every initiative designed to change the social system that favors the maintenance of their privileges."[95]
This situation of external domination and internal oppression is fundamentally unjust because it denies the
possibility of economic well-being and human dignity
to the majority of the people, and since peace is the
work of justice and not merely the absence of overt
violence,

> Peace will only come about when we cre-
> ate a new order that 'brings greater
> justice among men [sic]' . . .. Peace
> is not there for us; we must construct
> it.[96]

Among the "pastoral conclusions" which appear at
the close of the document, the church's ministry is re-
directed toward efforts to "defend the rights of the
poor·and the oppressed," to "support all the efforts of
the people to create and develop their own grassroots
organizations, to regain and consolidate their rights,"
and to "denounce the unjust action of the great powers
around the world against the self-determination of the
weaker nations."[97] In order to espouse the cause of
the poor effectively, however, the church is called upon
to break its own dependence upon the existing political

and economic structures which offer patronage and special privileges and to become a truly authentic "church
of the poor."

If, as Robert McAfee Brown concludes, the Medellin
conference signalled that "the 'reformism' of Vatican
II is taking a step toward a more 'revolutionary' recognition that structures deaf to the cry for justice may
need to be overthrown,"[98] this shift is attributable,
in part, to the new understanding gained of the Latin
American situation when viewed from the perspective of
a dependency theory of development and underdevelopment.
With its open criticism of developmentalist policies and
declaration of the fundamental injustice of the present
social order, Medellin marked a turning point for those
Christians who argued that "the decade of developmentalism is over and we are now inaugurating the decade of
liberation. Because liberation is the new name of development."[99] An additional consequence of this new
understanding further differentiates the theology of
liberation movement from the papal position on social
change, as Gustavo Gutierrez acknowledges:

> Our new vision, attentive to struc-
> tural factors, will help Christians
> to avoid the fallacy of proposing a
> personal change, detached from con-
> crete conditions, as a necessary pre-
> requisite to any social transforma-
> tion. If any of us remain wedded to
> this fallacy, in the name of some
> hazy humanism or disembodied spiritu-
> alism, we shall only prove to be ac-
> complices in the continuing postpone-
> ment of the radical changes that are
> necessary. Such changes call for
> simultaneous work on both persons and
> structures, since they condition each
> other mutually.[100]

The target of Gutierrez' criticism is the Christian social doctrine characteristic of much of the progressive
Vatican II social teaching which not only "accentuated
the sphere of faith and distinguished it from the plane
of worldly action"[101] but restricted the church's engagement in the world to a task of effecting a spiritual
conversion of individuals to Christian values.

This line of criticism was extended at the Santiago

conference of Christians for Socialism in 1972. The traditional image of the church as somehow positioned "above" social conflicts and possessing a uniquely global vision of humanity which allows it to embrace all persons without taking any particular political stance itself was challenged as politically naive and theologically false. In the Final Document of the convention, the argument was made that the church, if it wishes to contribute effectively to human liberation, must seriously question the ideology

> . . . of the prevailing system [which] imposes a 'spiritualistic' idea of man [sic]. It explains his behavior and history as if they were grounded mainly on moral ideas and attitudes, as if the ills of the world were based solely on ideological or moral deviations of a purely individual cast. Without at all denying the creativity and the moral worth of the individual person, we feel that the prevailing culture diverts attention away from scientific study of the economic and social mechanism which fundamentally govern the movement of history. It conceals the fundamental role of structures in the oppression of individuals and nations. It hides the basic impact of the economic factor, of class relationships in particular, on man's [sic] political, cultural, and religious life. Hence it sloughs off the idea of seeking change through a transformation of the economic system.[102]

For the liberation Christians who assembled at Santiago, the task before the church was to abandon any attempt to remain non-partisan or to preserve the "purity" of faith apart from its historical mediations and instead to participate actively in the struggle of the Latin American poor for freedom.

In its analysis of the problem of underdevelopment throughout the continent, the Final Document concludes that

> The economic and social structures of

> our Latin American countries are
> grounded on oppression and injustice,
> which in turn is a result of our
> capitalist dependence on the great
> power centers,

and that only by constructing a new society that is
qualitatively different from the present unjust order,
namely, a socialist society "without oppressors or oppressed," will "everyone have the same possibilities
for human fulfillment."[103] This new society will not
come about, however, by appealing to the good will of
those in power or by the generosity of the affluent
minority. What is required is a critical socio-economic
theory which discloses the mechanisms of oppression and,
above all, participation in the political struggle to
effect a transformation of the private property system,
to allow participation of the poor and marginalized in
decision-making processes, and to break the dependence
of their economies on foreign interests. In a less
cautious manner than that exhibited at Medellin, the
participants at Santiago explained further that

> Recognition of the class struggle as
> a fundamental fact enables us to arrive
> at an overall interpretation of the
> structures of Latin America. . . .
> Socialism presents itself as the only
> acceptable option for getting beyond
> a class-based society. . . . Only by
> replacing private ownership of the
> means of production do we create ob-
> jective conditions that will allow for
> the elimination of class antagonism.[104]

At the conclusion of the document, the participants
identified that the historical context "for a living
faith today is the history of oppression and of the
struggle for liberation from this oppression."[105] Although not necessarily accustomed to thinking and living
in the world in terms of conflict and confrontation,
Christians who have become engaged in the liberation
struggle now perceive, in Hugo Assmann's phrase, "the
world in conflict." As Phillip E. Berryman suggests,

> This experience of conflict--at first
> glance not a theological theme--is a
> primary datum for liberation theology.
> . . . This separates them from the

92

North Atlantic postconciliar notion
of a reconciliation with the world.
Simply to be reconciled to this world
is to accept complicity in oppression.
When the church comes to take on the
preoccupations of the world, it finds
a divided world, a 'rich world and a
poor world, with opposed interests
because the wealth of one and the
poverty of the other are correlatives.'[106]

Along with this awareness of a world divided by class
interests is a sobering recognition that "the class
struggle is a fact and neutrality in this question is
not possible" and, further, that

In a radically divided world, the
function of the ecclesial community
is to struggle against the profound
causes of the division among men
[sic]. It is only this commitment
that can make of it an authentic sign
of unity. Today, in Latin America
especially, this unity implies the
option for the oppressed; to opt for
them is the honest, resolute way to
combat that which gives rise to this
social division. . . . This perspective is, among other things, changing
the focus of the concerns of ecumen-
ism.[107]

The noticeable shift in focus for liberation Christians is to assert that in the contemporary world situation faith is expressed, above all, as political commitment and historical agency toward liberation from oppression and that the truth claims of Christian theology
must be verified historically. Hugo Assmann has observed that when Christians come to understand faith as
the practice of liberation,

. . . they effectively embody a shift
of the basic reference-point of their
faith, which is no longer a body of
doctrine, or a form of worship (both of
which remains important, but in a com-
plementary role), but the territory oc-
cupied by the historical process of
liberation.[108]

93

Participants at the Santiago conference further identified how this new starting-point for understanding their faith has also led them to a distinctive theological methodology:

> Reflection on the faith ceases to be abstract speculation outside of commitment in history. Revolutionary praxis comes to be recognized as the matrix that will generate a new theological creativity. Thus theological thinking is transformed into critical reflection in and on liberation praxis—in a context of permanent confrontation with the exigencies of the gospel.[109]

The purpose of such theological reflection is not to deduce a "Christian politics" from theological premises or to elaborate principles abstracted from the historical context which are then "applied to" various situations, but rather to engage in an ongoing process, as Osvaldo Luis Mottesi describes,

> . . . [of] critical reflection from within the action itself, upon the action that is provoked and realized because of the commitment. Its purpose is to enrich, perfect, orient and energize the praxis . . . to make more effective the Christian option for the poor, which is expressed by means of a liberating praxis at all levels and in all situations.[110]

What theologians of liberation argue is that among the fundamental methodological differences between this way of doing theology within the context of liberation praxis and the approach taken from within the dominant theological tradition, not the least of these is that liberationists recognize that

> The pastoral activity of the Church does not flow as a conclusion from theological premises. Theology does not produce pastoral activity; rather it reflects upon it.[111]

Furthermore, the differences which exist between the

94

progressive "theology of development" and liberation theology are, first, political and only secondarily theological. Jose Miguez Bonino contends, moreover, that the chasm which exists between these theologies is, in fact, much wider than the ecclesiastical documents tend to suggest and that there are two issues which cause the divide:

> One is the reluctance of Church authorities to admit an ideological option, particularly one related to Marxism. . . . Back of this is the fear of breaking the unity of the Church: a Church which understands itself as the Church of both the conservative and the progressive, the reactionary and the revolutionary, of the right and of the left cannot commit itself ideologically. The other point is the fear of calling the oppressed and exploited to work out their own liberation. This is due to two reasons: the fact that the hierarchies are more closely linked with the dominant classes and tend to address their exhortations to them, and the fear to incite a class struggle which may lead to violence. But these two points are precisely the decisive ones for a revolutionary consciousness. Unless the qualitative leap is taken, we are still moving within the realm of reformism and liberalism.[112]

This same conclusion, that the fundamental theological confrontation today is between progressive developmentalist theology and liberation theology, has been reached not only by Miguez Bonino but by Enrique Dussel, Gustavo Gutierrez, Hugo Assmann, and Beatriz Couch, as well.[113] In the next two chapters, we shall analyze more closely the contours of that confrontation and its significance by examining, first, the attempt by Denis Goulet to construct an "ethics of development" in relation to liberation theology. As we shall discover, although Goulet is highly critical of what the Latin Americans have labelled as "developmentalism," his own sensibilities remain much closer to those represented by the Second Vatican Council than to those of the libera-

95

tion theologians with whom he assumes affinity. As we highlight several problematic aspects of his ethical methodology, we shall question whether he has, in fact, escaped the limitations of ethical idealism as he intends. In the fourth chapter, we shall return to an analysis of selected liberation theologians and consider the grounds upon which Goulet's own implicit criticism of liberation theology might be sufficiently answered.

NOTES

1. C. I. Itty, Introduction to To Set at Liberty the Oppressed, by Richard D. H. Dickinson (Geneva: World Council of Churches, 1975), p. viii.

2. Samuel L. Parmar, "Issues in the Development Debate," in Dickinson, p. 165. My emphasis.

3. Gustavo Gutierrez, "Liberation Praxis and Christian Faith," in Frontiers of Theology in Latin America, ed. Rosino Gibellini (Maryknoll: Orbis Books, 1979), p. 22.

4. Rene Laurentin, Liberation, Development and Salvation, trans. Charles Underhill Quinn (Maryknoll: Orbis Books, 1972), p. 18.

5. Ibid., p. 26.

6. Mater et Magistra, para. 157, in The Gospel of Peace and Justice: Catholic Social Teaching Since Pope John (Maryknoll: Orbis Books, 1976). Subsequent citations from papal social teaching are from this source.

7. W. A. Visser't Hooft, ed., The New Delhi Report (Association Press, 1962), esp. pp. 94-99.

8. C. I. Itty, "Are We Yet Awake? The Development Debate Within the Ecumenical Movement," The Ecumenical Review (January 1974), p. 6.

9. Ibid.

10. Alistair Kee, ed., A Reader in Political Theology (Philadelphia: The Westminster Press, 1974), p. 69.

11. Robert McAfee Brown, "From Detroit to Nairobi and Beyond," Radical Religion, Vol. 2 (1976), p. 45.

12. Itty, "Are We Yet Awake?," p. 6.

13. Populorum Progressio, para. 14.

14. Ibid., para. 20 and 21.

15. Norman Goodall, ed., The Uppsala Report 1968 (Geneva: World Council of Churches, 1968), p. 49.

16. M. M. Thomas, quoted in Itty, "Are We Yet Awake?," p. 10.

17. Charles Elliott, "An Esoteric Critique of Cartigny," in In Search of a Theology of Development (Geneva: Committee on Society, Development and Peace, 1969), p. 21.

18. S. L. Parmar, "Goals and Process of Development and Objectives of Development Projects," in Fetters of Injustice, ed. Pamela H. Gruber (Geneva: World Council of Churches, 1970), p. 43.

19. Ibid., p. 42. My emphasis.

20. Marie Augusta Neal, A Socio-Theology of Letting Go: The Role of a First World Church Facing Third World Peoples (New York: Paulist Press, 1977), p. 63.

21. Samuel Parmar, "Some Thoughts on Strategy," Risk, Vol. 3 (1967), p. 112.

22. David M. Paton, ed., Breaking Barriers: Nairobi 1975 (Grand Rapids: William B. Eerdmans, 1976), p. 123.

23. Itty, pp. 12-13.

24. Jose Miguez Bonino, Doing Theology in a Revolutionary Situation (Philadelphia: Fortress Press, copyright (c) 1975), p. 16. Used by permission of Fortress Press.

25. `Ibid., My emphasis.

26. Gustavo Gutierrez, A Theology of Liberation, trans. and ed. by Sister Caridad Inda and John Eagleson (Maryknoll: Orbis Books, 1973), pp. 26-27.

27. Paton, pp. 121-122.

28. Visser't Hooft, p. 94.

29. Ibid., p. 107.

30. Ibid., p. 275.

31. Parmar in Dickinson, p. 166.

32. Julio de Santa Ana, "What Development Demands: A Latin American Position," in Dickinson, pp. 141-143.

33. ISAL (Commission on Church and Society in Latin America), "Christians, Churches and Development," Risk, Vol. 5 (1969), p. 44.

34. Visser't Hooft, p. 275.

35. Arend Theodoor van Leeuwen, Development Through Revolution (New York: Charles Scribner's Sons, 1970), p. 108.

36. ISAL, p. 44.

37. Dickinson, pp. 61ff.

38. Robert McAfee Brown, Theology in a New Key: Responding to Liberation Themes (Philadelphia: The Westminster Press, 1978), pp. 39-40.

39. Santa Ana in Dickinson, pp. 142 and 143.

40. M. M. Thomas and Paul Abrecht, eds., World Conference on Church and Society: Christians in the Technical and Social Revolutions of our Time (Geneva: World Council of Churches, 1967), p. 18.

41. Ibid.

42. Ibid., p. 16.

43. Ibid., p. 91.

44. Ibid., p. 60.

45. Ibid., p. 80.

46. Ibid., p. 142.

47. Ibid., p. 66.

48. Ibid., p. 143.

49. Ibid., p. 142.

50. Ibid., p. 140.

51. Ibid., p. 142.

52. Ibid., pp. 84, 138, and 86.

53. Ibid., p. 87.

54. Parmar in Dickinson, p. 176.

55. World Development: The Challenge to the Churches (Geneva: Exploratory Commission on Society, Development and Peace, 1968), p. 24.

56. Ibid., p. 27.

57. Ibid., p. 49.

58. Goodall, p. 46.

59. Ibid., p. 48.

60. Ibid., p. 46.

61. Beatriz Melano Couch, "New Visions of the Church in Latin America: A Protestant View," in The Emergent Gospel: Theology from the Underside of History, eds. Sergio Torres and Virginia Fabella (Maryknoll: Orbis Books, 1978), p. 204.

62. Goodall, pp. 48-49.

63. Ibid., p. 67.

64. Trutz Rentdorff, "A Theology of Development?," in In Search of a Theology of Development, p. 206.

65. Goodall, p. 48.

66. van Leeuwen, p. 112.

67. Paton, p. 136.

68. Brown, Theology in a New Key, p. 48.

69. Hugo Assmann, Theology for a Nomad Church, trans. Paul Burns (Maryknoll: Orbis Books, 1976), p. 134.

70. Gustavo Gutierrez, "Liberation Praxis and Christian Faith," p. 22.

71. Mater et Magistra, para. 163, 171-174, and 158.

72.   *Pacem in Terris*, para. 125.

73.   Ibid., para. 159 and 160.

74.   *Gaudium et Spes*, para. 4.

75.   Ibid., para. 21.

76.   Ibid., para. 42; cf. para. 76.

77.   Ibid., para. 64.

78.   Ibid., para. 69.

79.   *Populorum Progressio*, para. 20, 22, and 76.

80.   Ibid., para. 23, 24, and 31.

81.   Ibid., para. 57.

82.   Ibid., para. 26.

83.   Ibid., para. 48, 49, 61, and 51.

84.   Ibid., para. 49.

85.   Ibid., para. 73 and 13.

86.   *Octogesima Adveniens*, para. 43.

87.   Ibid., para. 41 and 45.

88.   Christine E. Gudorf, "Contested Issues in Twentieth Century
      Papal Teaching: The Position of the Vatican in Light of Chal-
      lenges from Liberation Theology" (Ph.D. dissertation, Columbia
      University, 1979), p. 185. Cf. Christine E. Gudorf, *Catholic
      Social Teaching on Liberation Themes* (University Press of
      America, 1980).

89.   Francois Perroux, quoted in Laurentin, pp. 112-113.

90.   Osvaldo Luis MOttesi, "Doing Theology in the Latin American
      Context," *Church and Society*, Vol. 68 (January-February 1978),
      p. 9.

91.   Gutierrez, *A Theology of Liberation*, p. 134.

92.   Assmann, p. 37.

93. Medellin Document on Peace, in Between Honesty and Hope, is-
    sued by the Peruvian Bishops' Commission for Social Action
    and trans. by John Drury (Maryknoll: Maryknoll Publications,
    1969), p. 203.

94. Ibid.

95. Ibid., p. 202.

96. Ibid., p. 205.

97. Ibid., pp. 208-209.

98. Brown, Theology in a New Key, p. 55.

99. Quoted in Miguez Bonino, Doing Theology, p. 21.

100. Gustavo Gutierrez, Introduction to Between Honesty and Hope,
     pp. xvi-xvii.

101. Gustavo Gutierrez, "Freedom and Salvation: A Political Prob-
     lem," trans. Alvin Gutierrez, in Gustavo Gutierrez and Rich-
     ard Shaull, Liberation and Change, ed. by Ronald H. Stone
     (Atlanta: John Knox Press, 1977), p. 74.

102. "Final Document of the Convention," in Christians and Social-
     ism: Documentation of the Christians for Socialism Movement
     in Latin America, ed., John Eagleson, trans. John Drury
     (Maryknoll: Orbis Books, 1975), p. 171.

103. Ibid., pp. 161 and 162.

104. Ibid., p. 169.

105. Ibid., p. 173.

106. Phillip E. Berryman, "Latin American Liberation Theology,"
     in Theology in the Americas, ed. Sergio Torres and John
     Eagleson (Maryknoll: Orbis Books, 1976), p. 28.

107. Gutierrez, A Theology of Liberation, pp. 275 and 278.

108. Assmann, p. 138.

109. "Final Document," p. 174.

110. Mottesi, p. 8.

111. Gutierrez, A Theology of Liberation, p. 11.

112. Miguez Bonino, pp. 57-58.

113. Enrique Dussel, "The Political and Ecclesial Context of Liberation Theology in Latin America," in The Emergent Gospel: Theology from the Underside of History, ed. Sergio Torres and Virginia Fabella (Maryknoll: Orbis Books, 1978), p. 179; Gustavo Gutierrez, "Two Theological Perspectives: Liberation Theology and Progressivist Theology," in Torres and Fabella, p. 242; Hugo Assmann, Theology for a Nomad Church, pp. 49, 56, and passim; and Beatriz Melano Couch, "New Visions of the Church in Latin America: A Protestant View," in Torres and Fabella, pp. 198ff.

PART TWO:

RESPONSES AMONG CHRISTIAN MORAL THINKERS
TO THE ECONOMIC DEVELOPMENT DEBATE

CHAPTER III

DENIS GOULET'S RESPONSE TO THE DEVELOPMENT DEBATE:
A CRITICAL MODERNIST'S SEARCH FOR "MIDDLE GROUND"
AND HIS IMPLICIT CRITIQUE OF LIBERATION THEOLOGY

The ideological tensions between developmentalists
(or modernists) and liberationists which are so evident
in the economic development debates within the social
sciences (Chapter I) and in the ecumenical church movement (Chapter II) are no less at work among Christian
moral thinkers. Part Two offers an occasion to consider further evidence of this ideological split--and how
deeply it runs--by closely examining in this chapter
the writings of Denis Goulet, a North American and Roman
Catholic moral philosopher, and in the next those of
selected Latin American liberation theologians.

I. Denis Goulet's Search for a "Middle Ground" in the
    Development Debates

Denis Goulet's selection as a moral thinker of importance to reckon with in the development debates is
not surprising. Among North Americans he is unmatched
for his serious and sustained attention to problems of
global economic and social development, and he has
placed issues of economic justice at the heart of his
work. He also goes so far as to describe himself as a
development ethicist or, alternately, as a moral philosopher of development who is engaged in what he terms a
new "discipline in the making," a discipline which makes
"the value-laden, ethical questions posed by development
the central object of . . . study."[1]

One essay, published in 1975, illustrates briefly
several of Goulet's insights about and contributions to
the economic development debates. The very title of
this essay, "World Hunger: Putting Development Ethics
to the Test," encapsulates a claim that appears throughout his writings, that world hunger and, more generally,
the problem of global economic injustices are of such
magnitude and human significance to "unmask the quality
of our ethics" and lead us to ask, "Is our ethics pious
rhetoric or effective praxis?"[2] Discussion will be
forthcoming about his reasons for finding moralistic
responses so woefully inadequate, but at this point, it
is important to emphasize that Goulet is adamant that
new paths for development must be located to insure that

all persons across the globe may attain both "bread and dignity." This is not to say, however, that he is sanguine about the possibilities or the probabilities that movement toward more just economic and social relationships will come easily or without immense conflicts. Given the present power configurations within Third World countries and between rich and poor nations, he estimates that nothing less is necessary than to revamp "our global economic and political institutions . . . to allocate resources on the basis of priority needs" rather than on the basis of "effective purchasing power."[3]

At this point in his essay on world hunger, Goulet discloses his interest as a moral thinker to introduce the argument that, in an age of scarcity and global injustices, a world market system which legitimizes the greed of some while denying life-giving goods and resources to the many, must be reorganized in such a way to institutionalize "the primacy of moral over material incentives." And the overarching moral incentive for that reorganization, he goes on to explain, should be human solidarity, which he proposes is the highest ethical value, certainly higher than self-interest but also higher than either justice or charity.[4] Only by embodying human solidarity with all persons and nations in our economic, political, and cultural relationships can we find ways to move toward an authentic development "founded on reciprocal strength in bargaining positions." Goulet raises the global political and moral stakes to no less than creating a new world order, based on genuine and long-term "reciprocity and equity among [and within] nations."[5] Judging present realities against the measure of that vision of authentic development for all, Goulet moves to stand among those liberation Christians who view the world "from below" in his own insistence that "the international order must not be protected; it must be radically transformed."[6]

Another theme which Goulet introduces in this essay is not only the need for deep-seated structural changes but also the problem of effecting the transition to a new global order which would make economic and social development possible even for the poorest of the poor. Incremental steps are needed, he suggests, but palliative measures are at the same time insufficient and even counterproductive, in that they "block deep change by lulling people into accepting minor gradual improvements instead of adequate responses to fundamental problems."

Only those strategies which "open up new possibilities
for subsequent radical change" are adequate and could
be labelled under his suggestive rubric of "creative
incrementalism." Such creative incrementalism is of
particular importance to moral agents who understand
their ethical and political task as "the art of creating
new possibilities, of shattering existing parameters and
opening the way for new ones."[7]

Goulet's own perspective on and work in the midst
of the economic development debates comes into even
clearer focus when it is acknowledged how determined he
is to push all parties to the point of recognizing that

> In stark terms the ethical issues at
> play are reducible to two: Which
> social forces will be the stewards of
> the emerging world order? On what
> values will the new international
> order be built?[8]

Goulet's own response to these questions will occupy
our attention in this chapter. It is important to give
full credit to Goulet for his interest in emphasizing
the underlying value questions, but what is problematic,
for reasons to be elaborated in this chapter, are his
political sensibilities and the method by which he in-
terrelates his normative ethical analysis and his political reflections. In contradistinction to the liberation theologians we shall be discussing in Chapter IV,
whose ethical analyses are grounded in and informed by
their participation in social movements for economic
justice, Goulet himself is disconnected from such social
movements. As evidence from his own writings will indicate, he regards himself either as a "free floater" or
as a "friendly critic" positioned within the North American guild of development scholars. His intent is to
radicalize and push his professional colleagues in the
moral and political direction he describes in his essay
on world hunger. The issue of contention, however, is
whether Goulet has sufficiently taken into account the
radicality of the split between developmentalists and
liberationists or pulled off the quite precarious balancing act that would be needed to stand between the
two sides of the development debate. Such a balancing
act may, indeed, by possible, but it is made much more
difficult if, at the same time, the attempt is made to
press the value questions Goulet is so concerned to
bring to the surface of the debates.

As this chapter unfolds, we would do well to keep in mind Miguez Bonino's remarks cited at the close of the previous chapter. The Argentinian theologian has argued that two issues which mark the chasm between developmentalists and liberationists are the explicit declaration of an ideological option, particularly a socialist one, and the call to the poor and the oppressed themselves to become their own artisans of economic justice. As evidence will indicate, these issues are quite important to raise in making a critical assessment of Goulet's contributions as a moral thinker to the development debates because he has self-consciously declared his intent to construct a normative ethics of global development in dialogue with Latin American theologians of liberation. Although it is true, for reasons to be considered shortly, that he does not speak of himself as a liberationist, he does claim an affinity between his own work and that of both dependency theorists and liberation theologians. Upon close scrutiny, however, we find reasons that this claim is not fully warranted. In fact, throughout his writings there is an implicit critique of liberation theology. The burden of proof in this chapter will be to demonstrate that, contrary to his own self-perception, Goulet belongs on the modernization side of the development debates and, further, that only by examining his writings in light of the ideological tensions which characterize these debates can we account for this otherwise surprising conclusion.

Before we undertake our analysis, however, we should note also that Goulet wishes to distinguish himself by actively resisting identification with either the developmentalist or liberationist side of the current development debates. For reasons to be enumerated in this chapter, he wants to locate, represent, and stand firmly in the "development center" as a non-ideological advocate for global economic justice. His is a search for a "middle ground" from which to mediate between the two ideological opponents of the debate. To be sure, he is fully cognizant not only of the conflictual dynamics of these debates but also of their ideological character. As early as 1968 he contended that

> I do not believe that what we know, or
> think we know, about development amounts
> to the voice of reason delivering pure
> imperatives, categorical or hypothetical.
> I do indeed fear that ideological and

other impurities of various sorts
have contaminated our discourse
regarding the issues of wealth and
poverty in the world. This contam-
ination has prevented us from planning or acting very wisely.[9]

He has also argued that "the impurities of various
sorts" which trouble him are to be found, in his judgment, on both sides of the debate.

Although he credits modernization theorists with
correctly identifying development as a dynamic, conflictual, and multidimensional process by which underdeveloped nations attempt to accomplish the difficult transition to modern forms of social life, he also argues that
modernists have more often than not been subject to an
ethnocentric bias in assuming that the advanced industrialized nations should serve as the model for Third-
World development. In The Myth of Aid and again in The
Uncertain Promise he has also acknowledged, for example,
that North Atlantic development experts and planners
have too readily and uncritically accepted a theory of
international trade which has "had as its purpose, according to [Gunnar] Myrdal, 'the explaining away of the
international equity problem.'"[10] He has, therefore,
found reasons to suggest that "profound and basic
changes in world economic structures are necessary before genuine development can become possible for the
world at large,"[11] and that it is necessary to grant the
dependency theory of development "some plausibility."
In reaching this conclusion, however, he cautions
against those who "endorse [a] simplistic 'scapegoat'
theory of underdevelopment" by succumbing to what he
regrets as "a growing tendency on the part of the poor
to blame rich classes and nations for their own backwardness."[12]

We shall return to examine the adequacy of Goulet's
reading of a dependency theory of development and underdevelopment, but the point to keep in mind is that because he finds deficiencies as well as important insights to be gained from both parties to the development
debates, Goulet attempts to find his way to a "middle
ground" which will allow him not only to appropriate the
"best of both worlds" but also to offer what he envisions as an objective and, therefore, non-partisan view
of development issues. Throughout his writings he is
insistent that global development not be perceived as

either parochial or "politically divisive" concerns. The process of development, which he describes variously as the human ascent, the "ascending spiral of human growth," and "the historical quest for new values, new institutions, and a new culture in each society,"[13] involves for him the construction of the "good life" for all persons in their given societies and, in his judgment, must be understood as an historically unfinished task for so-called "developed" as well as "underdeveloped" countries. In his plenary address before the American Society of Christian Ethics in 1974, he, therefore, made a quite characteristic claim that "we are all of us underdeveloped nations struggling to find some valid basis for defining our real needs and our essential relationships."[14]

In order to avoid what he determines to be an "unnecessary politicization" of development issues, Goulet suggests that it is only by adopting the "moral point of view" that "some valid basis for defining our real needs and our essential relationships" can be attained, and he also contends that a consensus must be reached through moral persuasion within and among nations that

> . . . for developed and underdeveloped
> societies alike, basic questions are
> neither economic, political, nor tech-
> nological, but moral. What is the good
> life and the good society in a world of
> mass technology and global interdepen-
> dence?[15]

Moreover, as a moral philosopher, Goulet takes as his own project the elucidation of a normative ethical theory of development which will enable him to speak and work "for the benefit of men's [sic] universal needs, not for any particular interests,"[16] and, thereby, to arrive at a form of rational discourse which is not ideologically bound and, more specifically, does not "resort to persuasive political definitions, thereby pre-empting all the intellectual ground upon which descriptive and evocative definition might find their place."[17]

Goulet is also convinced for another reason of the inherent wisdom of not falling to one side or the other of the development debates. He surveys the history of those debates and concludes that

> Arguments over the root causes of under-

110

development have now raged for 30
years. Prevalent in all this discussion is the recurrence of intellectual
cycles, at the crest of which some new
theory or focus captures the attention
of students and practitioners of development and becomes, in effect, a new
'fad.' For a while it was institution-
building, then liberation; at other
times integrated rural development or
upgrading human resources. With time,
however, each of these usually recedes
and becomes integrated into the existing
wisdom about development's multiple dimensions.[18]

What Goulet understands himself to be offering is a more
"integrated" and, therefore, adequate perspective of the
issues at hand than either developmentalists or liberationists have provided but, at the same time, one which
pays special attention to the critical insights of dependency theorists and liberation theologians. He argues for the validity of what he calls "the new liberation vocabulary," especially because it seeks to "unmask
the hidden value assumptions of the conventional wisdom"
and also "lays bare structures of dependence and domination at all levels." He also insists that the "competing terminologies of development and liberation are not
equally subject to distortion,"[19] and that the term "development" does, indeed, have a pejorative connotation
because it does not

. . . evoke asymmetrical power relations operative in the world or the
inability of evolutionary change models to lead, in many countries, to
the desired objectives.[20]

Despite the fact that he declares his own alignment with the critical perspective of dependency theorists and grants the preferability of the language of
liberation, Goulet also makes an argument for his retaining the "professional" development terminology in
his own writings, and he gives two reasons for doing so.
These reasons, we should note, are offered by him as a
way to protect his ideological neutrality and preserve
the integrity of the "moral point of view." Methodologically, Goulet states his preference for the use of development language to describe what he calls the "uni-

111

versal human project" of cultural transformation because
he finds that liberation motifs focus almost exclusively
upon negative conditional requirements of overcoming
domination and cultural dependence without providing
clear indication of the positive, universal and uncondi-
tional goals of that process. The question inevitably
arises, he argues, "liberation for what?," and he suggests that the development vocabulary is more amenable
for addressing theological questions about the requirements for the good life and the good society. Liberationists, he goes on to say, also tend to dwell too narrowly upon political and economic issues and upon the
necessity of overcoming alienating material conditions.
As a moral philosopher, Goulet contends that there must
necessarily be some vision of the good to motivate human
agency, and "when used normatively, 'development' proposes images of the good society, prescriptions for ob-
taining it, and symbols for generating enthusiastic allegiance to it."[21]

The second reason Goulet gives for retaining the
development terminology follows from a strategic consideration. He contends that "in spite of its absolute
superiority, . . . the language of liberation remains,
for many people in the 'developed' world, tactically
unmanageable."[22] He fully agrees that development language and theory need to be redefined and demystified,
but he finds it politically valuable and even necessary
to maintain dialogue with the "development guild" in
order to be able to act as a subversive within the ranks
to "open up new perspectives and render the leap into
'liberation' possible for many people."[23] He, therefore, wnats to preserve his professional credibility,
as it were, in order to mobilize change within advanced
industrialized societies. Furthermore, as he understands the issues, unless the "liberation vocabulary"
is able "to transform itself from the rallying cry of
victims alone into the victory chant of all men [sic]
as they empower themselves to enter history with no
nostalgia for pre-history," full human development will
not occur. Solidarity, which he ranks as the highest
ethical value, must indicate solidarity of all persons
in all societies in order to be realized, and development must ultimately signify a global goal coexistent
with the "goals . . . of existence itself: to provide
all men [sic] with the opportunity to live full human
lives. Thus understood, development is the ascent of
all men [sic] and societies in their total humanity."[24]
Therefore, he finds the development language more at-

tractive politically and at least initially a more inclusive and universally applicable terminology.

Goulet's preference for the "development lexicon"
is not, by any means, sufficient reason for labelling
him a modernist, but as we proceed with our analysis,
we will need to question whether he has, in fact, provided an ideologically neutral view of development or
located a "middle ground" above the cleavage which radically separates developmentalists and liberationists.
Similarly, there are reasons to question the accuracy
of his own self-assessment of his commonality with the
liberationist perspective. We shall proceed by first
examining Goulet's self-understanding of his work as a
moral philosopher. He identifies certain methodological problems which confront ethicists who wish to reflect upon issues of economic development. In the process of suggesting ways to address those problems, he
also identifies the ground upon which he finds his own
rapprochement with theologians of liberation. As we
move on to consider his placement within the social
scientific debates, we shall find reasons for describing
him as a critical modernist but, nevertheless, a modernist. Then after an analysis of several more problematic
aspects of his ethical methodology which further differentiate his from a liberation perspective, we shall conclude with observations about his location of the Vatican II side within the ecumenical debates.

II. Goulet's Self-Interpretation: A Moral Philosopher
     Constructing a Normative Ethics of Global Develop-
     ment in Dialogue with Latin American Theologians
     of Liberation

Denis Goulet's own stated intention as a moral
philosopher of development is to offer a model of socio-
ethical reflection which will correct the inadequacies
he perceives among development scholars and planners
and among professional ethicists who have failed, in his
estimation, to make the ethical questions posed by development primary to their study. Although he is quite
certain of the need, even of the demand for a normative
ethics of development, he, nonetheless, questions whether moral philosophers are capable of supplying answers.
That doubt persists for him even though he identifies
himself as working with the tradition of moral philosophical inquiry. Of particular concern to him is what
he calls "the very bankruptcy of conventional wisdom on
development" and, even more, the deepening "chasm be-

tween ethics and economics." As he assesses the contemporary situation, he finds, on the one hand, that
economists are no longer willing or else they judge
themselves less than competent "to evaluate ends or
ideals." Scholars in the development field back away
from raising normative ethical issues and narrowly re-
strict their lines of inquiry within boundaries set by
distinct disciplines. On the other hand, he argues that
"neither ethics nor theology [has] provided norms or
direction" for reflecting upon the dynamics of social
change or been able to restore the once-existent links
between economic science and moral philosophy.[25] Professional ethicists, he notes, have tended to ignore
issues of economic justice. Goulet has, therefore,
reached the conclusion that

> By and large, normative questions have
> been ignored or badly answered, by de-
> velopment experts and ethicists alike.
> By development experts because most of
> them flee value-laden questions, brand-
> ing them unscientific or impressionis-
> tic. Ethicists, in turn, have rarely
> looked to development processes and con-
> flicts as the raw materials of their
> moral reflection. By remaining outside
> of social change dynamics, however, they
> risk imprisoning themselves within
> sterile forms of moralism which are use-
> less when not positively harmful.[26]

The project which Goulet lays out for himself, from his
vantage point as one trained as a development expert
and as a moral philosopher, has a dual purpose--to correct defective models of development and "to thrust debates over economic and social development into the
arena of ethical values."[27]

      As a development scholar, Goulet identifies him-
self on the dissenting side of the debate among social
scientists, and in the preface to The Cruel Choice, he
states that

> My basic contention is that prevailing
> images of development are defective
> and that the standard view of its pro-
> per means and goals is erroneous. Not
> ethical theorists alone, but all those
> concerned with development must con-

sider new possibilities.[28]

He adds that his own sympathies lie with the dependency
theorists who argue that underdevelopment is not a state
of backwardness caused by a lack of "modern" technological, economic, and cultural conditions but rather that
"underdevelopment [is] the by-product of development itself" and that "structural vulnerability [is] the key
to understanding underdevelopment and fostering development."[29]

He takes special care to refute the view that development is an economic process only or that high rates
of economic growth automatically "produce" social well-
being. Rather, he understands development as a multidimensional "movement toward economic and social modes
of existence characterized by relatively high levels of
material living and rational control over environment."[30]
He also contends that many of the policies and economic
blueprints paraded about as developmental are aimed
rather at the domestication of the Third World by "societies already developed [which] seek . . . not to upset
their own positions of privilege."[31]

As a moral philosopher, Goulet is also not reticent
to acknowledge two distinct problems which confront
those who would wish to "bring normative unity and value
synthesis to the complex human experience of development."[32] One problem that he describes is the problem
of abstractness, for lack of a better term, which arises
for moral philosophers whenever "they take refuge in
concepts alien to the real experiences which alone can
provide raw materials for their ethical reflection on
development."[33] The temptation and inclination to moralize about development processes can be overcome,
Goulet suggests, only if ethicists abandon any attempt
to remain outside of social change dynamics and instead
allow themselves to undergo what he calls the experien-
tial "shock of underdevelopment." Rather than view underdevelopment as a "problem" to be solved, ethicists
should realize that underdevelopment is a global reality
which encompasses all persons and societies, a reality
which is also

> . . . more of a 'mystery' than a 'prob-
> lem'. . . . In mystery . . . it is impos-
> sible to situate oneself outside the
> dilemma; a problematic element is pres-
> ent, but the viewer himself is part of

115

the problem. . . . Therefore, if he
chooses to treat the matter as a
mere problem extrinsic to himself,
he is condemned to misunderstand it
and not solve it.[34]

A second and no less serious problem for Goulet
focuses on the issue of accountability. Not only must
ethicists view development as a dynamic historical process in which they are participants as well as observers, but they should also understand that "allegiance
systems [are] at the heart of ethics" and, as he goes
on to argue, that their critical task is not to "pose
ideal goals, and pass judgment on the means used by
others to pursue these or other goals," but rather "to
promote the values for which oppressed and underdeveloped groups struggle: greater justice, a decent sufficiency of goods for all, equitable access. . . ."[35]
Advocacy, he insists, is integral to and perhaps the
very raison d'etre of ethical inquiry.

Goulet is quite clear that his own agenda is to
provide a normative ethics of development which takes
the contemporary world-historical situation as the appropriate context and horizon for assessing moral obligation and which is also fully grounded in the commitments of moral agents to struggle for global justice.
He also judges that his work as an ethicist is similar
to and compatible with that of Latin American liberation
theologians. In his address to the American Society of
Christian Ethics, for example, he carefully delineated
some of the common ground upon which he assumes their
rapprochement has occurred. On that occasion he stated:

New modes of philosophizing are needed
in which theoretical construction is
linked vitally and organically to the
praxis, not merely of individual thinkers, but of living communities struggling to gain greater justice and more
equitable development. The example of
Latin American theologians of liberation such as Gutierrez, Assman [sic],
Segundo, Dussel, and others is helpful.
Their approach . . . 'situates' scholarly activity in its proper historical
matrix--that of social transformation
amidst concrete conflict.[36]

116

Elsewhere Goulet added that he also fully shares the conviction of liberation theologians that

> . . . development ethics must cope with structures of differential wealth and power among societies. Were it otherwise, ethics would be reduced to mere preachments addressed to the 'good will' and generosity of the powerful, and to the escapist sentiments of the powerless.[37]

What remains problematic, however, especially given Goulet's own self-interpretation, is that he offers a normative ethical theory which is not grounded within any specific struggle for liberation nor informed by a socio-historic analysis of the political and economic dynamics which shape our historical situations. Moreover, contrary to his own intentions, he also tends toward an idealist position by attempting, as he explains, "to influence development decisions otherwise than through power--namely be appealing to certain normative values."[38] The problem here, from a liberationist perspective, is not, by any means, his appeal to normative values or his interest in moral suasion, but rather that he fails to honor his promise of also providing a political analysis of the dynamics of economic development and attending to the power relations which either enhance or frustrate movement toward authentic development.

Even before we examine specific methodological problems in Goulet's writings, however, we may begin to account for the actual divergence between his work and that of liberation theologians by clarifying his placement within the social scientific debates over development. There are distinct reasons to suspect that contrary to his explicit self-identification with and sympathy toward the liberationists' perspective on global economic issues, Goulet remains a critical but, nonetheless, "unrepentant" modernization theorist.

III. Goulet's Placement within the Social Scientific Debates over Development: A Critical Modernist

Denis Goulet has professed his interest in and supposed compatibility with neo-Marxist dependency theorists. Therefore, to identify him as a critical modernist requires justification. Such justification is especially called for in light of the fact that he expends considerable energy throughout his writings in order to counter precisely those social scientific theories of development which mask the realities of domination and exploitation in "underdeveloped" nations, favor perpetuation of the status quo, and propose palliatives rather than substantial changes in the world economic and political orders. It is also true that he incorporates some of the more important insights of the dependency theorists in his analysis. He does not hesitate to argue, for example, that economic development policies which bypass the issue of power inequalities within and among nations more often than not exacerbate rather than ameliorate the conditions of underdevelopment which they intend to correct. He, therefore, stands in full agreement with the critics of "developmentalism" who contend that

> Recommendations which sound good turn out to be palliatives because they ignore structures of dependence and uncritically share the value assumptions of those who have a vested interest in maintaining control over the dynamisms of development now operative.[39]

He also identifies the problem of world development in graphic and unambiguous terms, namely, that "sociologically speaking, we are witnessing worldwide stratification; economically, a polarization between rich and poor nations."[40]

What places Goulet decisively on the modernization side of the social scientific debates over development is his uncritical acceptance of certain foundational assumptions of modernization theory, his ahistorical view of social change, and his quite apparent distrust of a neo-Marxist class analysis of the global dynamics of development and underdevelopment. Before elaborating on these points, however, we should first understand what kind of reading Goulet acutally gives to dependency theorists. Rather than finding that they offer a radically distinct interpretation of the world-historical situation or provide a fundamental critique of conventional theories of development as modernization, he instead minimizes the cleavage between the two theoretical perspectives. He also seems to assume that the theory of dependency arose only as a supplementary corrective to but not as an alternative for the theory of modernization which continues to shape First-World policies and strategies. What is also important to recognize and quite telling is that throughout his writings Goulet cites dependency theorists only at those junctures in his argument where he wishes to reinforce his own claims that modernization theorists have erred by offering a distorted view of the proper goals and the appropriate means to assure authentic global development. Two examples will illustrate this point.

Goulet frequently invokes liberationists, for example, whenever he wishes to challenge those modernization theorists who take for granted that the advanced industrialized nations are the necessary model for Third World countries to emulate in their own development. His argument is that modernists have wrongly projected an "affluence" image of development as a process aimed at the attainment of high levels of economic growth and mass consumption, and that this false image has been disseminated throughout the world by those who mistakenly assume that they are bearers of not only "modern" but superior values. As he explains,

> The dominance imagery equates, at least implicitly, the abundance of goods with the fullness of good. Quite logically, men [sic] come to be valued in monetary terms, and all other values are, in practice, subordinated to money. . . . There is, in short, a profoundly materializing force at work in the Western myth of the abundant life. When this myth is taken seriously by modernizing elites in the Third World, it easily generates anti-development.[41]

Although he does not mention Daniel Lerner by name, Goulet is taking aim at Lerner and others who too uncritically assume that the goal of the development process should be to transform individuals in Third World countries into the Americanized "cash customer, the radio listener, the voter."[42] He strongly objects to the identification of development as a process of Westernization or Americanization and argues at length that cultural diversity is a universally valid and indispensable value to be defended because "the human potential is too rich to be expressed adequately in a single form."[43]

If Goulet is prone to cite liberationists from the
Third World in order to credit them for sharing and re-
inforcing his own critique of the ethnocentric biases
of development planners and decision-makers, he also
has nothing but praise for their efforts to "unmask the
alienations disguised by the development lexicon: the
alienation of the many in misery, of the few in irre-
sponsible abundance."[44] He also argues that they rightly question, as he does, the means proposed to effect
social change in the Third World no less than the goals
of the development process which the affluent nations
impose on others.

> A second source of anti-development
> is the mode in which much technical
> assistance and financial aid has been
> accompanied, for the most part, by
> disdain for the 'beggar' and a haughty
> sense of donor superiority injurious
> to the dignity of the recipient. A
> complacent sense of cultural superior-
> ity has generally prevailed on the part
> of those possessing the technical skills
> needed in poorer lands.[45]

Goulet insists that authentic development, normatively
understood, is a cultural process which signifies not
only the attainment of certain benefits, including a
sufficient level of economic well-being for all persons,
but also the possibility of empowering persons to maximize their capacities for self-determination and self-
actualization. He particularly wants to chastize development scholars for underestimating the significance
of the dialectical nature of the relationships between
goals sought and the means used in the development process:

> . . . how development is obtained de-
> termines whether men [sic] are liber-
> ated or alienated; the manner is as
> important as the matter! The benefits
> of development could probably be ob-
> tained in some elitist, technocratic,
> oligarchic mode. . . . [But] to achieve
> the benefits of development at the cost
> of sacrificing human freedom and criti-
> cal intelligence is to negate the very
> good life and good society development
> seeks to produce.[46]

120

Goulet suggests that the emergent critiques of elitist patterns of relationship between developed and underdeveloped nations and the concern of Third World countries to control their own autonomous development are extremely well placed, especially since it is his own judgment that cultural autonomy is a primary, if not the ultimate, goal of the development process. He finds supporting evidence for that judgment from those Third World countries in which economic and "technological gains are [being] subordinated to the cultural creation of a new man [sic], capable of autonomy,"[47] and he enjoins liberationists as allies in challenging the "conventional wisdom" of modernization theorists by declaring that

> . . . the basic question is not modernization, improved standards of living, levels of industrialization, or even the rapidity of change, but rather the degree of control men [sic] can wield over their destinies. . . . The real problem for us, underdeveloped nations all of us, is to find ways and means of building new models of culture within which men [sic] can be equally responsible and equal participants. . . . Culture, therefore, not economics, technology, or politics, is the primordial dimension in development. And the central problem of culture is not its content but the degree of control men [sic] exercise over the speed, direction, and modality of cultural evolution.[48]

From a liberationist perspective, however, Goulet can be criticized at this point not so much for what he has said but for what he has failed to say. The quest for cultural autonomy and human freedom for self-development is without any doubt an indispensable dimension of the liberation struggle, but dependency theorists insist that the very possibility of regaining cultural freedom is intrinsically linked to and dependent upon the actualization of political and economic autonomy in the Third World. The problem with Goulet's assertion that "culture . . ., not economics . . . or politics, is the primordial dimension in development" is that he tends too quickly to reduce underdevelopment to a cultural problem and to downplay the significance of institutional and, therefore, political dynamics. Although he recognizes that authentic development will become possible for the Third World "only if world institutions are radically altered," he indicates little readiness to explore those necessary changes and instead moves rapidly to emphasize his own concern for "deep and far-reaching attitudinal changes" and his central claim that "a new pedagogy of values is . . . a prerequisite to the reconversion of world institutions."[49] His almost exclusive preoccupation with cultural realities and disregard for political problems is highly suspect from a liberationist perspective, but what is no less problematic is Goulet's consistent failure to take seriously the argument liberationists make that the dependency theory of underdevelopment must be read, first and foremost, as a socio-economic analysis and critique of the dynamics of global capitalism which have created the conditions of poverty and cultural dependency in the Third World and not simplistically as a "friendly" critique challenging nothing more than the ethnocentric and elitist biases of certain modernization theorists.

This failure makes Goulet vulnerable to a critique brought forth by Gustavo Gutierrez. In A Theology of Liberation Gutierrez warns of a strategy of cooptation employed by those who attempt to undercut the validity and neutralize the impact of the liberationists' critique by their acknowledgement of only minimal points of agreement with the dependency analysis. As Gutierrez explains,

> The theory of dependence met a new pitfall a short time ago: the danger of being accepted--nominally at least--by representatives of the prevailing system. It is the old policy of domesticating terms and ideas, weakening them, and causing them to lose their subversive character with regard to the status quo. Nun comments that 'it is indeed significant that in the past few years dependence has become a habitual topic for discussion in organizations, conferences, and documents approved by the system. This phenomenon can be explained in several ways. The first is tactical. In the face of such a massive and open penetration, it is advisable to reassure

public opinion by acknowledging part
of the problem and thus silencing the
critics. Meanwhile nothing really
effective is done to change the situation. . . .'[50]

That warning is applicable to Goulet, for although he
declares his own affinity with a dependency theory of
underdevelopment and insists that the concept of vulnerability is the "key to understanding and promoting development,"[51] he does not provide a political and economic analysis of those structural relationships which
shape the existing global dynamics of development and
underdevelopment. In backing away from a structural
analysis, he moves toward speaking of vulnerability
more in psychological categories.

Consider, for example, Gouelt's appropriation of
the argument that underdevelopment is a reality created
and perpetuated by the historical expansion of a capitalist world economic order:

Underdevelopment is an historical by-
product of 'development.' This statement must not be understood in a simplistic mode. Raymond Aron warns that
'the state of high development of some
countries is neither a cause nor a
condition of the underdevelopment of
other countries.' Nevertheless, the
condition of underdevelopment in its
totality is a consciously experienced
state of deprivation rendered intoler-
able because of newly acquired information regarding the development of other
societies and the existence of technical means for abolishing misery.[52]

Along with modernization theorists, such as Daniel
Lerner, Everett Hagen, and Albert O. Hirschman, Goulet
characterizes underdeveloped countries as traditional
and static societies which are only now in the process
of "awakening" to the modern world and of passing
through a difficult transition period of acculturation
to those modern values and attitudes diffused from the
"outside" world. He singles out what he describes as
the "consciously experienced state of deprivation" in
the Third World as the opening stages of this passage
toward modernity, and he explains that this quest for

development is now universally sought:

> A certain number of people in every
> society--no matter how static or tradi-
> tional it may seem--have now acquired
> the psychic mobility which is the first
> motor propelling developmental changes.
> Initially it is aspirations which change;
> later, initiatives are taken to alter
> the incentive systems operative in soci-
> ety, perhaps even the social structure
> themselves. This complex phenomenon--
> partly psychological, partly societal--
> has been variously labelled the 'revo-
> lution of rising expectations,' the
> 'emerging consciousness of the Third
> World,' or the 'awakening of the under-
> classes.'[53]

As a modernist, what Goulet emphasizes is what happens
to "the minds of men" and women in the experience of
development so that it is not always clear whether the
more significant shift taking place in the Third World
is the introduction of factories, for example, or the
appearance of new attitudes toward those factories.[54]

In keeping with the modernist perspective, Goulet
also qualifies the argument that the developed nations
have "caused" underdevelopment by speaking of their
transmitting, through a network of global communications systems, an affluence image of the "good life"
to the Third World. He contends that this image is so
powerful and pervasive that it has shattered the traditional worldviews of those pre-industrialized societies
whose "internal equilibrium" had previously been maintained by the adherence of their individual members to
certain "core values," to internalized social norms and
values which managed to control "the instincts of acquisitiveness and accumulation." His own explanation
of the modernication process, along with his concomitant accounting for the persistence of underdevelopment
in the Third World, is instructive of his modernist
sensibilities:

> The equilibrium between acquisitve
> desires and effective access to re-
> sources has been ruptured in most
> societies. This balance is expressed
> facetiously as follows: 'One shouldn't

want what he can't get.' The psychology of needs in 'traditional'
societies has always been based on
this principle. . . .

. . . Curbing desire was good because to do otherwise would unleash
forces of greed which could only
cause disruptive competition for
limited goods. The problem changes,
however, when demonstration effects
from outside begin to challenge the
fundamental assumptions of this
society's symbolic and normative
systems. For the first time, the
majority of men [sic] begin to
think unthinkable thoughts: (a)
maybe there is enough wealth for
all to have as much as they want;
and (b) maybe it is not bad for
me to want more than I have been
wanting.

. . . Demonstration effects remove
the curbs on desire <u>before providing</u>
<u>men [sic] with the means to expand</u>
<u>resource availability</u>. . . . Once it
becomes evident to them that it is
possible to desire more, they will,
by and large, begin to want more.
Even while they remove the brakes
from their own desire mechanisms,
however, they remain ignorant of the
technological requisites for multi-
plying available resources. . . .
They lack the effective ability to
generate additional wealth for themselves. . . . It is not easy to
understand the complex requirements
for being able to satisfy those wants.
Thus men's [sic] desires are tampered
with before they can realistically
satisfy these desires. <u>This, I hold,</u>
<u>is the main reason why development</u>
<u>objectives are so frequently unreal-</u>
<u>istic</u>.[55]

As this passage indicates, Goulet's diagnosis of
the problem of underdevelopment is not dissimilar from

that of the modernization theorists we examined in Chapter I. He, too, stresses that underdevelopment is essentially a "state of mind" which results from an imbalance "between the will and the way to modernize," and he does not dissent from those who theorize that the primary obstacles to development are located not only internally within the underdeveloped countries themselves but, ultimately, "back where all difficulties of human action belong: in the mind."[56] Moreover, even though he appears to be willing to concede that the advanced industrialized nations are implicited in the problems of underdevelopment, he moves rather quickly to suggest that their involvement proceeds mainly from the fact that "it is the rich who have tampered with the poor man's [sic] desire mechanisms and made him want to 'make it.'"[57] It is also noticeable that his analysis of vulnerability of the underdeveloped nations speaks more to the disequilibrium brought about by "the reconstruction of motivational and symbolic forces in men's [sic] lives"[58] as societies undergo their transition toward modernization than about structural consequences of neocolonialism.

What distinguishes Goulet's interpretation of underdevelopment from that of other modernists is his own stated ambivalence about "modernity" as the goal of the development process. In The Cruel Choice he identifies his own professional training within and personal compatibility with "the French school" of development thinking and with the work of Francois Perroux, Louis Lebret, and their disciples. These development scholars have, in his judgment, "always constituted, in some respects, a heretical minority" and an alternative to those modernists who equate development with high rates of economic growth or with industrialization and technological advancements. As he explains,

> [Their] position centers on qualitative improvement in all societies, and in all groups and individuals within societies. Although all men [sic] must surely have enough goods in order to be human, they say, development itself is simply a means to the human ascent. . . . According to these men and their disciples, social change should be seen in the broadest possible historical context, within which all of humanity is viewed

126

as receiving a summons to assume its
destiny. Their ideas have influenced
United Nations agencies in some measure, but they have made their greatest
inroads in religious writings on development: papal encyclicals, documents
issued by the World Council of Churches
and the Pontifical Commission on Justice and Peace. . . . The single geo-
graphical area where the French school
has achieved considerable penetration
is Latin America.[59]

Goulet also emphasizes that in contradiction to North
American modernization theorists, in particular, the
French school not only "stresses ethical values" but
further distinguishes itself "because of its historicity
and its insistence on norms for social goals."[60] He
places himself within this stream of development schol-
arship and declares himself no less committed than
Lebret and others to advancing the argument that

. . . the true task of development is
to create new civilizations. This is,
quite literally, the mandate: to create, in diverse cultural and historical settings, new civilizations where
the good life and the good society become real possibilities not just for
the affluent few, but for all humans
whose need for creativity and meaning
is no less acute or urgent than their
hunger for bread and dignity.[61]

If Goulet breaks rank with other modernists by insisting that the task of development is not the accumulation of wealth but rather the creation of new civilizations in which the human need for both "bread and
dignity" is recognized as the right of all persons, he
gains further distance by arguing that the advanced industrialized nations, no less than the developing nations, are presently suffering from what he calls the
universal "crisis of underdevelopment." He makes the
claim that

. . . development, at its deepest level, is not a matter of self-sustained
growth or modernization of social systems, but primarily a crisis in norms

and meanings.[62]

Third World countries are experiencing this crisis because the "virus of acquisitiveness" has spread from
rich to poor nations, disrupted "the delicate balance
between social restraints on desire and effectively
available resources," and undermined "the norms of need-
satisfaction which have allowed countless societies to
survive."[63] The affluent countries are also in a crisis
situation, however, because they relentlessly pursue the
goals of modernity, that is, prosperity and material accumulation, at the expense of other human values and
"have falsely assumed that men's [sic] most significant
needs are their material needs."[64] Therefore, as Goulet
interprets our world-historical situation, the fundamental problem confronting both so-called "developed"
and "underdeveloped" nations alike is a false, materialistic conception of the goals of development, namely,
the equation of the "good life" with the acquisition of
materal goods. Moreover, as he states his case, the
cause of underdevelopment throughout the globe is ultimately to be found in the loss, in the modern world, of
a normative vision of the good life to guide human action. As he explains,

> We must probe beyond definitions and
> diagnose the causes of underdevelop-
> ment. Underdevelopment is not due
> primarily to insufficient resources,
> rigorous climate, excessive popula-
> tion, technological backwardness, or
> insufficient aid. Underdevelopment
> flows from the central decisions any
> society takes as to its essential
> needs and its vital relationships.
> These are ancient moral questions:
> what relationship exists between
> goods and the good life, what is the
> basis for a just society, and what
> stance ought societies to take towards
> nature and towards that second nature
> we call technology?[65]

Even though Goulet presents himself as a critical
modernist in arguing that as long as nations pursue affluence as the goal of the development process, only
modernity of "pseudo-development" is possible, he, nonetheless, remains a modernist for assuming that "the decisive element in all this is patently the conception

one has of development itself."[66] He will argue, for example, that for rich as well as poor nations, "what needs to be overturned is their very conception of what development is,"[67] and, furthermore, that

> The locus of challenge, in short, must shift from infatuation with material growth, quantity, and merchandizing manipulation to the ambition of assuring the achievement of integral growth.[68]

In addition, along with Albert O. Hirschman and others, he concludes that while "the enterprise [global development] is technically feasible, . . . gigantic obstacles to success lie in the realms of will, spirit, and values,"[69] or, alternately, that "the single most important resource for development is human will, collectively and responsibly mobilized."[70]

Because he locates the problem of development and underdevelopment "in the realms of will, spirit, and values," Goulet proceeds to identify his primary task as a development ethicist as that of determining "how development can be guided by values and how value transformation can indeed become the main road to development."[71] If he is certain that a "<u>psychic</u> revolution" is necessary and sufficient to "confront and transform social structures,"[72] he is no less certain that a "new wisdom" about development issues is needed to overcome what he perceives to be the limitations of both capitalist and socialist approaches, as now historically evidenced:

> Communist and capitalist development models alike share a form of materialism which easily 'alienates' man [sic] . . . in things, in abstractions, or in power. It is, therefore, not surprising to see experimental 'third ways' proliferate . . . in the Third World. . . .[73]

Goulet's own interest in Latin American liberation theology follows from his reading that liberation theologians, whom he calls Christian prophets of development" or prophets of "a new moral order," are involved in a search similar to his own for an "experimental 'third way'" and are seeking both "a liberating vision of material goods" and a non-ideological path "to 'humanize' and 'Christianize' social change."[74] In the next section, we shall examine aspects of Goulet's ethical methodology which clearly differentiate his work from that of the liberation theologians with whom he attempts to align himself. However, it is already evident that Goulet's placement within the social scientific debates raises questions about his supposed affinity with liberationists. Has Goulet not failed to remove himself sufficiently from a criticism that dependency theorists have made of modernization theorists and "culturalists" who "reduce the problem of development to one of acquiring relative values" and from whom "man [sic] and the structures that exploit and oppress him remain relegated to a secondary plane or are totally erased from consideration"? More to the point, despite his own critical sensibilities, and his intention to pay attention to power dynamics and to institutional structures which inhibit authentic development, Goulet remains on the modernization side of the debate, minimizes the conflict at hand, and speaks almost too comfortably as a "culturalist." The problem here, as Goulet himself concedes, is that

> For the 'culturalist,' . . . exploitation, the immediate cause of poverty, nowhere fits into the conceptual scheme, nor does the solution necessarily require any basic structural change in society: The solution will come through the adoption of proper values. . . .[75]

IV. Problematic Aspects of Goulet's Ethical Methodology

As mentioned earlier, Goulet identifies two particular problems which confront the moral philosopher who wishes to reflect upon issues of economic development, the problem of abstractness and inclination to moralize about development concerns and the problem of accountability and effective advocacy. In this section we will question whether he has, in fact, overcome these limitations of doing moral philosophical inquiry which he has described as so problematic. As we shall discover, Goulet employs an ahistorical method for constructing his ethics of development and does not explicitly incorporate an historical perspective in his analysis; moreover, because of the way in which he separates out ethical questions from political considerations, he tends to obscure his own interests in advocacy. Several rath-

130

er problematic aspects of his ethical methodology may become apparent by examining his understanding of (a) the task and historical role of the development ethicist, (b) the relationship between value transformation and socio-economic and political change, and (c) the need for a "theology of history" which bears "witness to a transcendent absolute beyond history."

Before we examine these specific issues, however, we should keep in mind that Goulet operates with certain epistemological presuppositions which are quite distinct from those of the Latin American liberation theologians. To characterize the differences at hand, we should consider how Carter Heyward has differentiated the epistemological positions of subjective idealists and Marxist realists:

> Idealist epistemology is an Enlightenment-conditioned theory of knowledge, which holds that all knowledge is literally 'in the mind of' the knower. All knowledge is dependent upon the autonomous reason and sense perception of the individual theologian whose ideas are themselves the shapers of reality. Karl Marx challenged this theory with his epistemologically revolutionary thesis that the purpose of knowledge is not to understand the world but to change it; and that the world is not changed by ideas (central to the idealist position), but rather ideas are changed by the work of people in the world.

> Marxist epistemology is thus grounded in a post-Enlightenment recognition of the social reality of specific groups (classes) of people who, in their daily work, give shape to ideas, or expressions, of social reality (including religion and theology). The idealist emphasis is on the individual theologian and her power of right perception. For Marx, the emphasis is on the community as context for the theologian's work, and on her involvement in the work of the community. The idealist stresses primarily herself,

her own ideas. The Marxist attempts
to articulate the meaning of the
work of her people.[76]

As we shall note, in his ethical analysis Goulet proceeds primarily as a subjective idealist for whom, as
he states, "the accountability here invoked need be only
to reason itself."[77] In the next chapter we shall detail more closely how liberation theologians operate on
the basis of a Marxist understanding of knowledge and
how they, in ways distinct from Goulet's, argue that
more is necessary to effect authentic development for
all persons than an adequate conception of the "good
life" or a shared consensus about normative values.

(A) The task and historical role of the development
ethicist. It is quite accurate to say that Goulet is
highly suspicious of so-called "objective" social scientific analysis, and he perceives himself as an able
critic of the ideological biases of development experts
and social planners. When he turns to ethical inquiry,
however, his own methodology is that of a moral philosopher detached from any direct participation in history
and operating in the mode of a non-partisan, critical
observer. As he details the tasks of the development
ethicist, he contends that "the most important contribution . . . is to build a coherent theoretical framework in which partial and fragmentary ethical constructs
can be unified around a few central and inter-related
analytical concepts." In constructing a universally ap-
licable normative theory of the good, the ethicist
should attempt, moreover, to isolate the invariant requirements of the good life and reflect upon those fundamental needs and "common values which all societies
desire." The analysis of the general human condition
is to be undertaken from a distinctively universal point
of view "for the benefit of men's [sic] universal needs,
not for any particular interests," and even though development ethicists are specialists in the development
discipline, they are called upon to operate simultaneously as "generalists attempting to produce a synthesis
of the whole of reality; and as bearers of values."[78]
In his understanding the task of the ethicist is essentially theoretical and conceptual in seeking to clarify
and analyze value assumptions inherent in decision-making and in presenting alternative normative schema persuasively through rational discourse.

Although Goulet speaks of ethicists as "bearers of

132

values," he flees the particular and historical in as-
piring to reach the universal. This bias for the universal over against any particular concretization of
values is consistent with his claim that "only those
values can be truly human which can be truly universal."[79] Goulet argues that

> Moralists may--indeed they must--as-
> pire to universality, not some ready-
> made universality, but a tentative
> model of partial universality in the
> making. . . . A normative system must
> emerge.[80]

This normative system he finds necessary in order to
comprehend that the development process itself is "above
all, a task of forging new values and new civilizations"[81]
and a universal quest for the common good.

What should be emphasized, however, is that Goulet
does not make an a priori claim that universal goals or
values exist. He recognizes the fact that there may be
"cultural absolutes" which are ethnocentric in character. Once he has made that concession, however, he
quickly proceeds to assert that there do, in fact, exist
trans-cultural universals which are not bound ideologically but which arise because they reflect certain basic
and incontrovertible universal human needs.[82] His argument follows that

> Such goods need not enjoy identical
> relative importance in all societies,
> it is simply required that they be
> present in all. . . . These are prop-
> erly universalizable goals inasmuch
> as their forms and modalities can vary
> in different times and places. Never-
> theless, these goals relate to funda-
> mental human needs capable of finding
> expression in all cultural matrices at
> all times.[83]

Goulet is ambiguous, however, about whether human needs
change and how they are historically conditioned. As
a moral philosopher, he speaks of the goals of development as coterminous with the goals of human existence
as such, and he proceeds analytically to describe basic
ethical values ahistorically apart from societal structures which either enhance or frustrate human needs.

In a similar manner, he can also view "Christianity as embodying certain universal human values, notwithstanding its historical development in a particular cultural matrix."[84]

Following his ahistorical method of analysis, Goulet speaks rather abstractly about universal values. His is a highly generalized theory of obligation disconnected from any particular historical activities, locations, or agents. What is even more curious, however, is his depiction of the historical role of development ethicists and planners. He speaks of them as professional "witnesses of the human species, disengaged from their nations." Such ethicists, Goulet argues, are able to "speak 'heretically' on behalf of universal human interests," and they transcend particular loyalties to nation-states and corporate interests by assuming a status as citizens-of-the-world whose ultimate commitment is to universal development objectives. In elaborating on the role of intellectuals, Goulet quotes Louis Lebret's suggestion that "it is even worth asking whether it is not appropriate to establish an 'Order' of experts, analogous to the professional Order of lawyers and medical doctors."[85]

The question immediately arises about the accountability of such experts and the inherent elitism of such a professional grouping of development planners. Does Goulet not speak rather naively about the role of the "free-lancer" who is deliberately uprooted from any particular cultural and political community and who attempts to speak "universally" although certainly "with varying degrees of sympathy for some political cause"? Although he acknowledges that the "free-floater needs links to a new humanity in gestation,"[86] he is disappointingly vague about how development ethicists should be related to particular communities and whether they should remain "detached observers" or engaged change agents.

Goulet's attempt to locate a universal reference point for speaking as an ethicist and his arguments for the desirability of operating out of a non-partisan, "free-floating" position outside of any historically located communities are quite compatible with the modus operandi of the moral philosopher who views the world dispassionately. Whether such an attempt is possible or desirable is another question. Since Goulet is seeking to construct an ethics of development in rela-

tion to liberation theology, he might well attend more
carefully to the claim often made by Third World liberation ethicists that theory must be critically and dialectically interrelated with praxis. More to the point,
in Doing Theology in a Revolutionary Situation, Jose
Miquez Bonino reiterates a persistent claim of Latin
American theologians for liberation, namely, that there
is no privileged position from which to stand above or
outside the world and view reality. An "engaged faith,"
he contends, must reject any assumed impartiality in the
historical struggle for liberation. Furthermore, theological-ethical inquiry must necessarily begin concretely with reflection upon the particular historical situation in which one is located and then attempt to generate new possibilities for reconceptualizing and acting
upon that reality. Miquez Bonino's critical point, over
against Goulet, is that any analysis of the situation is
"unavoidably related" to and cannot adequately be considered apart from one's political commitments and, further, that the categories and methods of analysis must
not be "developed in abstraction or in pure objective
contemplation, but in the very effort to overcome the
present situation and move forward to a new society."[87]

    (B) The relationship between value transformation
and socio-economic and political change. Goulet does
not hesitate to acknowledge that development is a "two-
edged sword" fraught with dangers as well as possibilities for restructuring societal and global economic
conditions to allow for authentic human development.
"As symbolic catch-word," he suggests, "it promises a
better life and greater opportunities for all. In practice, however, it usually benefits the fortunate few and
strengthens the privilege of those who keep the masses
in their misery." Development ethicists must, therefore, assess realistically the nature of the task and
the constraints they must deal with in order to "move
beyond moralism and devise ethical strategies that can
work."[88]

    As he understands his task as an ethicist, however,
Goulet does not attempt to elaborate specific political
strategies, nor does he provide an analysis of the
structures of domination which impede the development
process in underdeveloped countries. As he says,

        It should be obvious that what I pre-
        sent is no detailed blueprint for
        strategies to be employed . . ., but

> merely a perspective within which the
> means selected for achieving stipu-
> lated ends become amenable to ethical
> appraisal.[89]

The ethicist provides "a set of conceptual standards for
judging ends and evaluating means,"[90] and the theoretical nature of this task is in keeping with the stance
of the moral philosopher who provides an ethical analysis of events and issues in the mode of a detached observer rather than a participant. Moreover, Goulet is
insistent that the ethical task is quite different from
the political although our ethical commitments should
lead us to political engagement and inform those actions.

It should not be assumed, however, that Goulet altogether avoids discussing political issues and strategies. In his analysis of the issue of world hunger, for
example, he does argue that the political task is no
less than to restructure the international economic
order, but he fears reducing development concerns to
questions of political and economic changes alone. He
understands the development crisis as, above all, a
universal crisis in human values, and what is at stake
in the human quest for development is not merely providing certain material benefits for people or restructuring policial and social conditions but empowering
persons to become "true creators of their own history."[91]
Therefore, the means adopted for achieving social goals
become as important, if not more important, than the
goals themselves. As we noted earlier, Goulet is insistent that

> . . . how development is obtained de-
> termines whether men [sic] are liber-
> ated or alienated; the manner is as
> important as the matter![92]

He is no less adamant that the "good life" is to be
judged, above all, in terms of the ability of persons
to maximize their capacities for self-determination and
self-actualization. Freedom is the essence of human
beings, and Goulet argues that coercive measures employed to effect social change are actually counterproductive since persons must be self-motivated and free
to make ethical choices and act upon them. Otherwise,
even though material conditions may be altered, in the
same process human subjecthood will not be affirmed.

Because Goulet defines liberation most fundamentally in terms of personal value transformation and self-
actualization through expressions of self-authenticated
agency, he emphasizes the importance of persons "con-
versions" and transformations in discussing what he iso-
lates as the ethical dimensions of the development process. For example, he advocates that people in industrialized societies should adopt measures of voluntary
austerity to allow for identification in solidarity with
peoples in the Third World and also to offer "a witness
to spiritual value, to personal worth, to human commu-
nion."[93] As an ethical strategy, voluntary austerity is
not to be judged according to its political consequences, nor should there be an organized attempt to enforce
austerity upon people without their consent. His rea-
soning is that

> Were we to do this we would exteriorize
> and institutionalize what is essentially
> an inner spiritual liberation. . . .
> Whether it has overt political reper-
> cussions or not, voluntary austerity is
> self-validating because it is gratuitous,
> because it is human.[94]

Although Goulet seems to be speaking for an "ethics
of intentionality" which disregards the consequences of
actions, what seems more plausible is that his distinction between ethics and politics betrays an idealistic
tendency to over-emphasize attitudinal changes and alterations in consciousness and to disregard the realities of institutionalized power dynamics. This bias is
apparent, for example, when he discusses the Chinese
model of development. He addresses almost exclusively
the issues of consciousness-change and cultural revalua-
tions without relating these aspects of the Chinese cultural revolution to changes in either the socio-economic
or political orders. In The Myth of Aid he explains
that

> Its [China's] effort to achieve pro-
> gress toward autonomous, mass-parti-
> cipation development gives primacy to
> cultural factors (creating new values
> in the 'new man' [sic]) over mere eco-
> nomic efficiency. This occurs in
> spite of China's formal adherence to
> an ideology which views culture as a
> mere derivative expression of material

137

infra-structures.[95]

Because of his own theory of development and underdevelopment which focuses almost exclusively upon the attitudinal changes and disruption of "value universes" which cause as well as accompany a people's "transition to modernity," Goulet can speak as if the Chinese revolution was undertaken principally in "the realm of ideas" by signalling an alteration of what he has described elsewhere as "men's [sic] inner environment comprising the world of their aspirations and motives."[96] Furthermore, he invests ideas and value commitments with such an autonomous power to shape historical realities and effect social change that he even credits what he calls "the power of ethics" with the capacity "to counter the power of wealth, of politics, of bureaucratic inertia, of defeatism, of social pathology."[97]

Unfortunately, what Goulet fails to do throughout his analysis is to describe the dialectical relationship between personal and social change. Since he does not provide any socio-historical analysis of the structures of domination or explore the impact of structural conditions upon consciousness, he appears idealistic and unnecessarily naive in considering the possibilities of reordering ethical priorities and values, especially within advanced industrialized societies. He is also so confident that executives in multinational corporations, for example, can be enlisted as "stewards of the transition" toward authentic global development that he even speaks of adopting a strategy of "winning 'defectors'" which "relies on appealing to the multiple loyalties of those presently serving global elitist constituencies."[98] He contends that this strategy will be sufficient to "win over" elites although not sufficient, by itself, to transform the inequities of the present world economic system:

> All institutional actors described
> herein harbor within their confines
> some individuals with the requisite
> dual loyalties [to their particular
> communities of interest and to a
> global community in the making].
> Therefore, institutional actors can
> change under the impact of human
> wills. International bureaucrats
> can discover numerous ways to become
> accountable to concrete communities

of need, even if they have at times divorced themselves from local allegiances to cultural origins. Similarly, enlightened personnel in transnational corporations can, in virtue of their loyalties outside the firm, pressure their own institutions to adopt radically different roles in a future order.[99]

From a liberationist perspective, this strategy of appealing to the good will of the powerful is highly problematic. Samuel Parmar has identified one questionable aspect of this kind of approach which "ignores vital questions about the nature and causes of poverty of the many and prosperity of the few" and also fails to analyze the relationship between power inequalities and the persistence of poverty:

> Decision-makers, many of whom are sincere and well-meaning and eager to help in development, are seldom free from the demands of the system which they operate. At best they can bring about some modification in rules and relationships, but they cannot be initiators of radical change, because such change undermines their power-base.[100]

Dependency theorists are no less doubtful of the adequacy of a social-change strategy which reduces the problems at hand to a question of attaining "proper" motivation. As James Cockcroft, Andre Gunder Frank, and Dale Johnson have argued,

> . . . political analysis involves the search for power relationships that reside in the structural relations between economic and social institutions, social classes, and the state. In this way, actors are agents of objective institutional, class, and power relationships that exist in society. The roles that individuals perform in various institutional involvements and in the political sphere are not determined merely by their personal motives nor

139

> by interpersonal-situational factors.
> Roles are fundamentally shaped by in-
> situtional arrangements and by basic
> structures of class and power.[101]

Because of the way in which Goulet defines and separates
ethical and political issues and in keeping with his
ahistorical approach to ethical issues, he bypasses the
need to analyze the power dynamics of the institutional
matrix within which development decisions and policies
are made. He also underestimates the urgency of political as well as personal changes. If this criticism
is accurate, then Goulet himself has provided grounds
to question the validity of his own methodology, for he
has argued that development ethics must deal with issues
of power and

> . . . cope with structures of dif-
> ferential wealth and power among
> societies. Were it otherwise, ethics
> would be reduced to mere preachments
> addressed to the 'good will' and gen-
> erosity of the powerful, and to the
> escapist sentiments of the powerless.[102]

(C) The need for a "theology of history" which
bears "witness to a transcendent absolute beyond history." As we consider Goulet's discussion of history
and theology, we should first attend to a basic ambi-
guity underlying his description of the historical quest
for development both as an ongoing process and as a terminal state. According to his ethical model, the telos
provides purpose and direction for human activity, and
Goulet argues that it is universally true, irrespective
of time or location, that persons project some vision
of the good life and the good society and seek to realize that goal. Within history the development process
remains necessarily open-ended, and he will contend
that because of the dialectical nature of the struggle
for liberation and development, the final outcome is
totally unpredictable. When he emphasizes the process
character of development, he states the following case:

> The great ascent may fail. Similarly,
> the take-off into self-sustained growth
> may never come or prove lasting. One
> errs if he imagines development to be
> a necessary progressive movement. . . .
> The only certainty is that development

140

for the world at large is uncertain,
notwithstanding pronouncements which
seem to assume that it is inevitable.
In my opinion, development can succeed only if the world realizes that
it can fail.[103]

Although Goulet does argue that there is no guarantee for the ultimate success of the development project,
he alternately presents a "theology of history" which
assumes that there is, in fact, a definite culminating
stage in history at which point humankind reaches its
final phase of development. The telos here is not only
guiding the process but also locating history's finis.
The issue, moreover, for Goulet is not whether there is
an inevitable end to history but whether a fixed term
or "perfection" is arrived at within history or whether
the action of a transcendent God beyond history must
necessarily "crown and transfigure a work humanly com-
pleted."[104] As he argues, the Christian cannot take
history itself as an ultimate, final end, for "what
makes human history important is its unrelenting drive
toward transcendence"[105] and its witness to a transcendent Absolute beyond history.

Not only does Goulet presuppose a certain understanding of religion, namely, as faith which posits a
God beyond history, but he also suggests that Christians
face a particular dilemma in attempting "to be present
to history without abdicating their specific witness to
a transcendent absolute beyond history."[106] He argues
that religion must be able to provide both a stimulus
for engaging in historical struggle and a caution against
restricting the full dimensions of liberation by en-
closing it "within purely finite borders." Accordingly,
theology has a two-fold task. First, theology must not
devalue the importance of commitment to projects within
history, but at the same time it must ascribe only relative ultimate meaning to "secular history." Second,
theology must provide "a cosmic vision of final human
destiny" and of "reality open to supra-historical transcendence."[107] His contention is that only "a conception of secular history with a theology based on a
transcendent theology" can motivate human engagement in
liberation struggles and overcome any tendency toward
escapism from history by "inciting faith in the future
and offering . . . pressing reasons for commitment in
the present."[108]

Goulet self-consciously constructs his theology of history as an alternative to any Marxist analysis of reality, which he interprets primarily as a philosophy of history. His criticism of Marxism focuses on what he takes to be its atheistic rejection of a transcendence beyond history and its mechanistic view of historical inevitability. Goulet's own position, however, describes history as the inevitable ascent toward complete human development, and, furthermore, he seems to assume that persons are willing to struggle against alienating conditions only if there is an assurance of ultimate success. On this point he seems to misunderstand liberation theologians who not only insist that history does not follow a pre-determined course, but who also argue that the question of perfectability in history--or beyond--is a misplaced debate and a quite inappropriate question upon which to concentrate. As Rubem Alves states, for example, Christianity is not to be understood as

> . . . a belief in the possibility of a perfect society but rather the belief in the non-necessity of this imperfect order. It does not claim that it is possible to abolish sin, but it affirms that there is no reason to accept the rule of the sinful structures that now control our society.109

Moreover, it is not self-evident that a theology of history such as Goulet offers is necessary to motivate human agency, for liberating praxis begins not with any prior acceptance of a goal to be realized in the future or with any assurances of ultimate victory but with the awareness in the present that conditions are not inevitable but alienating and to be opposed. The language of liberation theology is spoken more in terms of new possibilities rather than in terms of historical inevitabilities or of certain assurances.

One final question is whether Goulet has avoided the "theistic trap" of setting up a two-world dualism. Does he, in fact, succeed in his stated intention to identify a new form of religious praxis which can answer the Marxist critique of those alienating forms of religion which "abolish history" and "make ultimate significance reside in seomething a-historical"?110 He continues to insist that Christians "betray religion" if they "forego meta-historical transcendence."111 We must

142

agree with Miguez Bonino that as one who still stands within the Roman Catholic tradition, Goulet may yet suffer

> . . . from the still strong influence of the Scholastic view of the relation between nature and grace in which the latter becomes a superstructure built on the basis of the former, with the corresponding danger of mystic absorption of the human into the divine order.[112]

The danger of dualistic thinking is that it tends to undercut precisely the kind of historical engagement in the struggle for liberation which Goulet affirms. If he has not supplied sufficient means in his own writings to avoid this danger, we can at least agree with him fully that the issues at stake here are of great importance "not in high theory or speculation but in the realm of politics."[113]

From our analysis it is apparent that Goulet's own method hinders him from taking the direction in which he wants to work as a moral philosopher, especially since he is so adamant that, in regard to issues of liberation and global development, there can be no neutrality or retreat to a non-partisan zone. Insofar as he continues to view the world as a moral philosopher, however, he presents himself from the stance of a detached observer rather than that of an agent engaged in liberation struggles, and he tends to define ethical criteria in abstraction from the particular concrete conditions and conflicts of persons located in history. Whether wittingly or not, he has fallen prey to the "ideology of liberalism" that the ethicist can--and should--maintain a neutral position, free from "unholy alliances" on the right and left, and invoke norms which are available from a privileged position outside the historical situation. Therefore, he has at least asked the right question about whether moral philosophers are able to supply an adequate ethics of development if they fail to ground their ethical reflections historically and take more seriously their obligations as advocates for global justice.

V. Goulet's Placement within the Ecumenical Debates: A Progressive Developmentalist on the Vatican II Side

At first glance Goulet does not appear to be an immediate party to the ecumenical church debates over global development. After all, he describes himself as a philosopher of development whose project is to offer a decidedly "public ethic" which addresses an audience not only of Christians but also of those outside that faith experience. Moreover, even though he argues that ethical obligation must be grounded in a theory of value, that is, of the good, he distinguishes himself from other Christian ethicists by not depending on criteria from theology or from revelation to ground his understanding of the good. For him, basic human good is universally recognizable and arrived at by virtue of human self-knowledge and critical reflection on the conditions and processes of human development, and as an ethicist he appeals to ethical norms which all "reasonable" persons can share.[114]

It is also true, however, that Goulet acknowledges that certain theological assumptions inform and shape his work in some very fundamental ways. He would also be the first to admit that he has not stayed on the sidelines of the theological fray over development issues, for he has declared his intent to develop his own ethics of development in dialogue with Latin American theologians of liberation. In A New Moral Order he is quite explicit about his praise for and identification with what he calls the "new breed" of Third World Christians whose commitments to social justice have led them to aim, in his words,

> . . . to prove to the world--and especially to those who were engaged in social militancy before they were-- that they are serious about liberation, about 'the combat for development,'

and, furthermore,

> . . . [whose] contributions can be traced, in my opinion, to [their] loyal attachment to fundamental (though not fundamentalist) Christian ethical postulates.[115]

Goulet is also at his polemical best on those occasions in which he criticizes, for example, "so basically religious a writer as [Peter] Berger" for the latter's misreading of Paulo Freire in Pyramids of Sacrifice but especially for Berger's assuming that even a pessimistic reading of humanity and history can somehow "absolve Christians from full, incarnational insertion in the task of 'redeeming time.'"[116] Goulet is also as insistent as anyone else involved in the ecumenical debates that Christian ministry should aim at improving the situation of those who are least well-off and most powerless to determine their own lives and, more to the point, that "in concrete societies today, churches must decide whether to legitimate existing establishments, or become creative architects of new possibilities."[117]

Despite the fact that Goulet finds himself attracted to the liberation side of the development debates, he provides what amounts to an implicit critique of liberation theology. That critique arises from Goulet's judgment that liberation Christians have jeopardized the integrity of Christian faith by yielding to a Marxist and, therefore, materialistic understanding of human nature and of the dynamics of history and by their ideological reduction of religion to a political option. It is with liberation theologians in mind that Goulet has stated, for example, that

> Many contemporary Christians are tempted to betray their own peculiar trust by reducing their religion to being merely one other instrument for transforming the world.[118]

Because he assumes that Marxism and Christianity are two quite distinct and incompatible conceptual systems, he has also made the following generalization:

> Theoretical dialogues between Marxists and Christians as well as the practical collaboration between both categories prove conclusively that Christians are, by definition, bearers of a message of transcendence. . . . Indeed, one ceases to be a Christian in any meaningful sense if one reduces salvation or redemption to its purely historical dimension.[119]

He has also invoked the theological authority of no less than Reinhold Niebuhr to insist that, properly understood, that is, "in the absolute sense," there is "no such thing as 'Christian socialism.'"[120]

In order to decipher Goulet's understanding of what "being a Christian in any meaningful sense" involves and to give an accurate accounting of his critique of liberation theology, we need to recognize that his own theological and political sensibilities are more in accord with the Second Vatican Council than with the Latin Americans with whom he seeks to dialogue. One important clue to placing him within that dominant theological tradition is found, for example, in his interest to determing "whether there is a specifically Christian way of 'making history'" and in his affirmative response that Christians are called upon to assume a peculiarly "spiritual" task above politics:

> The most 'religious' way to make history . . ., even at the service of 'radical' transformation of societal structures, is by using the 'poor means'. . . . Those who have done the most to 'humanize' and 'Christianize' social change are the prophets who have resisted the enticements of power. . . .[121]

An additionally significant clue is Goulet's claim that the historical project which Christians should undertake is that of

> . . . creating a new civilization of theocentric humanism and promoting 'infravalent' secular and historical ends, that is, constructing a common good at once political, cultural, educational, economic and familial.[122]

Both these statements bear the noticeable imprint of Goulet's two principal mentors, Louis Joseph Lebret and Jacques Maritain, whose own work, in turn, gave fundamental shape to the progressive developmentalist position of the teaching magisterium.

Lebret, the French Dominican priest and development scholar who founded the interdisciplinary research center, Economy and Humanism, in 1941 and the Institute for Research and Training in Development (IRFED) in 1958, was the primary author of the papal encyclical, Populorum Progressio, and the one who first spoke of global development as the universal human ascent. Goulet studied and worked with Lebret in the late 1950's and early 1960's, and in speaking of him as the pioneer of the discipline of development ethics, Goulet credits the Dominican with the insight which is fundamental to his own work, namely, that

> Underdevelopment, in Lebret's view, is not mainly an economic problem; neither is it simply the inability of social structures to meet the new demands of formerly passive populations. Above all else, underdevelopment is a symptom of a worldwide crisis in human values.[123]

What is particularly important to recognize is that Goulet shares Lebret's disenchantment with both capitalist and socialist models of development, for the reason that each subscribes to the myth of mass consumerism as the goal of the development process. Goulet also endorses what Rene Laurentin has summarized as the message of Populorum Progressio, that authentic development will come about only as the result of "a conversion from economic materialism . . . to cultural humanism: a humanism that is open to man's [sic] divinization."[124] Lebret himself was explicit about the need for and the possibility of this new spiritual awakening, which would be the necessary and sufficient "last revolution":

> The Christian message, through . . . its great commandment of love, has a greater potential for civilization than any other. When any group of people comes to understand this, that group becomes fraternally united. When the people who claim to embody a Christian civilization put it into practice, the world will straighten itself out.[125]

As Laurentin has observed, Lebret was subject at this point to a kind of "clerical wishful-thinking" in maintaining "the naive conviction that an idea, simply because it was formulated or promulgated, was going to become a part of life and would even structure it."[126] Furthermore, because of Lebret's own fundamental mistrust of political movements and the fact that he was "fearful that he was not capable of correct political

147

analyses, nor of integrating the political dimension with the theory and practice of development,"[127] he often spoke as Goulet does that what Christians need in order to respond adequately to development problems is nothing more than "tough minds and tender hearts, or, as Lebret used to say, 'intelligent love.'"[128] Both men skirt the issue of political confrontation between rich and poor and talk only of the power of moral suasion.

If, according to Lebret, the church's role is that of "civilizing" through its teaching of Christian values and through motivating the individual to act in the world to institutionalize those values, Goulet advocates a quite similar strategy of personal value transformation as the means to effect social change. Because Goulet also diagnoses the fundamental problem of underdevelopment as a false, materialistic conception of the "good life" and argues that the primary obstacle to global solidarity is "the lure of material riches," he turns to religion "to teach men [sic] detachment from things."[129] Moreover, he remains at best skeptical of those Christians involved in socialist movements because he has appropriated Lebret's reading of Marxism as primarily a philosophical worldview or metaphysic antithetical to "the" Christian understanding of human nature and history rather than as a socio-economic analysis and critique of capitalist economic development. Goulet details Lebret's position in the following passage which is also descriptive of his own:

> Notwithstanding his evident sympathy with Marx's view of the nonalienated society, Lebret rejected what he took to be a truncated model of humanism which considered spiritual and personal excellences only in their bastardized expressions. . . . He believed that to imprison human destiny within the confines of an immanentist view of history is to close the door to genuine transcendence; in effect, it diminished the stature of man [sic].[130]

As a philosophical idealist, what Goulet finds most objectionable is what he regards as the inadequacies of a Marxist anthropology which denies that the human person is more a spiritual than a material creature, and he quotes Arnold Toynbee approvingly that

148

> Genuine growth . . . resides in a
> process of overcoming material ob-
> stacles and releasing the energies
> of society [and of the individual]
> to respond to challenges that are
> internal rather than external, spir-
> itual rather than material.[131]

In maintaining the dominant theological tradition's
antithesis between spirit and matter, a distinction
based on a natural-supernatural dichotomy, Goulet reflects, as well, the influence of Jacques Maritain, who
likewise insisted upon "the primacy of the spiritual"
and characterized human freedom in these terms:

> Man [sic] must gradually win a
> freedom which, in the social and
> political order, consists above
> all in his becoming . . . as in-
> dependent as possible of the con-
> straints of material nature. In
> short, the human person, so far
> as he is made for God and for
> participation in absolute goods,
> transcends the earthly society
> of which he is a member.[132]

By his own strong affirmation of the power of ideas to
reshape history and in keeping with his voluntaristic
appeal for persons to undergo a fundamental value transformation, Goulet also tends to convert persons into
Platonic beings subject to and determined by ideas and
values but not conditioned by concrete realities or vulnerable to suffering from political and economic inequities. Values take on a kind of autonomous existence in
his understanding of the ways in which persons and
their communities are shaped and reshaped. From a liberation perspective this "ideological inversion" of
social reality and ethical-political consciousness is
highly questionable. As Pablo Richard has countered,

> 'It is not the "gospel values" which
> upon incarnating themselves transform
> man [sic] and society, but it is
> rather man [sic] as historical sub-
> ject who transforms social reality in
> the measure in which he struggles to
> overcome all alienation and oppres-
> sion. Man [sic] is creative subject

149

of his history and not the object of
a world of values which "ought to
be" incarnated. Only by taking off
from praxis and not from the "gospel"
will theology be able to overcome
this inversion of subject-object, in
which the ideological character of
Christianity is rooted, and which
deeply impedes Christians from taking
up the social praxis of liberation.'[133]

What is no less questionable, however, for liberation Christians is Goulet's determination that the contemporary religious task is best described as that of
creating a new global civilization of theocentric humanism, a task which Maritain described as the construction of a "New Christendom" or, in his own words,

. . . a 'secular' Christian civilization, in which temporal things, philosophical and scientific reason, and
civil society, will enjoy their autonomy and at the same time recognize
the quickening and inspiring role
that spiritual things, religious faith,
and the Church play from their higher
plane. Then a Christian philosophy of
life would guide a community vitally,
not decoratively Christian, a community
of human rights and of the dignity of
the human person, in which men [sic]
belonging to diverse racial stocks and
to diverse spiritual lineages would
work at a temporal common task which
was truly human and progressive.[134]

As Gustavo Gutierrez has argued, this program to build
a profane Christendom, a society inspired by Christian
values, not only perpetuates "a certain ecclesiastical
narcissism" but, more importantly, maintains a "distinction of planes" approach which not only distinguishes
faith and world realitites but assigns a politically
neutral role to the church. As Gutierrez has queried,
however, in the contemporary Latin American situation,

. . . can it honestly be said that
the Church does not interfere in
'the temporal sphere'? Is the Church
fulfilling a purely religious role

when by its silence or friendly relationships it lends legitimacy to
a dictatorial and oppressive government? . . . Concretely, in Latin
America the distinction of planes
model has the effect of concealing
the real political option of a large
sector of the Church--that is, support of the established order. . . .
The dominant groups, who have always
used the Church to defend their interests and maintain their privileged
position, today--as they see 'subversive' tendencies gaining ground in
the heart of the Christian community--
call for a return to the purely religious and spiritual function of the
Church.[135]

Gutierrez does, indeed, recognize that Maritain's
ideal of a New Christendom was a progressive theological
proposal at the time of its articulation in the 1930's
and remained so even when the Second Vatican Council
adopted this perspective in presenting its Constitution
on the Church in the Modern World. Not only were Christians and most especially laypersons called upon to become active in promoting social justice, but the view
that the church acted in the world only to defend the
interests of the ecclesiastical hierarchy was criticized
and transcended. The argument which Gutierrez now wishes to make, however, is that in the present historical
context,

The distinction of planes banner has
changed hands. Until a few years ago
it was defended by the vanguard; now
it is held aloft by power groups, many
of whom are in no way involved with
any commitment to the Christian faith.
Let us not be deceived, however. Their
purposes are very different. Let us
not unwittingly aid the opponent.[136]

Given the fact that Goulet's intention is not to lend
support to any reactionary interests opposing authentic
development but rather to provide an ethical analysis
to promote efforts toward a more just global order, it
is disconcerting, to say the least, that he has not
questioned, in any straightforward or explicit fashion,

151

the adequacy and applicability of a theological perspective which, in Gutierrez's rather concise phrasing, has "lost its vitality and . . . become a hindrance to pastoral action."[137] While it is also true that Goulet is not entirely responsible for any and every misuse of his own work, the fact remains that his emphasis on cultural and not political dimensions of the struggle for economic justice and his criticism toward liberation Christians for their attraction to Marxist alternatives only camouflages his own commitment to conscienticize those in the affluent First World for whom he wishes to "render the leap into 'liberation' possible."[138] In the Third World the consequences of such a developmentalist, albeit progressive, position are even more dire, as this description of political realities in Latin America indicates:

> The military regimes now ruling most
> of Latin America share an aversion
> to 'politics.' Blaming 'politics'
> and especially leftist political ide-
> ologies for disorder, corruption,
> economic insolvency and other ills,
> the military leaders have banned the
> expression of competing demands, pro-
> mises and programs by political par-
> ties. . . . Out of their determina-
> tion to 'depoliticize' public life
> and their obsessive fear that an open
> and pluralist society may create con-
> ditions favorable to socialist alter-
> natives, right-wing military leaders
> have sought to impose a political
> order based on hierarchy, authority,
> obedience and the subordination of
> citizens' rights to the 'national
> interest.'[139]

Despite Goulet's concern, which we acknowledged at the beginning of this chapter, to place himself outside of the ideological debates over development and to locate neutral ground upon which "to transcend parochialism and provide transcultural 'human' answers to development questions,"[140] we have found ample reasons to suspect that he has not only fallen to one side of the debate but may well have even provided ammunition against those on the theological and political left with whom he has indicated his willingness to dialogue. Contrary to his own intentions, his is by no means a "neutral" or ideologically untainted "ethic of global development," but rather one which fails to move sufficiently beyond the limitations of the dominant developmentalist perspective.

In the next chapter we shall examine the emerging ethical-theological perspective of selected theologians of liberation from Latin America who offer a distinct alternative to this "progressivist" position. Their critique of and counterproposal to the liberal paradigm have arisen precisely to disclose how compromising a "centrist" position, such as Goulet's, can be within the dynamics of the economic development debate.

NOTES

1. Denis Goulet, A New Moral Order: Studies in Development Ethics and Liberation Theology (Maryknoll: Orbis Books, 1974), p. 2.

2. Denis Goulet, "World Hunger: Putting Development Ethics to the Test," Christianity and Crisis, Vol. 35, No. 9 (May 26, 1975), p. 132.

3. Ibid., p. 127. For Goulet's discussion of human needs and values, see especially his "Sufficiency for All: The Basic Mandate of Development and Social Economics," Review of Social Economy, Vol. 36, No. 3 (December 1978), pp. 243-261.

4. Ibid., pp. 128 and 126.

5. Ibid., p. 127.

6. Ibid.

7. Ibid., p. 130.

8. Ibid., p. 128.

9. Denis Goulet, "Discussion," in Neil H. Jacoby, The Progress of Peoples (Santa Barbara: The Center for the Study of Democratic Institutions, 1969), p. 35.

10. Denis Goulet, The Uncertain Promise: Value Conflicts in Technology Transfers (New York: IDOC/North America, in cooperation with the Overseas Development Council, 1977), p. 196; cf. Denis Goulet, "Domesticating the Third World," in Denis Goulet and Michael Hudson, The Myth of Aid: The Hidden

Agenda of the Development Reports (Maryknoll: Orbis Books,
1971), p. 13.

11. Goulet, Myth of Aid, p. 29.

12. Denis Goulet, The Cruel Choice: A New Concept in the Theory
     of Development, copyright (c) 1971 Denis Goulet, p. 30. Re-
     printed with the permission of Atheneum Publishers.
13. Goulet, New Moral Order, pp. 35, 42, and passim.

14. Denis Goulet, "Christian Ethics and World Development: A
     Critical Perspective," unpubl. ms. (January 1974), p. 9.

15. Goulet, Cruel Choice, p. vii.

16. Ibid., p. 181.

17. Ibid., pp. xx-xxi.

18. Denis Goulet, "Christian Ethics and Global Economics," Chris-
     tianity and Crisis, Vol. 38, no. 17 (November 13, 1978), p.
     273.

19. Goulet, Cruel Choice, pp. xvi, xv, and xx.

20. Ibid., p. xv.

21. Ibid., p. 19.

22. Ibid., p. xviii.

23. Ibid., p. xix.

24. Ibid., pp. xxi and x.

25. Goulet, New Moral Order, pp. 5-17.

26. Denis Goulet, "Beyond Moralism: Ethical Studies in Global
     Development," unpubl. ms. (June 1976), p. 5.

27. Goulet, Cruel Choice, p. vii.

28. Ibid., p. viii.

29. Goulet, Myth of Aid, p. 20.

30. Goulet, Cruel Choice, p. 14.

31. Goulet, Myth of Aid, p. 25.

154

32. Goulet, New Moral Order, p. 16.

33. Goulet, Cruel Choice, p. 10.

34. Ibid., pp. 24-25.

35. Goulet, Uncertain Promise, p. 219; "Beyond Moralism," p. 11.

36. Goulet, "Christian Ethics and World Development," pp. 10-11.

37. Goulet, Cruel Choice, p. 19.

38. Ibid., p. 335. Goulet's tendency to dismiss the significance of political realities and his inclination to reflect upon ethical issues apart from any analysis of power dynamics goes against his own better judgment, for he has argued, for example, that "development ethics is useless unless it can be translated into public action." He also cites the validity of the Marxian insight that ethical idealism is suspect insofar as it generates "prescriptive politics formulated in ideal terms and divorced from historically conditioned structures" (Cruel Choice, pp. 335 and 336-337). But because Goulet most often engages in ethical analysis split off from any critical political diagnoses, he disregards his own advice and seems to assume that the work of the ethicist is complete once normative values have been clarified and presented in a coherent theoretical framework. Therefore, his declared interest to investigate and influence development policies "otherwise than through power" remains legitimate but not sufficient from the perspective of liberationists who insist upon the need--always--for analysis of operative power dynamics in any social ethical inquiry.

39. Ibid., p. 64.

40. Ibid., p. 18.

41. Ibid., pp. 223-224.

42. Daniel Lerner, The Passing of Traditional Society, p. 50.

43. Goulet, Cruel Choice, p. 264.

44. Ibid., p. xxi.

45. Ibid., p. 224.

46. Ibid., p. 298.

47. Ibid., p. xvi.

48. Ibid., p. 272. Goulet's emphasis.

49. Ibid., pp. 294 and 295.

50. Gustavo Gutierrez, A Theology of Liberation, p. 96.

51. Goulet, Cruel Choice, p. 38.

52. Ibid., pp. 38-39.

53. Denis Goulet, "Sufficiency for All: The Basic Mandate of De-
    velopment and Social Economics," Review of Social Economy,
    Vol. 36, no. 3 (December 1978), p. 244.

54. Cf. Goulet, Cruel Choice, p. xiv.

55. Ibid., pp. 74-76. Goulet's emphasis.

56. Daniel Lerner, "Modernization," p. 390; Albert O. Hirschman,
    The Strategy of Economic Development, p. 11.

57. Goulet, Cruel Choice, p. 252.

58. Denis Goulet, "On the Goals of Development," Cross Currents,
    Vol. 18, no. 4 (Fall 1968), p. 388.

59. Goulet, Cruel Choice, p. xiv.

60. Ibid.

61. Goulet, "Sufficiency for All," p. 259.

62. Goulet, "On the Goals of Development," p. 387.

63. Goulet, Uncertain Promise, p. 23.

64. Goulet, Cruel Choice, p. 222.

65. Denis Goulet, "Ethical Strategies in the Struggle for World
    Development," unpubl. ms. (June 1974), p. 5. My emphasis.

66. Goulet, "On the Goals of Development," p. 398.

67. Goulet, Myth of Aid, p. 23.

68. Goulet, Uncertain Promise, p. 87.

69. Denis Goulet, _World Interdependence: Verbal Smokescreen or New Ethic?_ (Washington: Overseas Development Council, 1976), p. 19.

70. Goulet, _Uncertain Promise_, p. 44.

71. Ibid., p. 45.

72. Goulet, "Ethical Strategies in the Struggle for World Development," p. 28.

73. Goulet, "On the Goals of Development," p. 401.

74. Goulet, _New Moral Order_, pp. 85ff., 137; "Beyond Moralism," p. 24.

75. James Cockcroft et. al., _Dependence and Underdevelopment_, pp. 419 and 418.

76. Carter Heyward, "Speaking and Sparking, Building and Burning: Ruether and Daly, Theologians," _Christianity and Crisis_, Vol. 39, no. 5 (April 2, 1979), pp. 67-68.

77. Denis Goulet, "Is Gradualism Dead?: Reflections on Order, Change and Force," The Council of Religion and International Affairs (1970), p. 33.

78. Goulet, _Cruel Choice_, pp. 12, 87, 181, and 186.

79. Ibid., p. xxi.

80. Goulet, _New Moral Order_, p. 17.

81. Ibid., p. 35.

82. Goulet, _Cruel Choice_, p. 86.

83. Ibid., p. 87.

84. Goulet, _New Moral Order_, p. 96. My emphasis.

85. Goulet, _Cruel Choice_, pp. 178, 179, and 184.

86. Goulet, "Ethical Strategies in the Struggle for World Development," pp. 19 and 20.

87. Jose Miguez Bonino, _Doing Theology in a Revolutionary Situation_, p. 35.

88. Goulet, "Ethical Strategies in the Struggle for World Development," pp. 1 and 3.

89. Goulet, Cruel Choice, p. 169. My emphasis.

90. Denis Goulet, "World Hunger: Putting Development Ethics to the Test," Christianity and Crisis, Vol. 35, no. 9 (May 26, 1975), p. 132.

91. Goulet, "Ethical Strategies in the Struggle for World Development," p. 10.

92. Goulet, Cruel Choice, p. 298.

93. Denis Goulet, "Voluntary Austerity: The Necessary Art," Christian Century, Vol. 83, no. 33 (June 8, 1966), p. 751.

94. Ibid., p. 752. My emphasis.

95. Goulet, Myth of Aid, p. 61.

96. Goulet, Cruel Choice, p. 187.

97. Denis Goulet, "On the Ethics of Development Planning: General Principles and Special Application to Value Conflicts in Technology," unpubl. ms. (August 1975), pp. 28-29.

98. Goulet, Uncertain Promise, p. 227.

99. Ibid., p. 226. My emphasis.

100. Samuel Parmar in Dickinson, To Set at Liberty, pp. 176-177.

101. Cockcroft et. al, pp. 422-423.

102. Goulet, Cruel Choice, p. 19.

103. Ibid., pp. 107-108.

104. Denis Goulet, "Secular History and Teleology," World Justice, Vol. 8, no. 1 (September 1966), p. 14.

105. Goulet, New Moral Order, p. 132.

106. Ibid., p. 110.

107. Goulet, "Secular History and Teleology," p. 16.

108. Ibid., pp. 8 and 7.

109. Rubem Alves, "Christian Realism: Ideology of the Establish-
     ment," Christianity and Crisis, Vol. 33, no. 15 (September
     17, 1973), p. 175. Alves' emphasis.

110. Goulet, "Secular History and Teleology," p. 7.

111. Goulet, New Moral Order, p. 110. The issue of transcendence
     is discussed differently by the Latin Americans, as we shall
     be discussing in the next chapter.

112. Miguez Bonino, Doing Theology in a Revolutionary Situation,
     p. 144.

113. Goulet, New Moral Order, p. 128.

114. Cf. Goulet's discussion of solidarity as the fundamental
     moral category and this argument to justify his claim in
     "World Hunger: Putting Development Ethics to the Test," pp.
     126 and 131-132.

115. Ibid., pp. 84 and 85.

116. Denis Goulet, "Pyramids of Sacrifice: The High Price of
     Social Change," Christianity and Crisis, Vol. 35, no. 16
     (October 13, 1975), pp. 233, 234.

117. Goulet, "Beyond Moralism," p. 21.

118. Ibid., p. 22.

119. Goulet, "Christian Ethics and World Development," pp. 12-13.
     My emphasis.

120. Goulet, Cruel Choice, p. 312.

121. Goulet, "Beyond Moralism," p. 24.

122. Goulet, "Secular History and Teleology," p. 12.

123. Goulet, New Moral Order, p. 35.

124. Rene Laurentin, Liberation, Development and Salvation, p.
     210.

125. Louis Joseph Lebret, The Last Revolution: The Destiny of
     Over- and Underdeveloped Nations, trans. John Horgan (New
     York: Sheed and Ward, 1965), p. 198.

126. Laurentin, p. 183.

127. Ibid., p. 182.

128. Goulet, "Christian Ethics and Global Economics," p. 277.

129. Goulet, "World Interdependence," p. 29; Cruel Choice, p. 258.

130. Goulet, New Moral Order, p. 40.

131. Goulet, Cruel Choice, p. 18.

132. Joseph W. Evans and Leo R. Ward, eds., The Social and Political Philosophy of Jacques Maritain: Selected Readings (Garden City, New York: Image Books, 1965), p. 33.

133. Pablo Richard, "Socialist Rationality and the Historical Verification of Christianity," quoted by Phillip E. Berryman, "Latin American Liberation Theology," in Torres and Eagleson, eds., Theology in the Americas, p. 35.

134. Evans and Ward, p. 164. My emphasis.

135. Gutierrez, A Theology of Liberation, pp. 55 and 65.

136. Ibid., p. 65.

137. Ibid., p. 63.

138. Goulet, Cruel Choice, p. xix.

139. Patricia Weiss Fagen, "Human Rights in Latin America: Learning from the Literature," Christianity and Crisis, Vol. 39, no. 20 (December 24, 1979), p. 330.

140. Goulet, "On the Goals of Development," p. 391.

CHAPTER IV

LATIN AMERICAN LIBERATION THEOLOGIANS' RESPONSE TO THE DEVELOPMENT DEBATE: BREAKING WITH THE LIBERAL PARADIGM AND PROPOSING A "NEW WAY"

The parallelism noted thus far in our study of the ideological tensions and splits between developmentalist and liberationist parties to the economic development debate is not yet complete. On additional step must be taken to bring the argument forward and to allow us to proceed, in the concluding chapter, to an assessment of the normative socio-ethical significance of this debate. In this present chapter our attention turns to the emerging socio-ethical perspective of selected Latin American theologians of liberation. Our immediate purpose is to disclose how radically their discernment of the fundamental political, ethical, and theological issues at stake in the economic debate differs from that of progressive developmentalists such as Denis Goulet. The fact of the matter is that at the same time that Goulet offers us a liberal and even centrist perspective among Christian moral thinkers concerned with the problem of global economic justice, these theologians "from the underside of history" resolutely sound their voices from the left as if to answer contrapuntally the otherwise harmonious chords of the development response.

In positioning themselves to the left within the dynamics of the development debate, liberation theologians have undertaken a twofold task. The first task follows upon their perception of irrevocable inadequacies in the dominant developmentalist paradigm. They call for a critique of and break with this perspective and theoretical model as a necessary initial step toward moving effectively toward a global economy of justice. One concern in this chapter is to characterize and identify the significance of this critical moment which incorporates three distinct but inseparable "breaks." These breaks are experienced concretely as a political, methodological, and ecclesiastical rupture from the liberal developmentalist paradigm and progressivist "ways of doing business." Liberation theologians argue that these breaks are unavoidable if authentic economic development is to become even a possibility for the poorest of the world's poor. In their own words, Hugo Assmann has stated the liberationists' viewpoint that these breaks are not to be considered optional but rather obligatory in order to "improve the Christian's

161

qualifications both in the practical struggle for a more human world and in the intellectual struggle to interpret social realities."[1]

The second task before these theologians is constructive. They propose a "new way" for thinking and acting in solidarity with those struggling for economic justice within various social and ecclesial movements for human emancipation in Latin American and elsewhere around the globe. What accompanies their urgent appeals for a break with the dominant paradigm is a series of alternative recommendations for analyzing social realities and participating in politics as tranformative human moral agency, for engaging in Christian socio-ethical inquiry on terms which are neither idealist nor individualistic, and for discovering a concrete "spirituality of liberation" which more firmly grounds commitments to social justice and opens up new visions of emancipatory faithfulness. A second and equally important concern in this chapter is, therefore, to clarify this constructive moment on the liberationists' agenda which complements and only reinforces their argument for attaining critical distance over against the developmentalist paradigm.

To execute the design of this chapter and be able to specify the critical and constructive aspects of the emerging liberationist perspective, we shall give primary but not exclusive attention to the writings of three theologians-ethicists. From the Roman Catholic tradition, Gustavo Gutierrez is the recognized "pioneer" theologian and spokesperson for liberation Christians in his native Peru and on his continent, and Brazilian Hugo Assmann is both a sociologist and theologian. Jose Miguez Bonino is a Protestant liberation theologian from Argentina. Although differences exist among them, for our purposes we shall consider the more significant convergence these theologians have reached, on substantive as well as methodological grounds, in their critique of the dominant theological-ethical tradition and social scientific paradigm and in their constructive proposals for an alternative methodology for engaging in Christian socio-ethical reflection in our present world-historical situation.

The elucidation of this convergence will be our central preoccupation, but it is also well advised to read this chapter in correlation with the preceding discussion of Denis Goulet's "ethic of global development."

Our overall interest is to heighten and judge the significance of the differences between liberal and radical Christian ethical perspectives on global economic
issues. Although the differences between Goulet and the
Latin Americans will be made explicit only at some junctures in this chapter, we shall return in the concluding
chapter to examine them more closely. Intimations of
their nature and scope begin to appear early on, however, as we first turn to consider some preliminary observations about the historical context and sources of
this "new school" of liberation theology and its stated
intent to aim at "the elimination of all and every dualism."[2]

I. The Historical Context, Sources, and Intent of Latin
   American Liberation Theology

As we begin our examination, we might well take
note that in contradisctinction to Denis Goulet, Latin
American liberation theologians have offended the sensibilities of the guardians of theological propriety.
As far as the public record indicates, Goulet has not
alienated himself from the gatekeepers of the theological or development "guilds." He has certainly not done
so by speaking regularly of the need for specialists
of a new and, might we not also add, fully "respectable"
discipline of development ethics or by concerning himself with locating a nonpartisan middle ground between
contestants in the current development debates. The
Latin Americans, on the other hand, have abandoned any
claim to ideological neutrality. As the same time they
have insisted that theological-ethical inquiry is "no
longer the domain of the individual theologian [or the
professional], but rather of a politically committed
group."[3] What is perhaps their greatest offense, however, is the claim that these theologians seem increasingly prepared to make publicly and to defend, namely,
that Christian faith is rightly comprehended "only in
the struggle against oppressive structures and toward
emancipatory praxis."[4] Consequently, they make the
theological claim that

> Faith becomes virtually impossible
> when the horizon of transformation
> by revolution as a historical pos-
> sibility disappears. Then the Chris-
> tian message is deprived of its in-
> dispensable precondition and content.
> It has to be said once and for all

and very clearly that for those who
have understood the historical character of the Christian faith, the
loss of revolutionary vision implies
simultaneously the emptying of the
biblical theme of salvation and faith.
Nowadays, the major part of the churches believe in a different kind of faith
and a different kind of salvation.[5]

Although our immediate concern is to provide a context for our subsequent discussion and not to identify,
as others have done elsewhere, the ways in which either
"the offense has been taken" or various critiques
launched against the theology of liberation,[6] it does
seem worthwhile to consider, as we proceed, the accuracy
of an observation Phillip Berryman has made about these
theologians whose claims have become so controversial.
Berryman suggests that in the churches as well as within academia,

. . . the basic division comes not
over theories about liberation but
over a basic option for liberation
as a historical project, the building of a nonexploitative social
order, and especially 'taking sides'
in real struggle with all its risks.[7]

At the Theology in the Americas conference at Detroit
in 1975, Gustavo Gutierrez elaborated upon this point by
arguing that, in actuality, the fundamental theological-
ethical debate can be understood properly only as a debate about liberation itself and not about its theology
per se. For that reason, he also suggested that the
difficulties encountered today in doing theology can no
longer be approached as strictly theological, that is,
as internally generated, but rather as necessarily reflecting "the difficulties which we find in the first
act, which is the act of liberation and faith."[8]

To appreciate the depth and scope of these difficulties, as well as the dynamics of the ongoing debates,
we must first consider the socio-historical context
within which the theology of liberation has appeared and
the problems to which it is addressed. As we do so, it
is equally necessary to recognize, even at the outset,
that liberation theology is not simply a Latin American
"brand" of theology, as if all theologies were but par-

ticular instances of some form of universal discourse,
much less a "school of theology" in competition with,
say, North American or Western European theologies. As
Osvaldo Luis Mottesi explains from a liberationist's
perspective,

> The confrontation is not Latin Ameri-
> can 'versus' North Atlantic theology,
> as if the former were always synony-
> mous with liberation and the latter
> with oppression. Not everything that
> comes from Latin America is liberating,
> nor even necessarily Latin American.
> The dominant theology and culture of
> our lands have been imported from cen-
> ters of power, and therefore are op-
> pressive. We are dominated and depen-
> dent countries.
>
> On the other hand, not everything that
> comes from the North Atlantic is oppres-
> sive: in Europe and the United States
> there are theologies of liberation.
>
> It is essential to destroy the abstract,
> folkloric, chauvinistic myth surrounding
> Latin America. It is only a disguise,
> an ideological mask, which hides the
> real problem. As a Latin American I
> feel closer to the North American the-
> ologies of liberation than to the Latin
> American theologies of oppression.
>
> The root of the principle contradiction
> in the present theological confrontation
> must be sought in the oppression-libera-
> tion dialectic.[9]

What Mottesi and other liberation theologians have come
to insist upon, as this quotation indicates, is that
the distinctive character and quality of contemporary
theological-ethical reflection depends far less on its
origin geographically and much more on the stance taken
ethically "from the standpoint of a particular situation and by means of one option." More specifically,
they argue that what is most distinctive about "Doing
[liberation] theology in today's Latin American context"
is that it "implies living and thinking our faith within
and in opposition to oppression."[10]

That Latin America is an oppressed and not "merely" a poor continent is a discovery of particular significance for liberation Christians, for they have gained an understanding of their world-historical situation which leads them to conclude that

> . . . the existence of the poor is not fated fact; it is not neutral on the political level or innocent of ethical implications. Poor people are by-products of the system under which we live and for which we are responsible. . . . This is why the poverty of the poor is not a summons to alleviate their plight with acts of generosity but rather a compelling obligation to fashion an entirely different social order.[11]

No less significant and equally powerful is their ongoing exercise of cultural freedom to reinterpret their historical context precisely "from their perspective as citizens of poor and dominated countries."[12] In turning to view the modern world from their position on the periphery rather than at the center of the present world economic order, from the social location Gustavo Gutierrez speaks of as "the underside of history," liberationists have come to recognize, for example, that

> . . . the emergence of the modern world has meant very different conditions in different places. In Western Europe the modern process engendered political freedom and individual liberty. Elsewhere that same process meant new and more refined forms of exploitation of the common people. Their liberty will consist in liberation from oppression and spoilation inflicted in the name of 'modern freedoms and democracy' and by its bearers.[13]

For this reason, while developmentalists may continue to speak in terms of human progress, of gradual reforms, and of the need to integrate the marginalized into the structures of modern life, liberationists "start with a rejection of the existing situation, considered as fundamentally unjust and dehumanizing."[14] This difference

166

may not be over-emphasized. Liberationists find that they must speak, first and foremost, not of integration but of the need for emancipation from the structures of oppression which produce human suffering. That emancipation will then only gain fruition when it is possible to construct a new socio-economic order in which socially created inequality is minimized.

Because of the massive resistance mounted against such efforts to establish a more just and egalitarian society, especially during the past decade and a half, the Latin Americans also acknowledge that recent history within their countries demonstrates that

> . . . the world is not naturally open to change. On the contrary, we are witnessing a closing of ranks against change, and a climate of mounting repression.[15]

Appropriately enough, they, therefore, describe their historical context as a crisis situation. As Hugo Assmann explains the notion,

> In the Latin American context, the 'crisis' of society has been defined as a situation in which a society or nation has been led by its historical development to a point where its contradictions and incongruities are such that they cannot be resolved without producing basic changes leading to a new type of social order.[16]

What must be understood is that liberation theology arose out of and in response to this crisis situation and, more specifically, in the context of the persistent failure of development programs and reform movements to alter in any significant way the situation of oppression and misery throughout the continent. As we shall review later on, its emergence also coincided, not surprisingly, with the perceptual shift within the social sciences as the "mechanics of exploitation and domination" were reinterpreted in terms of a critical theory of economic, political, and cultural dependency.[17]

What should also not be underestimated is the importance of this newly gained self-understanding, of being "citizens of poor and dominated countries," as the indispensable pre-condition for the appearance of any liberation theology. At the Theology in the Americas conference in Detroit, Juan Luis Segundo spoke on behalf of his colleagues about the significance of this conscientization for their common work as theologians:

> We began our theology of liberation simply by being sensitive to our own oppression. . . . All oppression calls for a liberation. We, then, in Latin America began to think about liberation before thinking about a theology of liberation. I can say that this human (not precisely Christian) sensitivity to the fact that our people are oppressed was the basis for a praxis of liberation. And the liberation theology or, if you prefer, theologizing about liberation was only one part of a much wider task.[18]

Moreover, it is also essential to acknowledge, not only to be historically accurate but also to keep sight of the significant methodological departure at hand, that this theology of liberation followed upon but did not precede the appearance of various grassroots social movements aimed at human emancipation. Perhaps better stated, this theology arose out of and has continued to develop from within those movements anticipating and organizing for a more just socio-economic order.

Among liberation theologians a consensus has emerged that there could and, indeed, would not be a theology of liberation without these historical movements toward liberation, for it is precisely this liberation praxis which serves as the reference point and the very source for what Gutierrez and his compatriots recognize to be "a new kind of discourse about the faith and new forms of Christian community."[19] As he has explained,

> For many Christi s, active involvement in popular liberation struggles has created a wholly new way of living, celebrating, and communicating their faith. . . . They have come to that commitment by different paths, determined by class origin and personal philosophy, and have broken with their pasts in different ways. This is the major fact in the

recent life of the Christian community in Latin America. It is
the source and matrix of the effort
at theological clarification that
led to liberation theology, which
can only be understood in relation
to liberation practice. The popular liberation movement poses new
questions, theological as well as
socio-political, and these questions, rooted in liberation practice, are both starting point and
ultimate criteria for liberation
theology.[20]

These theologians also agree that theology is properly
understood as "an expression of the consciousness which
a Christian community has of its faith in a given moment
of history" and that liberation theology itself must be
seen as an attempt, undertaken collectively, to articulate and celebrate the experience of faith derived from
the commitment for liberation.

As may be expected, the forms of this theological
discourse vary, but Hugo Assmann has argued that in its
most authentic voice liberation theology sounds out "our
Christian babbling in Latin America" in the form of testimonies, testimonies which are often "fragmentary, provisional, without abstract theoretical consistency" but
which, nevertheless, preserve and communicate to others
"the testimonial offered by the commitment to a decided
struggle against captialistic oppression."[21] One reason
that liberation theology characteristically--and delib-
erately--takes the form of such fragmentary testimonies
is, as Beatriz Couch suggests, that

> They do not represent a complete, fin-
> ished product of a definite theological
> position; they are simply steps in a
> movement toward an increasingly criti-
> cal social awareness of the historical
> context and a theological search to
> illuminate it.[22]

Miguez Bonino has argued in a similar fashion that the
provisional character of liberation theology is intrinsic to the nature of the project at hand:

> To the extent that the theology of

169

> liberation is--and is made into--a
> new 'school,' a set of self-contained
> theological tenets or positions, it
> wil have its day and be gone. . . .
> But to the extent that we are here
> dealing with a task, the struggle for
> liberation, which lies as much ahead
> of us as ten or five years ago, which
> indeed in a certain sense always lies
> ahead of us, this task continues to
> be pertinent: a critical and commit-
> ted Christian reflection of the peo-
> ple who have made this struggle their
> own and who understand it as the con-
> crete witness to the freedom that has
> been promised. . . .[23]

This theology of liberation, which Gutierrez rightly insists "could not have arisen before the popular movement
had attained a certain maturity,"[24] is, therefore, necessarily in process, fragmentary, and open-ended because at this moment the popular movement toward liberation, in its political, economic, and cultural dimensions, is likewise very much in process and open-ended.
Liberation is still a project, not a product or finished
task.

There is an additional reason that liberation theology appears more often than not as "Christian babbling" or at least as unsystematic testimonials rather
than as polished theological treatises. This reason
concerns authorship. This theology is not primarily or
in the first instance the product of professional theologians, nor is it the "fruit of academic discourse."
Rather, what is quite distinctive about this theology
is that it is a collaborative enterprise, often undertaken "on the run," as it were, and the work of the
politically committed community in the very midst of its
struggles. Enrique Dussel contends that what is unique
about liberation theology over against academic-based
theology is precisely this fact, that liberation theology is "the expression of a grassroots ecclesiastical
and political movement, which is supported by thousands
of religious, priests, and laypeople in the most diverse
situations."[25] Moreover, because this theology attempts
to give voice to the hopes of the marginated and least-
well off members of society for the creation of a free
and just socio-economic order, its practitioners also
insist that theology will become authentically libera-

ting only as the poor themselves increasingly become their own theologians and speak with their own voices, or as Gutierrez states the case quite succinctly, "Without the poor as subject, theology degenerates into academic exercise."[26] From a liberationist perspective, therefore, theology is best understood not as a restricted domain or the private property of one class of persons but as the emerging and ever widening expression of a community's historical faithfulness and political commitment to embody a solidarity experienced, in Miguez Bonino's phrasing, as its "will to be a community," a community of human inclusivenenss and equality.[27]

Hugo Assmann speaks of this same "will to be a community" in more explicitly political terms, as evidenced by the historical resistance of the organized poor to development and developmentalism and by their revolutionary intent to embrace both "the struggle for a universal share of goods sufficient to ensure basic human dignity, and the struggle for free decision-making at all social levels."[28] Gutierrez has added to this observation the important qualifier that "what in the last instance sustains the liberation efforts of Latin Americans" is a particular vision, precisely the as-of-yet unrealized possibility "of a qualitatively different society in which [persons] will be free from all servitude, in which they will be the artisans of their own destiny. . . ."[29] This vision of human wholeness counterbalances but certainly does not cancel out the reality of the fundamental injustices and deep-seated divisions between social classes which characterize the Latin American socio-economic situation at present. It is precisely these divisions which the theologians understand to be primary data and the starting point for their reflection both nationally and globally. The liberation theology movement itself, as Sergio Torres has suggested,

> . . . grew out of an intuition that was increasingly felt by Third World Christians . . . [that] the division among rich and poor [is] the major phenomenon of contemporary history.[30]

The significance of that intuition has only increased in the past decade or so as more recognition has been gained of the seriousness and extent of this emergent split between economic groupings.

171

In addressing the reality of these socio-economic and cultural divisions and the shifting but deepening conflict between classes throughout the global economy, the Latin American liberation theologians do not intend to perpetuate, much less manufacture these divisions but rather to work effectively toward eliminating the causes for such splits within the human community.[31] In joining with others to struggle actively, that is, politically, toward creating this more just socio-economic and political order, they understand their common project as one of taking aim together in order to effect "the elimination of each and every dualism," most especially the radical divisions between the developed and underdeveloped, rich and poor, free and oppressed, powerful and powerless. Gutierrez has, furthermore, identified this task as coterminous with the primary task of contemporary theology, namely,

> . . . to elucidate the current state of these problems, drawing with sharper lines the terms in which they are expressed. Only thus will it be possible to confront the concrete challenges of the present.[32]

Because of their common understanding of their mutual task, liberationists have also come to a second and no less foundational intuition about their work which contributes to their sense of direction and gives shape to their self-identity. They now experience that the dominant theological tradition, represented by Vatican II and precisely the predominant tradition in which they have been educated and incorporated into the churches, is no longer adequate for addressing this world-historical situation politically and, therefore, theologically. After a conference of Third World theologians at Dar-es-Salaam in 1976, for example, Sergio Torres reported that those who had gathered agreed that "for a long time now, Christian communities on these three continents [Asia, Africa, and Latin America] have discovered that the universal discourse of theology does not interpret their reality."[33] They share the complaint that ecclesiastical documents, such as those of the Second Vatican Council, maintain an essentially liberal focus by presupposing a non-existent equality in society and either downplaying or ignoring the reality of class conflict within and among nations throughout the globe. They find that the Council's theological language is not only rather sanitized but also decep-

172

tively apolitical, even naive, as the documents speak
of a necessary openness or receptivity to the modern
world and a desire to engage in dialogue toward reconciliation with the "modern spirit." As Enrique Dussel
has noticed,

> It stresses becoming 'incarnated' in
> the world (without ever discovering
> the conflictual nature of that world,
> because it is considered good or posi-
> tive from an a priori viewpoint).
> This is the 'world' of the bourgeois,
> and the conflict is never discovered
> because the Christian has been educa-
> ted within the bourgeois ecclesiasti-
> cal culture.[34]

Gutierrez' critique of the Vatican II documents on global development is quite similar:

> . . . social conflicts are only treated
> in the general terms of the presence
> of misery and injustices in the world.
> . . . There is not serious criticism
> of the importance in our days of the
> domination monopolistic capitalism
> exercises over the popular classes, es-
> pecially those of poor peoples. The
> Council's concern was different; we
> are in the hour of dialogue with the
> modern world. The fact that society
> is not a united whole but is full of
> conflicts among social classes is
> something that is out of the field of
> vision.[35]

Not only does the dominant theological-ethical
tradition overlook or idealize the realities of social
oppression and conflict, but it also retreats much too
quickly to "a global viewpoint to the exclusion of a
historicity that may be partial, but is at least definite and real."[36] For this reason, Assmann has concluded that this dominant tradition, which is typically
the theological approach of the affluent world, has a
fatal tendency toward idealism because of its "inability
to be historically realistic" and most particularly because "its questions do not spring from the basic conflict inherent in the real situation."[37]

This lack of sufficient grounding historically is related to and provides partial accounting for what is perceived as an additional inadequacy of this dominant theology, its characterization of faith as affirmation. Affirmation is understood here not as dialectically related to protest and critique but as the acceptance (and acceptability) of a world that is already made, finished, and complete, and of a history already predetermined and, therefore, known. For liberationists faith is experienced, on the contrary, not as acceptance of the world as it is but rather in terms of generating new possibilities for a more just world and as the historical initiatives taken toward freedom, as transformative action for the construction of a "new and solidary world."[38]

If liberation faith is to be communicated, above all, in terms of these political and ethical commitments to change the status quo and to move toward more justice afforded to those least-well off in society, it is not surprising that liberation theologians have called for and engaged in a series of "breaks" with the dominant theological and political paradigms. As mentioned in our introductory comments at the beginning of this chapter, these breaks are considered necessary in order to arrive at a "new way" of doing theology which will accomplish two purposes more adequately: first, the critical task of "rereading of the history of Christian piety, action, thought--to 'unmask and expose the ideological misuse of Christianity as a tool of oppression,'" and, second, the constructive task of expressing and communicating the meaning of a "spirituality of liberation," or the realization that "personal involvement in the process of liberation constitutes a profound and decisive spiritual experience at the very heart of active political commitment."[39] The task of ideological critique is necessary because liberationists do not assume that the Christian faith as such is necessarily emancipatory, nor are they willing to assert the truthfulness of theologial claims apart from historical verification. The constructive task is no less urgent, however, for as Gutierrez has explained,

> If they [liberation Christians] are
> not always able to express in ap-
> propriate terms the profound reasons
> for their commitment, it is because
> the theology in which they were
> formed--and which they share with

other Christians--has not produced
the categories to express this option. . . .[40]

Liberation theology is, therefore, understood as an ongoing project to appropriate a language that will be
able to communicate authentically the liberation option
and the experiences of a truly emancipatory faith.

As we now proceed to investigate the proposed political, epistemological, and theological breaks from
the dominant tradition and an alternative perspective
on the development debate, we should also remain cognizant of the fact that from outside the socio-political
and ecclesial movement toward liberation, that is, from
within the dominant tradition, these breaks signify a
veritable negation of social scientific and theological
truth or at least a rejection of the customary ways of
"doing business." As we shall see, critics of liberation theology do, in fact, have the good judgment not
to minimize the seriousness of the challenge being made.
However, from within the "world of the other," from the
underside of history, these breaks mark a necessary
juncture toward the recovery of freedom and reappropri-
ation of the gospel as "good news to the poor," and,
therefore, bear a significance even apart from or, better yet, not wholly dependent upon the impact "from below" upon the dominant paradigm.

II. The Political Break: Critiquing Developmentalism
     and Discovering the "Primacy of the Political"

As early as 1971 Cesar Aguiar suggested that among
recent developments within the Latin American Christian
community, none was more noticeable or significant than
"the crucial fact about . . . its confrontation with
politics." In speaking about the increasingly active
involvement of laity and clergy in various political
movements for social change throughout the continent,
he singled out as particularly important the repercus-
sions of that political activism upon the internal life
of the churches, with the consequences that

> If in the early years of the present
> Church renewal, the key words divid-
> ing avant-garde members of the Church
> were 'preconciliar' and 'post-concil-
> iar,' today that avant-garde no longer
> divides along theological paths but

175

along political ones.[41]

The reality to which Aguiar was calling attention was an emergent ecclesiastical situation more and more difficult to ignore or misread. The church in Latin America could no longer be regarded properly as a "homogeneous reality without tensions or internal divisions," much less as an institution "outside history and above society," but only as a conflicted body divided "into politically irreconcilable positions."[42]

The fundamental political division within the churches Aguiar recognized to be the same as that which pertains within the wider society, the irreconcilable division between developmentalists and liberationists. Since, as we detailed in our first two chapters, this polarization is well evidenced by splits in interpretation and strategy formation in relation to issues of economic and social development, perhaps it will suffice at this point only to include Jose Miguez Bonino's summary characterization of the differences at hand between the Latin American parties to the development debates. Developmentalists are interested in promoting globally what he calls "the whole modernizing attempt," and they distinguish themselves by

> . . . understanding and describing
> the rise to power and wealth of the
> North Atlantic countries as a moral
> achievement due to certain conditions
> of character and the principles of
> democracy, free enterprise, and edu-
> cation. Any country, therefore, which
> would adopt these principles and ac-
> quire these qualities would naturally
> develop in the same way. More recent-
> ly, technology and planning have been
> added to the sacred order of develop-
> ment. What was not said or understood
> was that the rise of the Northern
> countries took place at a particular
> moment in history and was built on the
> possibilities offered by the resources
> of the dependent countries . . . [or
> that] Northern development is built on
> third-world underdevelopment.[43]

In order to account for the persistent failure of developmentalist policies and program to overcome conditions

176

of poverty and to allow for economic and social autonomy, developmentalists make characteristic turns in their arguments by identifying the problem alternately as a lack of resources, effort, or ability on the part of the developing nations or as a result of inadequate support from the developed Northern world.

Liberationists, on the other hand, no longer find these qualifications valid, nor do they accept the proposition that the deficiencies of developmentalism may yet "be corrected with greater skill, better intentions, a longer time, and harder work." They have turned a political and moral corner, as Miguez Bonino explains, in that they no longer regard the failure of developmentalism as merely accidental, but rather

> For a growing number of Latin Americans, . . . the reason for the failure lies deeper, in the very nature of the economic system. The Christians meeting in Santiago expressed it in this way. 'This unjust society has its objective basis in the capitalist relations of production that necessarily generate a class society.'[44]

In order to challenge effectively the injustices of this present socio-economic order, liberationists call for a radical break from the status quo, a dis-identification with its interests and modus operandi, and an organized move toward a new society. This new society would need to be a socialist society in which "a profound transformation of the private property system, access to power of the exploited class, and a social revolution that would break this dependence [of some nations upon others and some classes over others]"[45] would be possible. While advocating this political and economic restructuring, Miguez Bonino also identifies fundamental ingredients of a liberation perspective:

> . . . as a Latin American Christian I am convinced with many other Latin Americans who have tried to understand the situation of our people and to place it in a world perspective--that revolutionary action aimed at changing the basic economic, political, social and cultural structures and conditions of life is imperative in the world.

177

> Ours is not a time for mere devel-
> opment, rearranging or correction,
> but for basic and revolutionary
> change (which ought not to be
> equated necessarily with violence).
> The possibility for human life to
> remain human on our planet hangs on
> our ability to effect this change.
> Such a conviction can only partially
> be justified in discussion: convic-
> tions in the area of history can be
> theoretically explained but they can
> only be proved practically--by turn-
> ing them into history.[46]

Over against Denis Goulet's preoccupation and investment in cultural transformations as distinct from
political changes, liberationists insist that attaining
the practical proof Miguez Bonino is seeking, the turning of these convictions into history, is necessarily
a political as well as a cultural task. This conviction, rising out of their engagements in social justice
movements throughout Latin America, is in keeping with
the liberation understanding that "history is not primarily the unfolding of man's [sic] consciousness or of
his ideas but the dynamics of his concrete activity [to
transform nature and society]."[47] They understand all
too well that not all political engagement is liberating, however, and when liberation theologians speak of
the primacy of transformative action or of politics,
they are referring not to any action taken in the world
but to that way of being present to one another and
acting together to build a more just society in which
all persons may "live with dignity and be agents of
their own destiny."[48] They also propose that the most
accurate test for determining whether such action is
truly liberating is to judge its consequences for the
lives of the marginalized and least-well off members of
society. Their fundamental accountability is to these
concretely oppressed and not to a disembodied ideal of
a "new humanity in the making," of which Goulet speaks
throughout his own writings. Above all, liberationists
agree that they are morally obligated to question whether justice has been done and continues to be done to the
poor and oppressed. In the process of making such judgments, they also consider it quite necessary to avoid
what Gutierrez describes as "the pitfalls of an individualistic charity." If it is true that Christian praxis
aims at human liberation and is characterized by love

of the neighbor, then what must be understood, as well, is that

> . . . the neighbor is not only man [sic] viewed individually. The term refers also to man [sic] considered in the fabric of social relationships, to man [sic] situated in his economic, social, cultural, and racial coordinates. It likewise refers to the exploited social class, the dominated people, and the marginalized race. . . . Charity is today a 'political charity' . . .; it means the transformation of a society structured to benefit a few who appropriate to themselves the value of the work of others. This transformation ought to be directed toward a radical change in the foundation of society, that is, the private ownership of the means of production.[49]

Liberation theologians not only give normative ethical priority to justice understood in terms of this "political charity," but they also identify solidarity with the poor and marginalized and the commitment to the politics of liberation as exemplary Christian virtues. Again, in contradiction to Goulet, they have experienced and learned the value of this solidarity in their actual involvements in social and ecclesial movements for justice, rather than from the detached perspective of a "free-floater" who judges world-historical realities from a supposedly neutral and privileged position "above the fray." Moreover, it is precisely with this norm of radical social justice in mind that they have also come to insist that the politics of developmentalism is so woefully inadequate. Their overwhelmingly negative response to the question of whether justice toward the least-well off in society is possible within the existing global economic order follows upon their assessment that capitalism, both nationally and internationally, gives rise to and maintains relationships of domination and exploitation between the poor and the rich. They argue in explicit terms what Goulet will not concede even implicitly, that a capitalist socio-economic order is not "justice-producing" and, therefore, cannot be presumed to provide the solution for a problem of its own creation. For this very rea-

son, as well, we find that in the midst of an argument
for locating the primary source of poverty and underdevelopment within the structural dynamics of the existing
capitalist global economy, Miguez Bonino has also emphasized the importance of acknowledging that

> We are not dealing with particularly
> wicked people or with cancerous out-
> growths of a system which has to be
> cleansed and restored to health. We
> are simply facing the normal and un-
> avoidable consequences of the basic
> principles of capitalist production
> as they work themselves out in our
> global, technological time. The con-
> centration of economic power, the
> search for higher profits, the efforts
> to obtain cheaper labor and to avoid
> higher costs are of the very essence
> of that system.[50]

From this insight liberationists insist that as long as
developmentalist policies do not challenge the existing
capitalist framework of economic and political relationships between nations and among socio-economic groups
within nations, these policies will necessarily remain
"ineffective in the long run and counterproductive to
achieving a real transformation."[51]

If capitalist theories of socio-economic development are judged inadequate because they ignore or at
least underestimate the reality of structural dependency
which conditions the economy of underdeveloped nations,
they are, therefore, being faulted for misconstruing the
systemic and class character of the problem of global
poverty. Liberationists have found the neo-Marxist
theory of dependency better suited for clarifying their
present socio-economic situation and for assessing appropriate change strategies. Gutierrez has explained
the significance of this alternative theoretical framework in these terms:

> The perception of the fact of dependence
> and its consequences has made possible a
> new awareness of the Latin American re-
> ality. It is now seen clearly that in
> addition to economic factors, it is also
> necessary to take into consideration
> political factors. Development theory

must now take into account the situation of dependence and the possibility of becoming free from it. Only in this context can the theory make any sense and have any possiblity of being implemented. Studies made along these lines lead one to conclude that autonomous Latin American development is not viable within the framework of the international capitalist system.[52]

What Miguez Bonino has also pointed out is that this theory of dependence was "not developed in abstraction or in pure objective contemplation, but in the very effort to overcome the present situation and move forward to a new society."[53] Furthermore, this theory has remained subject to modification as new insights have been gained through efforts made at social transformation. For example, in keeping with an original insight that the dynamics of oppression change historically, liberationists pay close attention to the fact that

When capitalism developed in the Northern nations into other stages: industrial and then consumer capitalism, the role fo the dependent nations also changed: they were destined to provide raw materials and agricultural products frist and cheap labor and markets later.[54]

Because of these shifting dynamics and their political implications, dependency theorists are at present particularly interested in determining the novel role and impact of multinational corporations within the global economy and the consequence of their presence for countries, such as Brazil, which has become in Miguez Bonino's telling phrase, "a factory of multinational corporations."[55]

A second, quite significant modification in dependency theory has followed upon an awareness, also gained practically, that "dependence is not merely an external factor" conditioning the quality of life in poor nations but also an internal dynamic at work because of the class structure of these societies.[56] More often than not, a wealthy minority within underdeveloped nations benefits directly from maldistribution of income and resources and has remained politically an accomplice of foreign interests who likewise enjoy the advantages of

a "stabilized" national economy. Therefore, Gutierrez
has advised that

> . . . this theory [of dependency] as
> first propounded may not have empha-
> sized adequately that the primary
> confrontation is not between power-
> ful ('developed') nations or conti-
> nents and weak ('underdeveloped')
> ones, but between different social
> classes.[57]

Liberationists now insist, however, that the problem of
global poverty and of the persistence of underdevelopment may be rightly comprehended only within the historical context of class inequities and of the structural dynamics between rich and poor. Furthermore, to
"opt for the poor," that is, to be in solidarity with
the interests of the marginalized and dispossessed for
a more just society, necessarily requires much more than
a display of good will or noble intentions. As Gutierrez has argued,

> When we opt for the poor in a commit-
> ment to liberation, we are forced to
> realize that we cannot isolate op-
> pressed people from the social class
> to which they belong. If we were to
> do that, we would simply be sympathiz-
> ing with their own individual situa-
> tions. Poor and oppressed people are
> members of a social class which is
> overtly or covertly exploited by
> another social class. . . . To opt
> for the poor is to opt for one social
> class over against another; to take
> cognizance of the fact of class con-
> frontation and side with the op-
> pressed. . . .[58]

At this juncture perhaps we should state that if
liberationists perceive one deficiency of capitalist
development theory as its lack of sensitivity to the
reality of Third World dependency, they find a no less
serious inadequacy in that developmentalists do not
frame the problem of underdevelopment within the context
of national and international class struggles. Liberationists do not create the reality of class conflict
themselves, but they most certainly do make explicit

efforts to publicize its facticity and identify its
sources. In doing so, they differentiate the politics
of class struggle "from above," which is viewed as the
effort by the dominant and privileged few to maintain
the present economic order "beyond the time of its
ability to provide for the basic needs of all mankind
[sic]," and the politics of class struggle "from below."
This struggle from below Miguez Bonino has described as

> . . . finally, the effort of the op-
> pressed to break into a new form of
> economic and social organization in
> which work will be related to need and
> creation and not to profit. It is
> a struggle for the power to reshape
> society . . . a means for attaining
> a new and more just situation.[59]

The specific claim which liberationists make is that
only by advocating this politics of class struggle from
below can there be reasonable expectations of challenging "the appropriation by a few of the wealth created
by the work of the many" and, therefore, of eliminating
the actual causes of the deep societal divisions.

> Paradoxically, what the groups in
> power call 'advocating' class strug-
> gle is really an expression of a
> will to abolish its causes, to abol-
> ish them, not cover them over. . . .
> It is a will to build a socialist
> society, more just, free, and human,
> and not a society of superficial and
> false reconciliation and equality.
> . . . To build a just society today
> necessarily implies the active and
> conscious participation in the class
> struggle that is occurring before
> our eyes.[60]

As we discussed in the preceding chapter, this absence of class analysis is quite apparent even in the
writings of such a progressive developmentalist as Denis
Goulet. Goulet does not agree with the Latin Americans
on the central claim of the extent to which class dynamics give rise to and fundamentally shape social realities throughout the world economic order. He locates
injustices within the prevailing network of economic
and political relations, both nationally and interna-

tionally, but he remains convinced that non-palliative changes toward justice are possible within the confines of the present system. Liberationists are less hesitant in claiming that fundamental justice will become possible only after a socialist social and economic order has been brought into place. Where Goulet searches for modifications of parts to "clean up" and alter the whole, liberationists work diligently for a different pattern of organizing human relationships that will offset dominant dynamics of exploitation and oppression. Where they find compelling reasons for a decisive break from the old to allow for the new, Goulet finds reasons to hope that abuses from capitalism can be corrected and justice extended even to the most marginalized.

Any explanation for what generates these different judgments is only partial, but it does seem appropriate to point out, as Gutierrez has readily acknowledged, that the reality of class exploitation and oppression and, therefore, of class antagonisms is most often "endured and perceived first of all by those who have been marginated" by the socio-economic system which produces such deep divisions. This conflictual situation is likewise most often ignored or denied by those who benefit most from its perpetuation.[61] It just may well be that Goulet's own privileged social position and his detachment from any ongoing, concrete participation in liberation movements, North or South, offer at least some significant clues for his quite determined reticence to examine more seriously the urgency of the socialist option which liberationists insist is now no longer even debatable from their social location on "the underside of history."

It is precisely from within social and ecclesial movements organized throughout Latin America to work for a more free and egalitarian social order that liberationists have come to recognize the reality and extent of class conflicts. While pushing for the socialist option, they have also made certain discoveries about politics and about the primacy of the political. For reasons just mentioned, these discoveries have eluded Goulet, but their importance should not be underestimated for appreciating the distinctive character of the liberationist socio-ethical perspective. We turn now to review this distinctiveness as a way toward assessing their ethical methodology.

Gutierrez describes what he calls the "new under-

standing of politics" among liberationists in this manner:

> For a long time politics was viewed as
> one compartment of life. It was a
> sector of human existence, alongside
> of family, professional, and recrea-
> tional life. Thus, political activity
> was carried on in the free time left
> over from other occupations. Besides,
> it was thought that politics belonged
> to a sector of humanity especially
> called to that responsibility. But
> today those who have chosen a libera-
> ting commitment find <u>politics</u> to be
> <u>a dimension which includes and condi-
> tions all human activity</u>. It is the
> global environment and the collective
> arena of human fulfillment. . . .
> Every human situation has then a
> political dimension. To speak of
> [the] political dimension recognizes
> and does not exclude the multidimen-
> sional nature of man [sic], but it
> does reject all socially sterile com-
> partmentalization of life because it
> detracts from the real conditions in
> which human life unfolds. In the po-
> litical context, a person emerges as
> a free and responsible being, as a
> person in relation to nature and to
> other persons, as someone who takes
> the reins of his destiny and trans-
> forms history.[62]

This understanding by no means limits the political to
the former structures or machinations of governments
but rather operates on the assumption that "the realm
of politics is everything embraced by the term 'society,' and not only formal relationships with the
state."[63] Moreover, as liberationists take care to explain, perhaps to counter criticisms from Goulet and
other developmentalists, to speak of the universality
of the political is not to reduce human life experiences
to this one dimension, but rather to insist, as Hugo
Assmann does, that

> Every human act, even the most pri-
> vate, possesses not only a social

content (because it transcends the
individual), but a political content (because that transcending of
the individual is always related
to change or stability in society).[64]

Therefore, since all human activity has a political dimension, to acknowledge the primacy of the political is
both to recognize and take seriously, as Monika Hellwig
suggests, "the historical character of human existence"
and also to be "aware of the implications in all human
actions for the structuring of the lives and possibilities of others."[65] Furthermore, the political is recognized as the sphere for the exercise of critical human freedom, for it is only within and not outside this
sphere that "a person emerges as a free and responsible
being" and is enabled to display true subjecthood as an
historical agent participating in the decision-making
process and in the shaping and reshaping of social
structures.

Only in light of this rather comprehensive definition of the political do liberationists then proceed to
speak of politics in a more restricted sense as "an
orientation to power." In an unjust socio-economic
situation, such as their own, they identify the primary
political task as reordering power relationships in
order to construct an authentically human and humanizing
"polis," an egalitarian "society in which people can
live in solidarity" and in freedom.[66] It is with both
meanings in mind, however, that Gutierrez has concluded
that for liberation Christians, " . . . it is in the
framework of politics that Christians committed to the
poor and the liberation of the exploited classes will
ponder and live out their faith."[67] Faith is experienced as and within this process of human liberation,
whcih is necessarily political, and it is from the
singular vantage point of this faith experience that
liberationists view their break from the dominant tradition. Gutierrez explains the ethical-theological significance of this break as follows, and he could be addressing Denis Goulet as he does so:

In the past, concern for social praxis
in theological thought did not sufficiently take into account the political
dimension. In Christian circles there
was--and continues to be--difficulty in
perceiving the originality and specific-

ity of the political sphere. Stress
was placed on private life and on
the cultivation of private values;
things political were relegated to a
lower plane, to the elusive and un-
demanding area of a misunderstood
'common good.' At most, this viewpoint provided a basis for 'social
pastoral planning,' grounded on the
'social emotion' which every self-
respecting Christian ought to experience. Hence there developed
the complacency with a very general
and 'humanizing' vision of reality,
to the detriment of a scientific
and structural knowledge of socio-
economic mechanisms and historical
dynamics. Hence also there came
the insistence on the personal and
conciliatory aspects of the Gospel
message rather than of its political and conflictual dimensions.

. . . for [liberation] Christians
social praxis is becoming less and
less merely a duty imposed by their
moral conscience or a reaction to
an attack on Church interests. . . .
Social praxis is gradually becoming
more of the arena itself in which
the Christian works out--along with
others--both his destiny as a man
[sic] and his life of faith in the
Lord of history. Participation in
the process of liberation is an
obligatory and privileged locus
for Christian life and reflection.
In this participation will be heard
nuances of the Word of God which
are imperceptible in other existen-
tial situations and without which
there can be no authentic and fruitful faithfulness to the Lord.68

Some of these "otherwise imperceptible" nuances
are specifically theological and most especially the
liberationists' critique of the dominant religious tradition for dichotomizing being Christian and acting
politically. At this point, however, there are two ad-

ditional discoveries about the political which should be
mentioned. The first is the radical nature of liberation politics, and the second is the conflictual aspect
of building a more just social and economic order.
About the radicality of liberation politics, we should
recall Miguez Bonino's observation that liberation theology itself "rests on an analysis and interpretation
of the Latin American situation for which the transition
from developmentalism (or reformism) to liberation is
crucial" and his corollary claim that this theology
"make[s] no sense outside of such an analysis."[69] Hugo
Assmann has given corroborating evidence for this position by noting the parallel development of a theology
of liberation alongside a radical neo-Marxist sociology
of liberation which sought to challenge and displace the
liberal sociology of development which prevailed
throughout Latin America in the 1950's and early to mid-
1960's:

> Rooted as it is in the present histori-
> cal context of Latin America, the theo-
> logical and political theme of libera-
> tion is the obvious correlative of the
> sociological theme of 'dependence.'
> Just as the latter marks the beginning
> of a new line in social science in
> Latin America, breaking away from the
> scientific methodology and 'theoretical
> models' imported from North America
> and European schools, which were in-
> capable of facing up to the complexity
> and political connotation of the prob-
> lem in this form, so the theological
> and political theme of liberation
> ushers in a new context and a new meth-
> odology of Christian reflection on
> faith as a definite historical event.[70]

It is quite necessary to acknowledge the fact that liberationists have abandoned, without reservations or
hopes for retrieval, developmetalist politics and the
theoretical paradigm on which it was based. They have
also turned away from what Gutierrez speaks of as "a
simple reformist attitude regarding the existing social
order," because of the judgment that "by its very shal-
lowness this reformism perpetuates the existing system"
which produces human suffering in the first place.[71]
What they have experienced instead is an increasing
radicalization, both politically and theologically, as

188

we shall discuss in detail later, in the process of (1) appropriating and reassessing a neo-Marxist analysis of dependent capitalist development and underdevelopment and (2) attempting to work out an effective political strategy for creating a socialist alternative to the present status quo.

This process of radicalization has not necessarily been uniform among liberation Christians, but what is characteristic of their political transformation is, first of all, an insistence upon not separating what Robert McAfee Brown terms human and political concerns:

> To separate 'human' and 'political' concerns is to look at consequences rather than causes: we see the con-sequences of starving people and our instinct is to feed them and thus 'put an end to starvation.' But starvation will continue as long as the causes that bring it about are left unchallenged, for example, a system that increases rather than decreases the gap between rich and poor.[72]

In addition to placing and analyzing ethical issues within the appropriate socio-economic and political con-text, what is also characteristic is that in their search for locating the root causes of the misery and exploitation in the Third World and for determining how the capitalist political economy functions globally and regionally to produce both wealth and poverty, libera-tionists have come to an agreement not simply about the particular validity of the dependency theory of economic development. They have found this social scientific theory indispensable for clarifying their own social situation and identifying the structural dynamics by which the impoverishment of the poor in poor nations has been perpetuated. As Raul Vidales has gone on to explain, once this transition has been made from a de-velopmentalist to a liberationist social scientific perspective,

> . . . Latin American theology cannot view the sciences with indifference as if each and every one of them could provide the same help. It will opt for those analyses, postulates,

and diagnoses that are more closely
in line with the goal of discerning
and achieving a social order in
which human beings can live as true
adults. . . . For the very same
reason it will be thoroughly critical of those scientific and ideological systems which explicitly or
implicitly run counter to that ideal.[73]

Precisely because they are convinced that the choice of
analytic instruments is of such ethical significance,
liberationists will carefully differentiate, for example, among various usages of the term liberation, for
the employment of the "proper" terminology is not considered sufficient indication, in and of itself, of the
ethical commitment or the political and theological
colors being flown. Hugo Assmann's cautionary remarks,
therefore, are quite typical:

. . . not for a moment should its
analytical content or central seman-
tic axis be forgotten; any discussion of liberation must always go
back to its essence: denouncing
domination; perception of the mechanics of dependence; opposition
to 'development' and the capitalist
economic system; and a break with
the 'unjust established order.'[74]

Liberationists are also mindful of the political
significance of the choice of diagnostic tools and analytical instruments. In accord with Marx's dictum about
incorporating the interest to transform as well as understand the world, they most certainly have extended
their interest in social scientific analysis beyond arriving at an adequate interpretation of the present
socio-economic situation to that of examining and evaluating various options for action. The concern to determine effective strategies for social change in the
direction of establishing a more just social order is
not only pertinent to the work of liberation Christians
"in the field" but quite deliberately included in the
methodology of the theologians whose reflections rise
out of and in response to the actions taken to effect
human emancipation. Gutierrez speaks of the necessary
link between analysis and strategy in this way:

> . . . those who have committed them-
> selves to the struggle for a different
> society feel the urgency of acquiring
> the greatest possible knowledge of the
> private profit mechanisms of capitalist
> society. Only this knowledge will make
> their action effective. A vague and
> lyrical summons to defend human dignity
> which does not take into account the
> root causes of the present social order
> and necessary conditions for the con-
> struction of a just society leads no-
> where.[75]

Assmann is no less adamant that because "there can be
no real commitment to liberate one's country on the
general level alone," liberation ethics must, therefore,
"include the working out of a strategy (which must in-
volve choosing a particular political approach)," as
well as the ongoing reassessment of the effectiveness
of various tactical measures adopted.[76]

This concern for political effectiveness, no less
than the commitment to act as well as to theorize on
behalf of a new and more just world, has led Assmann
to assert quite accurately that the originality and distinctive character of liberation theology is not merely
its appropriation of social scientific theory but its
willingness to declare its advocacy of a particular
ethical and political system. As he explains,

> . . . we have not rejected the ideo-
> logical step entailed in choosing a
> particular ethical or political sys-
> tem. And when I say 'we,' I am not
> talking of a few committed individu-
> als. This is now the basic element
> of theological thinking in the the-
> ology of liberation. . . .

> As I see it, the novelty of
> this form of theology consists in
> its open use of ideology as a wea-
> pon in the struggle for the trans-
> formation of the New World, and at
> the same time its consciousness of
> the precarious nature of its word.[77]

Over against the dominant theological paradigm (and

Denis Goulet's perspective) which "tends simply to op-
pose faith and ideology" and to characterize all ideologies either as demonic or "from its nonconflictive
world vision . . . as a series of isms, a somewhat
idealist perspective,"[78] liberation theologians speak of
ideology both in a negative and positive sense. Negatively, an ideology is a perspective which masks and
distorts the reality of oppression and serves the interests of preserving the status quo. Positively, an
ideology is one of emancipatory struggle which defines
and projects a unified view of reality and offers what
liberationists identify as an historical project. An
historical project is considered different from "a vision which makes no attempt to connect itself historically to the present," but it is also less than a program or "a technically developed model for the organization of society." An ideology, understood in a positive sense, rightly functions, as Miguez Bonino has
discerned,

> . . . to force options in terms of
> the basic structures of society. It
> points in a given direction. . . .
> It is in this general sense that we
> speak of a Latin American socialist
> [ideology or] project of liberation.[79]

Furthermore, liberationists do not wish to delude anyone into thinking that a non-ideological perspective on
social reality is either possible or practicable, for
as Miguez Bonino has also explained, "every form of
praxis articulates--consciously or unconsciously--a view
of reality and a projection of it, an analysis and an
ideology. . . ."[80]

For these reasons liberationists recognize that the
decisive question has become not whether one has adopted
an ideological stance but rather which stance has been
taken and how it accords both with certain ethical values and with knowledge gained of historical realities.
Because of their own commitment to work for a socialist
alternative to the present status quo, they have also
not been able to avoid making a third discovery about
liberation politics, namely, its conflictual nature.
The possibility of moving toward a more just social order is dependent upon the nature and the outcome of the
confrontation "between groups with different interests
and opinions" and the "overcoming of every obstacle to
the creation of an authentic peace among people."[81]

More and more frequently in Latin America this confrontation has taken shape as the conflict between segments
of the religious community seeking to defend the interests of the poor and various repressive military dictatorships seeking to protect the privileges of a wealthy
minority of the population. In several nations Penny
Lernoux has observed that

> As the only institution capable of
> withstanding the military, the Church
> has become a surrogate for democracy,
> providing a protective umbrella for
> popular organizations, such as labor
> unions and peasant federations, which
> otherwise would succumb to repression.[82]

What is also becoming quite apparent to liberationists
is that these church people who have declared their political intentions to alter the socio-economic and political structures which produce poor people are now
themselves becoming subject of this repression and are
"starting to have the same fate as the poor." Furthermore, as Gutierrez has emphasized, "these Christians .
. . are not jailed, tortured and killed for their 'religious ideas,' but for their social and evangelizing
practices."[83]

In light of this contemporary experience, liberation Christians, such as Gutierrez, would want to qualify Aguiar's statement, which we noted at the beginning
of this section, about the significance of the churches'
confrontation with politics throughout Latin America.
First, what they consider even more important than the
fact of Christian involvement in politics is the particular alignment of Christians with the socialist movement for liberation. Moreover, they stand in agreement
with Assmann that, however regrettably, Christians on
the left do not have any sort of monopoly on politics.
On the contrary,

> . . . politics today is the essential
> road for Christian consciousness, al-
> most equally so for the left and for
> the right. The class struggle is be-
> coming more acute within the churches
> as it becomes more acute in society.[84]

What liberation Christians have also come to recognize is that their political engagement and collective

action to forge a radically different social order has
led them to a fundamental questioning and rethinking not
only about the existing society and political realities
but about the meaning of their Christian faith, as well.
That questioning, as we shall discuss in the next two
sections, has resulted in proposals for a methodological
and an ecclesiastical break to accompany the proposed
political rupture with the dominant theological paradigm.

III. The Methodological Break: Critiquing Ethical-
      Theological Idealism and Proposing a "New Way" of
      Doing Theology

      On more than one occasion Gustavo Gutierrez has
taken care to differentiate Latin American liberation
theology from other "progressive" theologies, such as
the theologies of development and of revolution, to
which he notes "it is at times linked and with which it
is erroneously confused." The first point of distinction remains political, that liberation theology, as we
examined in the previous section, presupposes "a different analysis of reality based on more universal and
radical political options." The second differences is
methodological, which Gutierrez explains as follows:

> The theology of liberation differs . . .
> above all in the very concept of the
> task of theology. [It] does not intend
> to provide Christian justification for
> positions already taken, and does not
> aim to be a revolutionary Christian ide-
> ology. It is a reflexion which makes a
> start with the historical praxis of man
> [sic]. It seeks to rethink the faith
> from the perspective of that historical
> praxis, and it is based on the experi-
> ence of the faith derived from the lib-
> erating commitment. For this reason,
> this theology comes only after that in-
> volvement, the theology is a second
> act. Its themes are, therefore, the
> great themes of all true theology, but
> the perspective and the way of giving
> them life is different. Its relation
> to historical praxis is of a different
> kind.[85]

The historical praxis of which Gutierrez speaks is that

transforming action aimed at human liberation and, more specifically, the liberation praxis of the oppressed to free themselves. While it is quite accurate to claim that liberation theologians have consistently maintained that "active commitment to liberation comes first and theology develops from it" and also to note that this theology takes form as critical reflection "on and from within the complex and fruitful relationship between theory and praxis," he contends that much more needs be said than the fact that liberation theology replaces the deductive with the inductive method. As he explains,

> It is not enough to know that praxis must precede reflection; we must also realize that the historical subject of that praxis is the poor--the people who have been excluded from the pages of history. Without the poor as subject, theology degenerates into academic exercise.[86]

Liberationists are well aware but do not seem overly troubled that this "theology of active witness to faith, of practice, of involvement in liberation struggles," as Gutierrez describes it, has been criticized as "intellectually less rigorous, and therefore less valid, than an academic, theoretical theology." They readily admit that liberation theology follows a different rationality, as it were, but they claim that its "way of knowing things," its epistemological approach, is not only legitimate but quite advantageous, as Gutierrez contends in the following passage:

> Reasoning from a concrete situation is quite different from (but no less rigorous than) reasoning from a priori "first principles"--unfamiliar though the ruling classes and their ideological dependents may have found it. Furthermore, participation in a concrete historical process--such as the lives of the oppressed--enables one to perceive aspects of the Christian message that theorizing fails to reveal.[87]

At the same time, however, liberationists acknowledge that from the perspective of the dominant theological tradition, this theology of liberation struggles has little or none of the familiar coloration of classical theology. The reason is precisely because it does not take either revelation or tradition as its fundamental point of departure. Rather, this theological discourse starts with questions from the world-historical situation and with human actions in particular socio-cultural contexts. Hugo Assman notes that while this critical reflection on human history may not automatically be presumed to be theological, he argues that it does, indeed, become theological

> . . . to the degree that it looks for
> the presence of the Christian faith
> in historical experience; it is this
> which distinguishes theology from
> other ways of reflecting critically
> on this experience. If reference to
> faith in history is laid aside, then
> there is no theology.[88]

Moreover, he insists that "pure theology," that is, theological reflection which "leaves various aspects of human activity out of account" and which abstracts from historical realities in order to safeguard its own "cradle of reflection" is by no means the equivalent of good theology, although this equation is often assumed within the dominant tradition. The distinctive charater of liberation theology follows from the fact that

> . . . we start with the supposition
> that the proper subject matter of
> theology is the complex totality of
> all aspects of human activity that
> can be critically understood. . . .
> Once theology decides to take a
> keen interest in all the elements
> that go to make up the complex whole
> of human activity, it will not take
> long to realize how unreal many of
> its earlier concerns have been, and
> how remote its language. The con-
> sequence of this will not be a sort
> of totalitarian theological take-
> over, but the humility of a practi-
> cal theology, one that listens more
> and speaks less, but when it speaks,
> says relevant things capable of mak-
> ing a deep impression of the critical

consciousness even of those who do
not share its beliefs.[89]

A liberation methodology has significant implications for engaging in Christian socio-ethical reflection, as well. Consider, for example, the difference
between these two modes of ethical inquiry. One mode
of doing Christian ethics claims authenticity as a truly
theological ethic because it begins with a revelational
starting point, offers typically a description of the
"mighty acts of God," and proceeds from there to consider the human response to these actions. Although there
are variations on this approach, it characteristically
presents "ethical dilemmas" by positing an ideal course
of action and then "asking afterwards for the degree of
'compromise' permissible to accommodate the actual conditions in which action has to be taken."[90] Miguez
Bonino has questioned the adequacy of such an idealist,
deductive, and ahistorical approach, and has countered
that ethical-theological reflection, properly understood, is not, in the first instance, "an effort to
give correct understanding of God's attributes or actions but an effort to articulate the action of faith."[91]
A liberation mode of ethical inquiry begins concretely
with reflection upon the world-historical situation in
which particular moral agents are located, and it attempts to generate new possibilities for reconceptualizing and acting upon that reality more effectively.
More specifically, liberation reflection arises out of
and follows upon the social practice of historical a-
gents to overcome conditions of oppression. Moreover,
such reflection is undertaken not for its own sake but
in order to refer back to that emancipatory activity
which it seeks to clarify and make more intelligible.
Therefore, as Gutierrez has pointed out, the distinctive
character of liberation theology and ethical inquiry is
not only that theory and practice are dialectically related, but that such analysis

> . . . will proceed from an option and
> a commitment. . . . This reflection
> starts from a commitment to create a
> just fraternal society, and must con-
> tribute to make it more meaningful,
> radical, and universal.[92]

Much more clearly than Goulet, these theologians insist
upon being rooted historically within social justice
movements and of offering theological-ethical reflection

from within and in reference to the politics of liberation, not from a so-called privileged position outside
or above the fray.

Liberationists not only agree with Miguez Bonino
that the purpose of theological-ethical reflection is
to "articulate the action of faith," but that they also
share Assmann's conviction that

> The real step forward only comes with
> a demand for all theology to concen-
> trate on the historical reality of
> men's [sic] actions (particularly
> those of Christians) in transforming
> the world, to such an extent that
> this becomes a constant point of ref-
> erence.[93]

It is because of the very practical nature of its concerns and the attention given to the historical demands
for liberation that liberation theology has about it a
rather painful and often unexpected concreteness, a concreteness which is maintained, in part, by its deliberate incorporation of social scientific insights and analysis. The inclusion of the social sciences means,
too, that the praxis of liberation about which the theologians speak is, in the words of Miguez Bonino,

> . . . not simply subjective or arbi-
> trary; it means that a situation has
> been analyzed and assumed by means
> of an interpretative synthesis. In
> this way, the socio-political analy-
> sis and the ideological option implic-
> it in it, which are included in the
> praxis adopted, are determinative in-
> tegrants of theological reflection.[94]

What is also included within a liberation method of inquiry is an assessment not only of the socio-historical
situation within which moral agents are called upon to
act, but also assessments of various options for action
and strategies which are judged in terms of effectiveness and in terms of their compatibility with the norm
of maintaining solidarity with the least well-off members of society. Hugo Assmann has noticed that this
concern for strategy considerations is noticeably absent from the dominant theological-ethical paradigm, or,
as he states his critique,

> The higher reaches of the ecclesiasti-
> cal hierarchy avoid the pitfalls of
> considering how faith can be worked
> out in practice by jumping clear over
> them and assuming that the question
> has already been answered. Sympto-
> matic of this is the repeated insis-
> tence, in documents like Populorum
> Progressio, that the 'specific con-
> tribution' of Christianity consists
> in providing a 'global,' 'integral'
> view of man [sic] and history.[95]

As a liberationist, Assmann makes a counter-proposal
that ethicists must necessarily concern themselves with
evaluating the implications for social action of any
and all faith claims, especially because "faith must be
understood as basically its practice, its working out
in history" rather than as doctrinal affirmations or
even in "the simple sense of 'practicing the faith.'"[96]

In addition to its concreteness and its explicit
employment of social scientific analysis, liberation
theology is also quite distinctive in its claims about
the nature of authority. For example, a theologian's
qualifications, or better stated, authority to reflect
and to speak for the community of the faithful, is
judged not in terms of his or her detachment from a particular situation or non-partisanship, but rather in
terms of the interests and commitment demonstrated and
the multidimensional involvement sustained over a significant time period in the ongoing process of overcoming oppression. Gutierrez details the importance of
this situational location of the theologian as follows:

> Theologians can only accomplish
> their goals in the Christian com-
> munity if they have included them-
> selves in the process of liberation,
> and involved themselves with the
> poor and the oppressed, Difficult
> questions are raised for theological
> reflection, making it quite clear
> that it is impossible to separate
> the theory from the social process.
> The theologian is not an idle spec-
> tator in this historical setting,
> watching it pass by, but a person
> who has an important living place

in society among the social classes
that confront him or her. From
this central point one thinks and
lives one's faith, and this condition enables the theologian to make
the word a more understandable
reality in reality. . . .[97]

Christian idealists downplay the importance of being
"grounded" historically, but liberationists insist there
is no privileged position <u>outside</u> of the socio-historical situation from which to view reality and to reflect
upon the faith commitment to liberaton, but rather that
the historical movement toward liberation itself provides the primary and, indeed, a quite privileged <u>locus
theologicus</u> for "a theology which does not stop with
reflecting on the world, but rather tries to be a part
of the process through which the world is transformed."[98]

From this theological perspective the insertion of
the ethicist into the historical movement for social
justice is judged indispensable, for access to the
knowledge to be gained is possible only experientially
from within these very movements of men and women struggling to live freely and in dignity. Through this practical engagement a new knowledge of reality is gained,
a knowledge geared toward the transformation of the
world. Gutierrez has explained the distinctive character of this liberation epistomology as follows:

We do not come to know history, which
is an indissoluable mixture of nature
and society, except in the process of
transforming it and ourselves. . . .
Knowledge of reality that does not
lead to a modification of it is really
an unverified interpretation, and interpretation that is not transformed
into truth. . . . Historical reality .
. . ceases to be the field for the application of abstract truths and
idealistic interpretations; instead
it becomes the privileged locale from
which the process of knowledge starts
and to which it eventually returns.
Praxis that transforms history is not
the degraded embodiment of some pure,
well conceived theory; instead it is
the very matrix of all authentic knowl-

edge, and the decisive proof of that
knowledge's values. It is the point
where people recreate their world
and forge their own reality, where
they come to know reality and discover their own selves.[99]

Liberationists also argue that truth is not essentially
conceptual, that is, located in a "realm of ideas" apart
from historical realities and waiting to be applied, but
rather that it is disclosed in the actions of historical
agents in the very midst of concrete events. They have
come to insist, therefore, that the truthfulness and
meaning of Christian faith itself "cannot be abstracted
from its historical significance" and its practical consequences precisely because faith, as Assmann emphasizes,

. . . can only be historically 'true'
when it 'becomes true': when it is
historically effective in the liberation of man [sic]. Hence the 'truth'
dimension of faith becomes closely
linked to its ethical and political
dimensions.[100]

Moreover, because faith appears only through historical
mediations and not as abstract truths independent of
the socio-historical situation, Assmann also reminds us
that it is impossible to appeal to norms outside of our
social praxis because

. . . we do not possess Christianity
'as such' in a way that enables us to
introduce it into discussion as an a
priori critical criterion. . . . It
is impossible to go straight to the
'heart of Christianity' because Christianity exists only in a series of
historical embodiments. . . .[101]

Among the implications of this epistomological perspective for the doing of social ethics, most certainly
one is that liberation Christians have a permanent task
before them of critically examining "the forms in which
the living of the faith has been translated throughout
history and is translated today into the political practice of Christians." Gutierrez has concluded that "to
do otherwise is to remain in an abstract and ahistorical

level. . . ."[102] In addition to remaining self-critical, sociologically speaking, of the complicity of the
church and other social insitutions in maintaining systems of oppression, Christians are also called upon to
acknowledge the fundamental historicity of the faith
and to accept the fact that theological truth is not
located in or limited to the past but that it emerges
in the present. Accordingly,

> . . . theological reflections carried
> out in another cultural context say
> very little to them. Such reflections
> transmit the consciousness which pre-
> ceding Christian generations had of
> their faith. Their expressions are a
> reference point for these committed
> Christians; they do not, however,
> rescue them from their theological
> orphanhood, because such expressions
> do not speak to them in the strong,
> clear, and incisive language which
> corresponds to the human and Chris-
> tian experience which they are liv-
> ing.[103]

Therefore, theological reflection, whether derived from
a different socio-cultural context, such as Western
Europe, or from another historical situation, such as
the early Christian churches, is not immediately available or able to be appropriated without critical examination. If liberationists focus primarily upon their
present and quite particular world-historical situation
and give the present more "weight" theologically than
either the past or the future, they do so not in order
to reject the validity of the biblical witness or to
disregard the significance of tradition, but, as Miguez
Bonino notes, in recognition

> . . . of the simple fact that we al-
> ways read a text which is already
> incorporated in a praxis, whether
> our own or somebody else's. There
> is no possiblity of extracting the
> text and projecting it objectively
> as a norm. There is only the pos-
> sibility of criticism from within
> ourselves or in dialogue with
> others.[104]

A final socio-ethical implication of this epistemological perspective is that additional support is given
to ground Assmann's suspicion, which we noted earlier,
of the inadequacies of a "pure theology" divorced from
human action and independent of any particular historical context. Jose Comblin has identified the fundamental problem with any such aseptic and detached theology
as its "incorruptibility," or, in his own words, as the
fact that

> It no longer says anything to anyone
> because it is now pure message, re-
> moved from every context that might
> give it some specific meaning. We
> end up with a pure message that says
> nothing to anyone. As soon as any
> theology is completely detached from
> every ideology, it ceases to say
> anything.[105]

It was in reaction against such a theology that Third
World theologians at their Dar-es-Salaam meeting stated
their intent to "reject as irrelevant an academic type
of theology which is divorced from action" but also
their preparedness "for a radical break in epistemology
which makes commitment the first act of theology and
engages in critical reflection of the praxis of the
reality of the Third World."[106] This epistomological
break is considered necessary because of the perceived
inadequacies of the traditional way of knowing and preserving theological truth (and relating this knowledge
to social action) and in recognition of the fact that
theological reflection is now being done in a distinctively different socio-cultural situation and in response to specific world-historical issues. As Gutierrez describes this shift,

> To engage in the revolutionary strug-
> gle is to enter into a different cul-
> tural world, where there is a new way
> of approaching truth and of relating
> it to historical practice, i.e., of
> linking knowledge and change, theory
> and practice.

> Faith has been lived and reflected on
> in another universe from that of the
> contemporary revolutionary experience.
> . . . [But] from now on, faith has to

> be understood in light of the his-
> torical praxis where people are
> struggling for a truly human life.[107]

As we have already considered during our discussion
of the political break with the developmentalist paradigm, liberationists most certainly question the validity of the dominant theological tradition because it
tends to idealize reality by downplaying the conflictual
nature of present world history. Assmann has charged
more specifically that the typical theology from the
affluent world demonstrates an inherent inability to be
historically realistic because "its questions do not
spring from the basic conflict inherent in the real
situation." Moreover, he argues that when theologians
from the North do consider world problems, they tend,
for the most part, to avoid political partisanship and
to offer only vague sociolocial analysis of issues as if
they are "afraid to name the organs of oppression openly." The most serious failing, however, from Assmann's
perspective is that North Atlantic theological ethical
reflection

> . . . concentrates almost exclu-
> sively on the desacralization
> brought into the man-nature [sic]
> relationship by technology, and ig-
> nores the primordial (political)
> aspects of the man-nature-man [sic]
> relationship, the man-mechanics
> [sic] of the domination relation-
> ship, and the whole question of
> 'principalities and powers.'[108]

Liberationists consider this insensitivity to the political dimension of socio-ethical problems as serious as
the related problem of the idealist temptation to ab-
stain politically. Both are only reinforced, they
claim, by a presentation of Christian faith in an abstract and ahistorical fashion as "the teaching of principles above specific political options,"[109] and by the
traditional, dualistic assumption that there is a plane
of faith proper (and, therefore, of theological truth)
separate from the plane of temporal realities. In order
to challenge these assumptions effectively, liberation
Christians have proposed that an epistemological break
with "the old way of knowing" is needed.

What liberation theologians have found so highly

problematic in the dominant theological paradigm is precisely the epistemological assumption that truth is "defined a priori independently of its verification" with its own attributed efficacy. As Assmann has detailed the traditional perspective,

> Basically truth was something to be
> accepted or not, and the purely in-
> tellectual act of accepting it or not
> in no way affected its status as
> truth. . . . Truth was something valid
> in itself, and once that was estab-
> lished, it could not be either vali-
> dated or invalidated by historical
> validations or invalidations. These
> could easily be dismissed as 'imper-
> fect applications' proper to the human
> condition, with no power to affect the
> absolute permanence of truth in it-
> self.[110]

The ideological significance, in a negative sense, of this dualistic notion of truth distinct from its historical efficacy in practice is that

> . . . the ideal truth, truth in it-
> self, is what matters, and a declara-
> tion of fidelity to this serves to
> cover the absence of any real truth
> on the historical plane. Dualism
> implies a contempt of man [sic] and
> his history, shifts the ethical axis
> to the plane of idealism, and so
> sets the whole area of historical
> reality free to be manipulated by the
> powers that be.[111]

Along with their rejection of the reality and supposed efficacy of a distinct "heaven of truth," liberationists also deny the validity of regarding truth idealistically as the "conformity of the mind to a given object," as Gregory Baum has accurately reported in the following passage:

> Such a concept of truth only con-
> firms and legitimates the world as
> it now exists. The world . . . is
> not a static object which the human
> mind confronts and attempts to under-

205

> stand; the world is, rather, an un-
> finished project which is being
> built by the people who make it up,
> and its reality tomorrow and in the
> future depends in part on what these
> people think and do. Knowledge is
> . . . a dimension of this world-
> building process . . . [and] the
> norm of truth must be taken from the
> kind of world knowledge helps to
> create.[112]

Methodologically, liberation theologians have, therefore, found good reason to question the adequacy of any
ethical analysis which takes as its fundamental point
of departure the abstract assertion of "basic principles
. . . cast in completely ahistorical terms."[113] They
also have come to recognize the need to disclaim the
possibility of distinguishing church teaching about
human nature and the meaning of history as "truthful,"
in the traditional sense of being timeless and unalter-
able knowledge, while suggesting that about socio-political issues there can only be a plurality of shifting
opinions. From a liberationists perspective, theological truth is not self-contained and complete in and of
itself but rather awaits historical verification.
Therefore, they have made the epistemological counter-
proposal that truth is better understood, as Rubem Alves
has argued, as "'the name given by the historical community to those actions which were, are, and will be
effective for the liberation of man [sic].'"[114]

It is in full keeping with this liberationist epistemology that Gustavo Gutierrez has argued that Christian proclamation must be historically grounded and politically verified.

> The proclamation of the word can only
> be understood from the point of view
> of the practice, of actions. In action
> our faith becomes truth, not only for
> others, but for ourselves too. By
> acting as Christians, we become Chris-
> tians.[115]

From their participation in various socio-political
movements for liberation throughout Latin America, liberation Christians have come to recognize the validity
of this epistemological presupposition, but they have

also discovered the need to reassess the nature and demands of Christian spirituality and the "life of faith"
in light of the requirements of a truly liberating praxis in solidarity with the most marginalized and oppressed. This reassessment, undertaken in conjunction
with both the proposed political and epistemological
ruptures with the dominant theological tradition, has
signalled a further break, an ecclesiastical rupture,
which we shall now examine.

IV. The Ecclesiastical Break: Critiquing Neo-Colonial
     Christianity and Discovering a "Spirituality of
     Liberation"

     At the same time that liberationists speak of the
possibility of a new society in which relationships of
exploitation and domination will be transcended or at
least minimized, they also envision the emergence of a
"new kind of person." This new person is one who will
be able to resist successfully the internalization of
oppression and who, in Gutierrez's words, will be "increasingly free of the bonds preventing us from shaping
our lives." Among these bonds are the "prevailing ideologies that have shaped our societies and ourselves,"
including those religious elements which have served
historically as sanction and justification for colonial
and then neo-colonial oppression in Latin America.
Therefore, Gutierrez's assertion that "religion must be
criticized insofar as it generates or reinforces oppression"116 is not debatable among liberation theologians who also proceed to speak of the need for self-
criticism, as well. The following statement issued by
Third World theologians is representative of this awareness:

               Theology is not neutral. In a sense
          all theology is committed, conditioned
          notably by the socio-cultural context
          in which it is developed. The Chris-
          tian theological task in our countries
          is to be self-critical of the theolo-
          gians' conditioning by the value sys-
          tem of their environment. It has to be
          seen in relation to the need to live
          and work with those who cannot help
          themselves, and to be with them in
          their struggle for liberation.117

     What liberationists are seeking in the Latin Ameri-

can Christian communities is a break with what may be
called the colonial and, more recently, the neo-colonial
mentality in order to allow for full commitment to the
historical process of liberation. This break signals
a conversion experience for liberationists, a conversion
with quite significant religious and political implications, as Gutierrez has noted.

> It is not a question of a withdrawn
> and pious attitude. Our conversion
> process is affected by the socio-
> economic, political, cultural, and
> human environment in which it occurs.
> Without a change in these structures,
> there is not authentic conversion.
> We have to break with our mental
> categories, with the way we relate to
> others, with our way of identifying
> with the Lord, with our cultural
> milieu, with our social class, in
> other words, with all that can stand
> in the way of real, profound, soli-
> darity with those who suffer, in the
> first place, from misery and injus-
> tice. Only thus, and not through
> purely interior and spiritual atti-
> tudes, will the 'new man [sic]' arise
> from the ashes of the 'old.'118

This conversion process is the pivotal experience
of a liberation spirituality. It involves a critical
examination and reordering of the Christian life in
terms of the contemporary faith experience of engagement in the movement for liberation. This examination
includes, mose specifically, a critical inquiry into
the ways in which the churches in Latin America have
participated in or even contributed to colonial and neo-
colonial oppression and how this history has shaped
Christian identity and forms of piety and service. As
Miguez Bonino has declared,

> A Christian can only understand him-
> self in Latin America when he dis-
> covers, analyzes, and takes a stand
> concerning these historical relation-
> ships of his faith. [Moreover,] the
> first 'break' in the new Christian
> consciousness is the affirmation that
> we are moving beyond a colonial and

a neo-colonial Christianity, with
all that this implies.[119]

The effects of colonial Christianity, including a
false sense of superiority bred among the faithful with
an accompanying insensitivity to oppression, are well
known to liberation Christians.[120] They are perhaps
even more concerned, however, about the more immediate
legacy of neo-colonial Christianity. Over the course
of the last several decades, neo-colonialism has given
rise to a developmentalist theology in the churches.
Admittedly, this theology has had a liberal facade and
a rather progressive social program.

> The liberal trends are in favor of
> the adaptation of the churches to
> the indigenous cultures and to the
> operation of parliamentary democracy
> within the framework of free enter-
> prise capitalism. Local religious,
> priests, bishops have replaced the
> foreign ones. The theology was thus
> adapted to suit the post-independence
> situation. However, there was not
> yet a fundamental alliance of the
> churches with the masses struggling
> for radical social justice.[121]

What Enrique Dussel also finds quite characteristic of
this developmentalist theology is its lack of "awareness of the problem of classes and of the dependence
that the Latin American continent was suffering under
the economic, political, and military power of the
United States."[122] Beatriz Couch has added that "theologically speaking, the transcendent nature of the
church was maintained," such that there was an explicit
rejection of the churches' assuming a political stance
concerning social justice issues since all political
options were considered relative. The problem with this
position, as Couch explains from a liberation perspective, is that

> If all political options are rela-
> tive, the church cannot take sides;
> the prophetic mission is reduced to
> condemn the actual oppressive struc-
> tures and then reject violence, yet
> there is not an open and frank in-
> volvement to bring about basic chang-

es in a situation of institutional violence whose daily death toll is criminal.[123]

More to the point, the transition from this neo-colonial theology to a liberation theology and faith is not accomplished or even possible until "engagement for revolutionary change is no longer an academic question but a mandate of Christian obedience, a sign of faithfulness."[124]

The urgency of effecting this transition is also indicated by the liberationists' unwillingness to dicotomize "being Christian and acting politically," As Gutierrez has explained,

> Henceforth it is in the framework of politics that Christians committed to the poor and the liberation of the exploited classes will ponder and live out their faith. . . . It is there where the proclamation of the gospel seems to immerse itself in the purely historical realm that theological reflection, spirituality, and preaching should now arise. For only in that soil can we preach a Christian message that is incarnated in our here and now.[125]

It is also from within this faith experience that liberation Christians have made several discoveries, which we will only briefly mention, about the contemporary role of the churches, about the dialectical relationship between personal and social change, and about the character of the contemporary theological crisis confronting the churches.

About the role of the churches, liberationists agree that, first of all, "the origin [of the church] is no longer seen as a set of foundational doctrines, structures, or norms but as the launching of a historical task . . .,"[126] the task of effecting human emancipation in history. Because of the political nature of that task, liberation Christians now question whether it is possible to speak any longer of only a "civilizing" function of the church, as if the primary function of Christian ministry was to promote certain "ethical, cultural, and artistic values and at the most . . . a

very general and uncommitted defense of the dignity of
the human person." They counter that the role of the
churches must now be seen to be "to conscienticize, to
politicize, to make the oppressed person become aware
that he is a man [sic]. . . ."[127]

About the dialectical nature of personal and social
change, liberationists have learned from their own practical experiences that social action to transform the
world changes the actors as well as their world reality.
One consequence of this understanding has been the
clarification of an anthropological perspective in which
the person as historical agent is seen fundamentally as
"a project of liberation that constantly emerges in the
fight against the objectifications given in nature, in
history, in society, in religion."[128] A second consequence is the move to criticize and move beyond what
Gutierrez labels as a "half-truth" influential in Christian circles for some time, namely,

> . . . that it did little or no good
> to alter social structures if the
> heart of human beings did not under-
> go any change. And this was a half-
> truth because it ignored the fact
> that 'hearts' can also be transformed
> by altering socio-cultural structures.
> Both aspects, in other words, are in-
> terdependent and complementary be-
> cause they are grounded on a common
> unity. The view that a structural
> transformation will automatically
> produce different human beings is no
> more and no less 'mechanistic' than
> the view that a 'personal change of
> heart' will automatically lead to a
> transformation of society. Any such
> mechanistic views are naive and un-
> realistic.[129]

About the contemporary theological crisis, liberationists recognize the fact that there is an almost
universal acknowledgement about some kind of a crisis
situation in theology and in the life of the churches,
but very little consensus about its nature or about an
appropriate response. They have noticed, too, that from
the affluent North,

> The explanations come easily: secu-

211

larization, lack of community participation, crisis in the culture, the
absence of theological giants such
as Barth, Tillich, and Bultmann.[130]

From their situation on the periphery of the global
economy, liberation theologians from the Third World
perceive the crisis in quite different terms:

There is a crisis in theology because there is a crisis in the culture of Western scientific ration-
alism. And there is a crisis in the
culture because there is a change in
the economic mode of production,
which has not been able to resolve
the injustices of the world and overcome the different forms of oppression. . . .[131]

It is in response to this crisis situation that liberation theologians hope and intend to make their contribution, a contribution containing at the very minimum a
determination "not to add to the process of diluting
the revolutionary implications that circumstances have
dictated [the process of liberation] should contain."[132]
Again, a significant reason for the proposed ecclesiastical break is to make it possible to reclaim a necessary
theological humility about the fact, as Miguez Bonino
suggests,

There is no divine politics or economics. But this means that we must
resolutely use the best human politics
and economics at our disposal.[133]

It also means that Christians must learn that their
faith is not a priori liberating or effective in the
struggle for socio-economic justice but only insofar
as they act in solidarity with the least-well off in
society and "commit [themselves] lucidly, realitically,
and concretely" to the praxis of liberation "not only
generously, but also with an analysis of the situation
and a strategy of action."[134]

This well-placed concern among liberation theologians and ethicists for appropriate analysis of social
realities and for effective strategies to maximize economic justice, especially for the poorest of the poor,

212

will be of particular interest to us as we turn now to
an overall assessment of the normative socio-ethical
significance of the economic development debate. It is
quite fair and necessary to say that the true import of
the debate itself will not come into view unless we review the dynamics and ideological character of this debate within the context of present dimensions of the
global economic crisis and only as we pay heed to the
liberationists' perception that this crisis is deepening. We also need to remind ourselves, at the same
time, that Latin American liberation theologians have
straightforwardly called upon us to employ a specific
measure for judging the value of both developmentalist
and liberationist contributions to the development debate and for considering the soundness of any recommendations for how we are to shape our ongoing work as
Christian social ethicists. All judgments and recommendations, they rightly tell us, must be informed by
a critical assessment of how well each side of the debate does, in fact, enable us to improve our qualifications, as Assmann was quoted saying at the beginning of
this chapter, "both in the practical struggle for a more
human world and in the intellectual struggle to interpret social realities."[135] That measure will be applied
in the next and final chapter.

NOTES

1. Hugo Assmann, "Statement by Hugo Assmann," in Theology in the
    Americas, ed. Sergio Torres and John Eagleson (Maryknoll:
    Orbis Books, 1976), p. 302.

2. Jose Miguez Bonino, Doing Theology in a Revolutionary Situa-
    tion (Philadelphia: Fortress Press, 1975), p. 70. Miguez
    Bonino identifies this intent to transcend dualistic thinking
    as the distinctive characteristic of liberation theologies.

3. Hugo Assmann, "Basic Aspects of Theological Reflection in
    Latin America," Risk 9:2 (WCC, 1973), in A Reader in Political
    Theology, ed. Alistair Kee (Philadelphia: The Westminster
    Press, 1974), p. 110.
4. Beverly W. Harrison, "Liberation Theology and Social Ethics:
    Some Theses for Discussion" (unpubl. ms., November 1977), p.
    1.

5. Assmann, "Statement by Hugo Assmann," p. 301.

213

6. For examples of critiques of Latin American liberaion theology, see the letters of Raul Cardinal Silva, Archbishop of Santiago, to Gonzalo Arroyo and the Organizing Committee of the Christians for Socialism Movement in Chile and their responses, in John Eagleson, ed., Christians and Socialism: Documentation of the Christians for Socialism Movement in Latin America, trans. John Drury (Maryknoll: Orbis Books, 1975), pp. 35-66. Robert McAfee Brown sketches eight types of critiques, some more substantive than others, in his Theology in a New Key: Responding to Liberation Themes (Philadelphia: The Westminster Press, 1978), pp. 101-131. Penny Lernoux provides a detailed account of the opposition movement within the Latin American Roman Catholic hierarchy, which reached a fevered pitch prior to the 1979 Catholic Bishops Conference (CELAM III) in Puebla, Mexico, in her introductory comments to John Eagleson and Philip Scharper, eds., Puebla and Beyond: Documentation and Commentary, trans. John Drury (Maryknoll: Orbis Books, 1979), pp. 3-27. Also, for a North American sociologist's critique of liberation theology, see Peter L. Berger, Pyramids of Sacrifice: Political Ethics and Social Change (Garden City, New York: Anchor Books, 1976). British theologian Edward Norman's Christianity and the World Order (New York: Oxford University Press, 1979), chastizes the Latin Americans for "politicizing religion," but Dorothee Soelle has responded that "Norman's book, in brief, has to be understood as a strategic move (conscious or unconscious) in the class struggle from above." Her critique of Norman, along with Roger L. Shinn's critical assessment and Peter Berger's more sympathetic reading, may be found in "Continuing the Discussion: 'A Politicized Christ,'" Christianity and Crisis, Vol. 39, no. 4 (March 19, 1979), pp. 50-57.

7. Phillip E. Berryman, "Doing Theology in a (Counter-) Revolutionary Situation: Latin American Liberation Theology in the Mid-Seventies," in Theology in the Americas, p. 58. Cf. Enrique Dussel's observation (supra, p. xxxvi) that the present conflict within the Latin American churches is not between conservatives and radicals but between progressives and radicals.

8. Gustavo Gutierrez, "Statement by Gustavo Gutierrez," in Theology in the Americas, p. 309.

9. Osvaldo Luis Mottesi, "Doing Theology in the Latin American Context," Church and Society, Vol. LXVIII, no. 3 (January-February 1978), p. 9. My emphasis.

10. Ibid. Mottesi's emphasis.

11. Gustavo Gutierrez, "Liberation Praxis and Christian Faith," in _Frontiers of Theology in Latin America_, ed. Rosino Gibellini, trans. John Drury (Maryknoll: Orbis Books, 1979), p. 8.

12. Sergio Torres, "Introduction," in _The Emergent Gospel: Theology from the Underside of History_, ed. Sergio Torres and Virginia Fabella (Maryknoll: Orbis Books, 1976), p. vii.

13. Gustavo Gutierrez, "Two Theological Perspectives: Liberation Theology and the Progressivist Theology," in _The Emergent Gospel_, p. 174.

14. Gustavo Gutierrez, _A Theology of Liberation_, trans. and ed. Caridad Inda and John Eagleson (Maryknoll: Orbis Books, 1973), p. 174.

15. Hugo Assmann, _Theology for a Nomad Church_, trans. Paul Burns (Maryknoll: Orbis Books, 1976), p. 65.

16. Ibid., p. 116.

17. Ibid., pp. 115ff.

18. Juan Luis Segundo, "Statement by Juan Luis Segundo," in _Theology in the Americas_, p. 280. Segundo's emphasis.

19. Gutierrez, "Liberation Praxis and Christian Faith," p. 2.

20. Gutierrez, "Two Theological Perspectives: Liberation Theology and Progressivist Theology," p. 227. Gutierrez's emphasis.

21. Assmann, "Basic Aspects of Theological Reflection in Latin America," p. 108.

22. Beatriz Melano Couch, "New Visions of the Church in Latin America: A Protestant View," in _The Emergent Gospel_, p. 220.

23. Miguez Bonino, _Doing Theology in a Revolutionary Situation_, p. xix.

24. Gutierrez, "Two Theological Perspectives: Liberation Theology and Progressivist Theology," p. 250.

25. Enrique Dussel, "The Political and Ecclesial Context of Liberation Theology in Latin America," in _The Emergent Gospel_, pp. 189-190. Dussel also notes that liberation theology arises out of a distinct historical praxis and that this grounding in a social and ecclesial movement further distinguishes it from European theology of hope and political the-

ology, for which there is "'still no ecclesial movement'" (Ibid., p. 190).

26. Gutierrez, "Two Theological Perspectives: Liberation Theology and Progressivist Theology," p. 247.

27. Miguez Bonino, Doing Theology in a Revolutionary Situation, p. 68.

28. Assmann, Theology for a Nomad Church, p. 33. Assmann's emphasis.

29. Gutierrez, A Theology of Liberation, p. 91.

30. Torres, "Introduction," p. vii.

31. Monika Hellwig accurately characterizes the liberationists' understanding of the goal of the liberation process, which is not "a mere effort to get the oppressed class into the oppressor position," but rather so to alter the structures of society "as to undo the oppression itself, not to pass it over into different hands" ("Response of Monika Hellwig to Avery Dulles," in Theology in the Americas, p. 102).

32. Gutierrez, A Theology of Liberation, p. 46.

33. Torres, "Introduction," p. 4. Robert McAfee Brown records a telling anecdote (Theology in a New Key, p. 77) about how North American theologians disclose their ethnocentric bias whenever they assume that their theology is normative and all others are derivative. He quotes the complaint of Latin Americans who rightly query, "Why is it that when you talk about our position you always describe it as 'Latin American theology,' but when you talk about your position you always describe it as 'theology'?" Cf. Gustavo Gutierrez's reflections on the universal character of theological discourse, in Teofilo Cabestrero, ed., Faith: Conversations with Contemporary Theologians, trans. Donald D. Walsh (Maryknoll: Orbis Books, 1980), pp. 96-97.

34. Dussel, "The Political and Ecclesial Context of Liberation Theology in Latin America," p. 181.

35. Gustavo Gutierrez, "Freedom and Salvation: A Political Problem," trans. Alvin Gutierrez, in Liberation and Change, ed. Ronald H. Stone (Atlanta: John Knox Press, 1977), pp. 53-54.

36. Assmann, Theology for a Nomad Church, p. 112.

37. Ibid., pp. 57-67. Cf. Beatriz Melano Couch, "New Visions of the Church in Latin America:" A Protestant View," in The Emergent Gospel, esp. pp. 198-209. Couch observes that liberal theologians of development in Latin America in the 1950's and early 1960's were consistently blocked in their efforts to transcend ethical idealism because they "lacked a historical understanding of the evolution of Latin America" (p. 204). With the emergence of a historically grounded, structural and critical perspective on underdevelopment dynamics which was developed and refined in the mid-1960's by neo-Marxist dependency theorists, theologians gained a new language and theory to name their socio-economic realities in terms of dynamics of dependency and domination. The social scientific breakthrough complemented the theological advancement from a theology of development to a theology of liberation, a process we detailed in Chapter II.

38. Miguez Bonino, Doing Theology in a Revolutionary Situation, p. xxvii.

39. Ibid., p. xxvi; Gutierrez, "Liberation Praxis and Christian Faith," p. 25.

40. Gutierrez, A Theology of Liberation, p. 203.

41. Cesar Aguinar, "Currents and Tendencies in Contemporary Latin American Catholicism," in Louis M. Colonnese, ed., Conscientization for Liberation (Washington, D.C.: U.S. Catholic Conference, 1971), p. 36.

42. Clodovis Boff, "The Illusion of a New Christendom: A Critique of the Preliminary Document of CELAM III," LADOC, Vol. IX, no. 1 (September-October 1978), p. 7.

43. Miguez Bonino, Doing Theology in a Revolutionary Situation, pp. 15-16.

44. Ibid., p. 26.

45. Gutierrez, A Theology of Liberation, pp. 26-27.

46. Jose Miguez Bonino, Christians and Marxists: The Mutual Challenge to Revolution (Grand Rapids: William B. Eerdmans Publishing Company, 1976), pp. 7-8. Miguez Bonino's emphasis.

47. Ibid., p. 92.

48. Assmann, Theology for a Nomad Church, p. 59.

49. Gutierrez, A Theology of Liberation, p. 202.

50. Miguez Bonino, Doing Theology in a Revolutionary Situation, p. 29.

51. Gutierrez, A Theology of Liberation, p. 26.

52. Ibid., pp. 87-88.

53. Miguez Bonino, Doing Theology in a Revolutionary Situation, p. 35.

54. Ibid., p. 27.

55. Ibid., p. 28.

56. Assmann, Theology for a Nomad Church, p. 115. Cf. Andre Gunder Frank, "Who Is the Immediate Enemy?," in Andre Gunder Frank, Latin America: Underdevelopment or Revolution (New York: Monthly Review Press, 1969), pp. 371-409.

57. Gutierrez, "Two Theological Perspectives: Liberation Theology and Progressivist Theology," p. 240.

58. Gutierrez, "Liberation Praxis and Christian Faith," p. 8.

59. Miguez Bonino, Doing Theology in a Revolutionary Situation, p. 119.

60. Gutierrez, A Theology of Liberation, p. 274. My emphasis.

61. Ibid.

62. Gustavo Gutierrez, Praxis of Liberation and Christian Faith, revised edition (San Antonio: The Mexican American Cultural Center, 1976), pp. 19-20. My emphasis.

63. Assmann, Theology for a Nomad Church, p. 30.

64. Ibid., p. 32.

65. Monika Hellwig, "Response of Monika Hellwig to Avery Dulles," in Theology in the Americas, p. 105.

66. Gutierrez, A Theology of Liberation, p. 47.

67. Gutierrez, "Liberation Praxis and Christian Faith," p. 12.

68. Gutierrez, A Theology of Liberation, pp. 48-49.

69. Miguez Bonino, Doing Theology in a Revolutionary Situation, p. 21.

70. Assmann, Theology for a Nomad Church, pp. 49-50.

71. Gutierrez, A Theology of Liberation, p. 48.

72. Robert McAfee Brown, Theology in a New Key, p. 176. Brown's emphasis.

73. Raul Vidales, "Methodological Issues in Liberation Theology," in Frontiers of Theology in Latin America, p. 42.

74. Assmann, Theology for a Nomad Church, p. 56.

75. Gutierrez, Praxis of Liberation and Christian Faith, p. 20.

76. Assmann, Theology for a Nomad Church, p. 131.

77. Ibid., p. 124.

78. Phillip E. Berryman, "Latin American Liberation Theology," in Theology in the Americas, p. 44.

79. Miguez Bonino, Doing Theology in a Revolutionary Situation, p. 38.

80. Ibid., p. 95. Cf. J. Philip Wogaman's discussion of ideology, "Can We Avoid Ideological Thinking?," in his The Great Economic Debate: An Ethical Analysis (Philadelphia: The Westminster Press, 1977), pp. 14-33.

81. Gutierrez, A Theology of Liberation, p. 48.

82. Penny Lernoux, "The Long Path to Puebla," in Puebla and Beyond, p. 18.

83. Gustavo Gutierrez, "The Power of the Poor in History," LADOC, Vol. 9, no. 6 (July-August 1979), p. 28.

84. Assmann, "Basic Aspects of Theological Reflection in Latin America," p. 109.

85. Gutierrez, Praxis of Liberation and Christian Faith, pp. 44-45; cf. Gutierrez, "Liberation Praxis and Christian Faith," p. 22, and Gutierrez, "Freedom and Salvation: A Political Problem," p. 83.

86. Gutierrez, "Two Theological Perspectives: Liberation Theology and Progressivist Theology," p. 247.

219

87. Ibid., p. 244. Cf. David Tracy, Blessed Rage for Order: The New Pluralism in Theology (New York: The Seabury Press, 1975), esp. pp. 242ff. Tracy characterizes liberation theology as a contemporary expression of "a practical theology in interdisciplinary conversation with empirical sociologists and economists" (p. 248), but Robert McAfee Brown notes that Tracy offers an oversimplified critique of this "practical theology" by claiming, for example, that Gustavo Gutierrez (p. 255) has offered critical reflection on praxis and especially the concept of development, but that the Peruvian "does not apply that same method to any of the major Christian doctrines which inform his important work." Brown provides contrary evidence to invalidate Tracy's reading of Gutierrez in his Theology in a New Key, pp. 109-110.

88. Assmann, Theology for a Nomad Church, p. 62.

89. Ibid., pp. 83-84.

90. Miguez Bonino, Christians and Marxists, p. 30.

91. Miguez Bonino, Doing Theology in a Revolutionary Situation, p. 81.

92. Gutierrez, "Freedom and Salvation: A Political Problem," p. 82.

93. Assmann, Theology for a Nomad Church, p. 58.

94. Miguez Bonino, Doing Theology in a Revolutionary Situation, p. 72.

95. Assmann, Theology for a Nomad Church, p. 120.

96. Ibid., p. 80.

97. Gutierrez, "Freedom and Salvation: A Political Problem," p. 184.

98. Gutierrez, A Theology of Liberation, p. 15.

99. Gutierrez, "Liberation Praxis and Christian Faith," pp. 18-19.

100. Assmann, Theology for a Nomad Church, p. 81.

101. Ibid., p. 60.

102. Gutierrez, Praxis of Liberation and Christian Faith, p. 49.

103. Gustavo Gutierrez, "The Hope of Liberation," _Worldview_ (June 1974), p. 35.

104. Miguez Bonino, _Doing Theology in a Revolutionary Situation_, p. 81.

105. Joseph Comblin, "What Sort of Service Might Theology Render?," in _Frontiers of Theology in Latin America_, p. 67.

106. "Final Statement: Ecumenical Dialogue of Third World Theologians, Dar-es-salaam, Tanzania, August 5-12, 1976," in _The Emergent Gospel_, p. 269.

107. Gustavo Gutierrez, "Theology and the Chinese Experience: Some Reflections," unpubl. ms., p. 104.

108. Assmann, _Theology for a Nomad Church_, pp. 57 and 92.

109. Berryman, "Latin American Liberation Theology," p. 37.

110. Assmann, _Theology for a Nomad Church_, pp. 76-77.

111. Ibid., p. 77.

112. Gregory Baum, "The Christian Left at Detroit," in _Theology in the Americas_, p. 404.

113. Gutierrez, "Liberation Praxis and Christian Faith," p. 4.

114. Rubem Alves, quoted in Assmann, _Theology for a Nomad Church_, p. 76.

115. Gustavo Gutierrez, "Revelation and the Proclamation of God in History" (mimeograph for the Chicago Jesuit Project for Third World Awareness, 1975), p. 14.

116. Gutierrez, "Two Theological Perspectives: Liberation Theology and Progressivist Theology," p. 241.

117. "Final Statement," in _The Emergent Gospel_, p. 270.

118. Gutierrez, _A Theology of Liberation_, p. 205.

119. Miguez Bonino, _Doing Theology in a Revolutionary Situation_, p. xxv.

120. For example, see "Final Statement," in _The Emergent Gospel_, pp. 266-267.

121. Ibid., p. 267.

122. Dussel, "The Political and Ecclesial Context of Liberation Theology in Latin America," p. 178.   Dussel's emphasis.

123. Couch, "New Visions of the Church in Latin America: A Protestant View," pp. 204 and 209.

124. Ibid., p. 211.

125. Gutierrez, "Liberation Praxis and Christian Faith," p. 12.

126. Miguez Bonino, Doing Theology in a Revolutionary Situation, p. 156.

127. Gutierrez, A Theology of Liberation, p. 270.

128. Miguez Bonino, Doing Theology in a Revolutionary Situation, p. 115.

129. Gutierrez, "Liberation Praxis and Christian Faith," p. 11.

130. Torres, "Introduction," p. xiv.

131. Ibid.

132. Assmann, Theology for a Nomad Church, p. 129.

133. Miguez Bonino, Doing Theology in a Revolutionary Situation, p. 149.

134. Gutierrez, A Theology of Liberation, p. 205.

135. Assmann, "Statement by Hugo Assmann," p. 302.

CONCLUSION

THE SIGNIFICANCE OF THE GLOBAL ECONOMIC DEVELOPMENT DEBATE FOR CHRISTIAN SOCIO-ETHICAL METHODOLOGY

"Things fall apart; the centre cannot hold."[1]

In this final chapter our attention turns to an overall assessment of the significance of the current debate over global development in the social sciences and within the ecumenical church movement. Of primary concern is to make some informed judgments about what we are to make of the conflicting perspectives identified and analyzed in the preceding pages, and to gather insights and implications especially from our critical examination of writings by Denis Goulet and Latin American liberation theologians. Our purpose in doing so is to suggest ingredients necessary for an adequate Christian socio-ethical methodology to enable us to become more effective advocates for an authentically emancipatory "economy of justice" globally.

Three tasks remain by way of concluding this study. First, it is necessary to pause and evaluate the meaning of the most recent twists and permutations within the development debate itself. The appearance internationally of multinational corporations and nationally of national security states portend rather momentous structural shifts in the world order. Among liberationists at least, the present global situation is recognized as one of crisis, for the very reason that the dominant capitalist "mode of production which has not been able to resolve the injustices of the world and overcome the different forms of oppression"[2] is presently extending and rigidifying its "global reach," to use the phrase of Barnet and Muller. As noted throughout this study, this contemporary crisis of the political economy, along with the collapse of the liberal consensus about the "rightness" of capitalist economic development theory and policies, provides the occasion for the development debate under examination.

Recent events and shifts within the dynamics of the debate offer additional confirmation of my thesis about the irreconcilable split between liberal and radical parties to this debate, but the specific point I wish to make here is that what is strikingly notice-

able at this historical juncture is that the "middle"
or "development center" is dropping out of the debate
and moving either to the left or to the right. Important background to these developments shall be given
by viewing the emergence of three ideologies of a "new
globalism" among First World governments, multinational corporations, and national security states.

A second task is to identify specific learnings
from and implications of the development debate for
engaging in Christian social ethical inquiry about
issues of global economic justice. Here special attention will be given to Denis Goulet's recent writings
and also to Miguez Bonino's argument that

> . . . it seems to many of us that
> it [neo-Marxist dependency theory
> of development and underdevelopment]
> has proved, and still proves to be,
> the best instrument available for an
> effective and rational realization
> of human possibilities in historical
> life. A Marxist praxis is both the
> verification and the source of pos-
> sible correction of the hypothesis.3

A third and final task is to consider the importance of the theological stakes which this debate and
the reality of global economic injustice raise for
Christian ethicists in their work as educators for
justice and to suggest directions in which to proceed
from here in order to maximize justice globally.

I. The Emerging Liberation Perspective as a
    Revolutionary Paradigm Shift

At the outset it is important to take stock of
the fact that liberationists perceive their emerging
perspective signals a revolutionary paradigm shift
away from the dominant developmentalist paradigm and
encompasses a social scientific, moral, and theological disjuncture from "business as usual." For reasons
to be enumerated in these concluding remarks, I share
their assumption that this radical paradigm shift is
necessary and valid. The impetus for their working
out an alternative perspective has been their recognition of the dimensions and scope of a global crisis.
In fact, the liberation call for social revolution has
been issued in light of the judgment that an "economy
of justice," especially one which would be authenti-

cally developmental and provide for the well-being of
those most marginalized, is not possible within a capitalist world order. Furthermore, because monopoly
capitalism, as economist Theotonio Dos Santos has suggested, is the "conditioning situation" of both the
affluent nations of the First World and the poor
nations of the Third World,[4] the changes that are
judged necessary to make economic justice possible are
not "merely" those of modifications within parts of
the system but rather a transformation of the conditioning situation itself into a new social and economic order.

Preparing the way for that socio-economic and
political transformation is the present signalling of
what Thomas S. Kuhn describes as a paradigm shift.
This shift occurs with a "community's rejection of one
time-honored scientific theory in favor of another
incompatible with it," with the "consequent shift in
the problems available for scientific scrutiny and in
the standards by which the profession determined what
should count as an admissible problem or as a legitimate problem-situation."[5] As we have observed in this
study, the liberation perspective is informed by a
neo-Marxist theory of dependency and grounded in a
social and ecclesial movement aimed at establishing a
socialist society. It arose precisely in response to
the perceived failure of liberal economic theory and
policies to explain adequately what is going on in the
world economy and to propose appropriate new strategies
to overcome economic inequities. This liberation
paradigm emerged as a critique of and alternative
paradigm to the dominant developmentalist paradigm.
Moreover, the very shift among Latin American liberation theologians from a developmentalist to a liberationist perspective has been identified by them as
"the crux of the matter."[6]

Because the Latin Americans also connect or, better yet, imbed the dynamics of a contemporary crisis
in theology and in the social sciences within the
encompassing economic crisis, they do not hesitate to
identify this shifting of paradigms as an indispensable component of a multidimensional conversion process
Part of this process may be described in Kuhn's terms
as a scientific revolution, but they also speak of a
theological and ethical liberation, as well.[7] This
revolutionary shift, in theology as well as in the
social sciences, has been

> . . . inaugurated by a growing
> sense, again often restricted to a
> narrow subdivision of the scien-
> tific [and religious] community,
> that an existing paradigm has
> ceased to function adequately in
> the exploration of an aspect of
> nature [or of an ethical issue] to
> which that paradigm itself had pre-
> viously led the way. In both politi-
> cal and scientific [and theological]
> development the sense of malfunction
> that can lead to crisis is prerequi-
> site to revolution.[8]

Furthermore, Latin American theologians argue that
their own political and theological project to struggle
for a new, non-exploitative social order and to engage
in a theological process that is authentically emancipatory and liberating can be read and understood adequately only in terms of the dynamics of this global
economic crisis and its accompanying paradigm shift.

What we may also notice, along with Kuhn, is not
only that the development debate is now being waged
between two competing paradigms, but that this debate
is also forcing a choice between two incompatible
modes of organizing community life and structuring
economic arrangements. Because of this awareness we
can, therefore, sense the massive conflict coming into
play between two quite distinct rationalities.
Although developmentalists often minimize the degree
and extent of this conflict, liberationists have
reason to agree with Robert Heilbroner, for example,
that liberal economists have, indeed, reached the
limits of rationality "with regard to the engineering
of social change" and that "many economic and social
problems lie outside the scope of our accustomed
instrumentalities of social change."[9] Within the
boundaries set by the capitalist paradigm of economic
development, liberationists conclude that the problem
of the increasing disparities between rich and poor
cannot be solved adequately, for as Michael Harrington
has argued, the capitalist world economy has itself
produced and continues to function quite well with
these inequities. The conclusion Harrington draws
from this realization is that

> We confront, then, a system of injus-
> tice, a complex global mechanism that
> reproduces its essential inequities in

226

good times and in bad and does so
purposefully (though not conspir-
atorially).[10]

Moreover, as he has gone on to add, "there is no possibility that the mechanisms that were designed to produce that inequality will provide the means for ending
it."[11]

To conclude that the developmentalist paradigm
will not enable us to solve the problem of global
inequity is not to say that the dominant liberal
theory of economic development has not been effective
or adequate for some problem-solving. As Alistair Kee
has noted, the developmentalist theory and the economic
policies it has generated have, indeed, served and
"suited the white north rather well."

> The idea of development was indeed
> enthusiastically proposed instead of
> revolution. It had about it the
> assurance of rationality, continuity
> with the patterns of the past, con-
> trol and measurable goals. Develop-
> ment was essentially about quantita-
> tive change along the well-trodden
> path of the north. It was less emo-
> tive and 'political' than revolution.
> Above all it promised that no matter
> what change took place the north
> would always be superior and the
> south always dependent. 'Development
> is the new name for peace' . . . But
> given the bad faith in the north,
> development became the guarantee that
> the new day would never dawn.[12]

To counteract what Kee has also accurately described
as "pessimism in the underdeveloped world at the
prospects for development" and the equally pervasive
"cynicism about the fine words contributed to the
debate by nations responsible for maintaining the
present inequities,"[13] liberationists have moved to
the foreground to contend that a different rationality, a socialist rationality, is needed now to make
a global economy of justice conceivable and possible
between and within nations, in the South as well as in
the North.

Given the irreducibility and the **intractability**

227

of the emerging debate between developmentalists and liberationists, what we might also learn from Kuhn is that

> When paradigms enter, as they must,
> into a debate about paradigm choice,
> their role is necessarily circular.
> Each group uses its own paradigm to
> argue in that paradigm's defense.

> The resulting circularity does
> not, of course, make arguments wrong
> or even ineffectual . . . . Yet,
> whatever its force, the status of the
> circular argument is only that of per-
> suasion . . . . As in political revo-
> lutions, so in paradigm choice--there
> is no standard higher than the assent
> of the relevant community.[14]

This insight certainly accords well with a claim recently presented in behalf of liberation theologians by Gustavo Gutierrez, whose concern is not only to address but to broaden "the relevant community" in responding to the cries of the victims of economic injustice throughout the Third World. Gutierrez suggests that the very universal character of Christian theology--and its credibility as an authentically universal language--is not given but rather depends upon the continual possibility of open discourse and the willingness to exchange ideas and concerns freely and persuasively. In his own words of explanation he has stated:

> For me theology has a certain claim to
> universality, in the sense that the
> experience reflected upon by a group
> of Christians is offered to the church
> community to see if other Christians
> recognize themselves in any way in
> that kind of reflection on faith . . . .
> And I believe that today in Latin Amer-
> ica there is an effort to think through
> our Christian existence on that conti-
> nent in revolutionary process, and
> that's what we offer to the rest of the
> church as an attempt to think through
> the faith. And it seems to me that
> other Christians who live in somewhat

different circumstances will find
in that reflection some points in
common and others not.[15]

Finding areas of agreement and disagreement is an
important exercise for any moral discourse, but
Gutierrez also points us toward the need for argumen-
tation, persuasion, and gaining as much "assent of the
relevant community" as possible. His claim is particularly suggestive for the work of a Christian social
ethicist, for he acknowledges that while theologians-
ethicists must necessarily remain grounded in the particular socio-historical context in which they live
and work, they must also seek to create a more inclusive community and to convince others of the need,
even of the moral obligation, to listen to alternative
views and to incorporate insights from as wide a range
of sources as possible. Enough is not said, however,
until we also take note that the liberationists' test
of the adequacy of any such "soundings" is whether the
voices and moral claims of those least well-off have
been heard and responded to fairly. What we may add
at this point, as we proceed with our concluding
remarks, is that a moral agent's objectivity, as it
were, and a theologian's credibility may well be guaranteed only insofar as he or she maintains "openness
to other critical claims," especially the claims
pressed by those struggling against injustice, in that
"other critical interpretations must be accepted as
'correcting' the possible subjective distortion of
'our group.'"[16]

Because of the ideological and conflictual nature
of the economic development debate, however, it is
understandable that "openness to other critical claims"
and distortion-free discourse are not arrived at
effortlessly. Moreover, any expectation that the
actual outcome or resolution of the economic development debate will be determined by the quality of our--
or others'--ethical discourse or by powers of persuasion alone is by no means to be taken for granted,
especially since the debate concerns lived-world realities within human institutions that pertain literally
to matters of life and death and also since it high-
lights opposing ways to structure fundamental social
relations. Kuhn's argument is well taken, then, that
this debate, as any debate over paradigm choices, is
not resolvable "by logic and experiment alone,"[17] and
most certainly not within the confines of a book.
Rather, the outcome is--and must be seen to be--pend-

229

ing because it is, in fact, dependent upon human moral
choices to be made and actions taken or not taken. In
the next two sections, however, we shall have reason
to wonder whether the debate will not be soon fore-
closed or made "academic" or at least foreshortened
and the issues at hand decided not by moral persuasion
and agency but rather by force. As we shall see, the
forces of reaction being mounted come primarily from
those on the right who are resisting, and resisting in
very powerful ways, the very social, scientific,
moral, and theological paradigm shift we have been
discussing. Before discussing the most recent developments and permutations within the global economic
debate itself and the pending collapse of the "development center," we first need to set the stage by
speaking of the appearance of ideologies of a "new
globalism" which are indicative of a counter-attack
against the emergent liberation position and paradigm
shift.

II. The Appearance of Countervalent Ideologies
     of a "New Globalism"

     The issue of how to resolve the crisis of the
global political economy and to prevent the production
and distribution of more injustices and suffering,
especially in the Third World, is fast losing its
character as an open question. In light of recent
structural shifts within the world economy and the
appearance of countervalent ideologies of a "new globalism," there are reasons to conclude that the economic crisis is deepening and that resistance to any
significant transformations of the world order is
increasing in order to block liberation efforts to
locate and put into place a truly global economy of
justice. One clear sign of this deepening crisis is
that the center itself is collapsing within the
dynamics of the development debate. To be able to
analyze this current state of affairs, we first need
to recognize that recent permutations in the debates
among social scientists and within the churches have
come about in response to conflicting sets of claims
being reasserted about the role of governments, corporations, and churches in economic development programs
and policies. Each of these claims is being presented
as an appeal for a new kind of globalism which will
make authentic development possible through the world.
That these claims are also ideological in character
should not be surprising to us after our extensive

examination of the developmentalist and liberationist perspectives on development issues.

There are two distinct senses in which development thinking has been and continues to be ideological. First, all social scientific and theological analyses are informed by and to varying degree shaped by "assumptions, beliefs, values, and orientations. In this sense, everyone has an ideology, a screen through which she or he perceives the social world." A second meaning of the term is more problematic, however, in that ideology, understood negatively, operates to mask the reality of inequities and exploitation and serves to preserve an unjust status quo. As Lee Cormie has explained,

> These [negatively ideological] theories reflect the experiences of 'freedom' and affluence of the upper classes, and their social interests in reproducing their privileges and power . . . .
>
> In these theories underdevelopment, poverty, alienation . . . are all interpreted as unconnected to the power and affluence of the upper classes, as the responsibility of those afflicted and not of economic, political, and social structures. Symptoms of the success of this ideology may be seen in the tendency among oppressed groups to internalize responsibility for their plight and to act out their rage in self-destructive and politically impotent ways.
>
> These theories make it impossible to understand the experience of oppressed groups, or to do anything to promote fundamental social change. These theories give us a picture of harmony where there is conflict, of progress toward equality where there are growing gaps in income, wealth and power between poor and working people on the one hand and the upper classes on the other. As such they are potent weapons in the hands of those who seek to reproduce the present order.[18]

Of particular importance to our assessment of the development debate are three examples of how the ideological defense mechanisms of the present unjust world economic order are currently producing just these kinds of "potent weapons" in an effort to resist any fundamental restructuring of the global economy toward equalization among and within nations. Only with this analysis before us shall we be able to examine in their historical context the most recent shifts within the social sciences and the churches vis-a-vis the development debates.

Our first example does not appear to be ideologically suspect at first or even second glance. The United Nations Independent Commission on International Development Issues, under the leadership of Willy Brandt, issued its report in 1980 under the title, North-South: A Programme for Survival. Brandt's introduction to the report is presented as "A Plea for Change: Peace, Justice, Jobs," and he acknowledges the deep-seated need for fundamental restructuring of relationships between rich and poor to make authentic development possible in the Third World. However, as an appeal for change "from the top down," by governments acting cooperatively and in their national self-interests to allow for peaceful--and at the same time profitable--economic exchange, the Report takes the following political position:

> None of the important problems between industrialized and developing countries can effectively be solved by confrontation: sensible solutions can only result from dialogue and cooperation. This demands a new perception of mutual dependence of states and people . . . .
>
> . . . all nations will benefit from a strengthened global economy, reduced inflation and an improved climate for growth and investment. All nations will benefit from better management of the world's finite resources . . . . All nations-- industrialized and developing, market or centrally planned economies-- have a clear interest in greater security, and in improved political

232

capability and leadership to manage
global problems.[19]

The vision of the world and the proposals for
moving toward a just world order which this Report
promulgates are certainly attractive in the appeal
made for a reduction of international tensions and for
constructive steps toward peace, but Brandt's Commission downplays the realities of class conflicts within
developing nations and also the dependence of the poor
South which makes it so vulnerable, economically and
politically, to the affluent North. To ask the dependent partners in an unequal relationship to recognize
"simple" common interests and to cooperate with the
more powerful partners is to assume falsely that in
such an imbalanced relationship differentials in power
and wealth are not determinative of any give and take.
The more accurate perception is that even when there
are mutual benefits growing out of a sustained relationship, more often than not those in the superordi-
nate position gain more. The rich do continue to get
richer and the poor poorer. Moreover, as long as the
affluent nations are able to set and change the rules
of the game to suit their own needs, the world order
will continue to be unfair to those who are in weaker
positions. What is quite telling is that Brandt and
his commissioners do not emphasize the potential salu-
tary effects of at least the kind of conflictual situation which would make possible a transformation of
this systemic inequality toward a more just peace.
Quite to the contrary, the report contains assurances
to the powerful that no fundamental restructuring is
in order and that newcomers from the Third World not
be viewed as "intruders and 'enemies of the system'"
but as clients eager to participate and be integrated
into the present world market.[20]

The Brandt Report is symptomatic of the ideological stance of "world harmony through government cooperation" which minimizes the problem of international
class differentials in wealth and power and discounts
the liberation struggles of peoples, often over
against their own governments, to break the bonds of
dependence and exploitation. A similar example from
the United States government is the Preliminary Report
of the Presidential Commission on World Hunger,
issued in December 1979. This Commission identifies
that "poverty is the root cause of hunger today" and
recommends, among its strategy considerations, that
"the United States make the elimination of hunger the

primary focus of its relationship with the developing countries, beginning with the decade of the 1980s."[21] Critics of this report have argued that reliance upon government officials and the effectiveness of increased foreign assistance to "solve" the problem of hunger is misplaced and incapable of making the systemic changes necessary for economic and social justice in the Third World. Frances Moore Lappe, Joseph Collins, and David Kinley have countered the Commission's findings by arguing that

> The basic fallacy embodied in the Commission's 'more US aid' prescription is the assumption that aid can be designed to reach the powerless even though channeled through the powerful. Official foreign assistance necessarily flows through recipient governments and these governments (particularly those the US chooses to aid) represent narrow, elitist economic interests. Foreign aid has not played a transforming role--transforming an anti-democratic economic control by a few into a participatory, democratic process of change. It cannot. Rather, official foreign aid reinforces the power relationships that already exist.[22]

Their insight, in keeping with the liberation perspective, is that international cooperation within present global political dynamics only serves to perpetuate and reinforce the skewed concentrations of political and economic power which block authentic development in the poor South.

One final observation is in order about this "world harmony through governmental cooperation" ideology. In recent times there are signs that even the cooperation which does take place between First and Third World nations is decreasing and that the possibility of armed aggression is increasing. To cite but one rather frightening example, after the Iranian Revolution and the seizure of hostages in the United States Embassy in Teheran, the United States government has demonstrated what Richard Falk describes as "a new willingness . . . to consider military intervention in the Third World." The revolutionary nationalism of which the Iranian Revolution is a prime example has provoked a shift in "a more rightist direction" among foreign policymakers in Washington, but, even more damaging, as Falk has observed, is that

> . . . the Ayatollah's provocation
> also . . . create[d] a moral foun-
> dation for an American crusade
> against revolutionary nationalism
> that is neither Marxist-Leninist
> nor pro-Soviet. The new mood
> supersedes the cold war rationale
> for intervention by one that is
> openly racist and imperial in its
> character. By this reasoning, the
> US is opposing Islamic fanatics on
> behalf of 'civilized values' and,
> besides, it must for practical
> reasons remove the growing threat
> from nationalism in the region to
> the oil lifeline of the West.[23]

As Falk has concluded, the governmental response of the United States toward Iran may well become a pattern of counterrevolutionary effort "to protect the world economic and political position of the Western alliance."[24]

To criticize the limitations of this "world harmony through governmental cooperation" ideology does not necessarily place us in the best of company, however, for ideologues of another type also speak of the need to transcend national governmental operations in order to secure global peace and economic development. Spokespersons for multinational corporations promise that through the operations of their transnational business interests and with the uninhibited flow of capital, goods, and technology, a truly "global market" will come to replace the "irrationalities" of international politics. As Richard Barnet and Ronald Muller have noted, the slogan of the multinationals is "world peace through world trade," and the ideology of this new globalism is that everyone, rich and poor, North and South, will benefit as corporations extend their production, distribution, and exchange activities around the globe.[25]

Even critics of the multinational corporations recognize that not all the evidence has been amassed as to whether the global corporation is in the business of exploitation or development, but analysts such as Barnet and Muller do have grounds upon which to argue

that multinational corporations are designed and now
function "for worldwide profit maximization, not the
development needs of poor countries."[26] Because these
economic enterprises concentrate vast wealth, power,
and technology into the hands of a few organizations
which are not politically accountable to any nation-
state, they are changing customary patterns of production, distribution of wealth and income, and even the
balance of political power within and among nations.
Barnet and Muller state their own thesis about the
multinational corporations as follows:

> . . . the global corporation, opera-
> ting under its present ground rules,
> is not the instrument to bring about
> economic redistribution. While its
> particular global strategy does
> indeed break down national frontiers,
> it strengthens class divisions. The
> global enterprise may spread wealth
> geographically, but it concentrates
> it politically and socially. Thus in
> the fulfillment of its global vision
> both justice and stability are
> eluded.[27]

In addition to the ideologies of a new globalism
justifying the privileged positions of governments and
multinational corporations on the world scene, a third
ideology is making its appearance, especially to
rationalize and defend the presence of military dictatorships throughout Latin America. The ideology of
the national security state has emerged with the
establishment of right-wing military regimes after a
series of reactionary coups in Brazil, Argentina,
Bolivia, and Chile. The military elite are now her-
alded as the agents of economic and social change, and
their leadership is claimed to have become necessary
for national security because of the repeated failure
of civilian leaders to promote economic development
and because of the need to protect the nation-state
from the threat of communism. All powers are concentrated in the state and its executives, who argue that
protest movements and liberation struggles for economic justice within the nation only weaken internal
security and must, therefore, be eliminated. The
logic which informs the ideology of the national security state is dependent upon the "science of military
strategy," and as Jose Comblin recounts the logic of
"total warfare" which preoccupies the thinking of
national security managers,

236

> Geopolitics shows how the present
> world is divided into two world-
> wide blocs or coalitions . . . .
> Latin American national security is
> identical with Western security,
> and especially with the national
> security of the United States . . . .
> They have all taken up the Brazilian
> doctrine that the war against commu-
> nism is the fundamental opposition in
> the present condition of the world.[28]

In the interests of maintaining national security and
strengthening ties with the powers of the North Atlantic, the military regimes also welcome the presence of
multinational corporations to enable economic growth
and modernization. Such economic development is
judged necessary so that "the state may acquire more
and better weapons to defend itself," but also to
reduce domestic tensions and promote "social harmony."[29]

The ideology of the national security state also
includes a specific and noticeably geopolitical role
for the churches. The churches are approached as
defenders of traditional values and as collaborators
in maintaining the prevailing social order of the West.
As Comblin explains, the national security state offers
the churches a new "Constantinianism with a view to a
new Christendom," a pact between church and state to
protect and promote each other's privileges and powers.
What is significant about this invitation, Comblin
notes, is that

> The ideological documents of the
> national security state show that
> the Christianity it seeks is essen-
> tially a cultural phenomenon.
> Probably its proponents do not even
> know that Christianity can be any-
> thing other than a cultural phenom-
> enon. What they call Christianity
> is the cultural inheritance of the
> past--a collection of beliefs and
> ritual patterns, laws and traditions
> --that is able to lend identity to a
> nation, a collection of symbols that
> can pull a whole people together in
> the same mindset and make them feel
> kinship. They never appeal to the
> gospel as a force that can criticize

237

an establishment, bring about new
realities, change social patterns.[30]

In soliciting the support of the churches for defending the legitimacy of the security state, the military
regimes also propose that the problem of freedom in
the contemporary world is not posed by realities of
domination, exploitation, and injustice but by the
external threat of communism and by the internal cultural resistance among the populace toward modernization and economic growth. The churches are, therefore,
called upon to educate the masses to awaken to the modern world and to promote those values of good citizenship which will make the nation-state secure from its
enemies, internal and external.

Although there may well be connecting links among
these three ideologies of a "new globalism" which we
have examined, the concern before us now is to review
recent shifts within the development debate itself
which have been taking place in response both to the
steady emergence of the liberation perspective and to
the resistance being mounted against any such radical
critique and counter-proposal to the dominant economic
world order.

III. Recent Developments within the Global Economics
Debate: When the crisis comes, "The Center
Cannot Hold"

Within this particular socio-historical and
political context, with the global appearance of
national security states, multinational corporations,
and the call for more governmental cooperation internationally to maintain present political and economic
configurations, certain twists, turns, and permutations are suddenly taking place within the economic
development debate itself. The development which is
especially significant among social scientists and
within the churches is the near collapse of the
"development center," or at least the current tendency
for those in the middle to move to the left or, more
often than not, to the right. What is disconcerting
from a normative socio-ethical perspective is that
allies in the liberal community who have been most
willing to join together issues of economic development with concerns about social justice are now gravi-
tating toward those on the political right who suppress the question of equity and who are more inter-

ested in proposing development strategies which serve
to maintain their own privileges and power in an
unjust world order.

To illustrate this trend among social scientists,
we may cite the recent writing of liberal economist
Sylvia Ann Hewlett, whose criteria for measuring even
minimal standards of socio-economic justice in the
Third World were cited in the Introduction to this
study.[31] In The Cruel Dilemmas of Development: Twentieth Century Brazil, Hewlett proposes that there is
little if any chance of escaping the difficult and
humanly painful tradeoff between the need for economic
growth and capital formation in developing countries
and the promotion of human and social well-being for
the vast majority of persons within these societies.
As she explains,

> It is a basic contention of this
> book that poverty and repression
> are grounded in the harsh reali-
> ties of economic evelopment. Most
> human rights violations, far from
> being the idiosyncratic preference
> of some evil ruler are integral
> parts of the development struggle
> . . . . In concrete terms, the
> impressive economic performance of
> Brazil (Turkey or the Philippines)
> in the modern period has depended
> upon massive poverty and political
> repression, and it would not have
> been possible under democratic
> governments pursuing egalitarian
> economic policies.[32]

On this score Hewlett now stands in agreement with
Robert Heilbroner, who has likewise suggested that in
Third World countries "the price of development is apt
to be political and economic authoritarianism," and,
furthermore, that for the resolution of social conflict
and economic crisis, "such governments may be unavoidable, even necessary."[33]

The reason Hewlett, the liberal economic theorist,
offers for the necessity of repressive political governments for effecting economic development is that
transformations of an order and magnitude needed in
poor countries are impossible without high levels of
capital savings and investments, and extracting a sur-

plus of capital "large enough to propel society to a new level of productive capability often means the forced restriction of consumption for the masses of the people."[34] It is disconcerting that she does not ask if capital accumulation could occur in another, less humanly costly way, but no less problematic is her stated contention that social injustice, in the form of chronic poverty for the majority of the population, and political repression are to be accepted as unpleasant but ordinary consequences of the "normal" development process itself. As Hewlett in her own words explains, "the former is a direct ressult [sic] of the capital accumulation process; the latter is the apparatus of control necessary to prevent effective revolt on the part of the oppressed."[35]

It is quite true that the suppression of dissent has been a major goal of the national security state apparatus in Brazil, as Hewlett acknowledges, and she rightly identifies, for example, the cause of a period of violent repression from 1968 to 1973 as "very simply, the Brazilian military was determined to wipe out the Left, because it feared a socialist revolution similar to the one in Cuba."[36] She has also noted that a fundamental reason for the relative relaxation of repressive governmental measures within Brazil is that the opposition of the radical Left has now been muted or eliminated altogether. In light of these developments, however, what Hewlett cannot show us is that economic development programs have also taken place during this time frame which have improved the life situations of those Brazilians who still suffer in poverty. Rather, she attempts to provide what only appears as an empty word of encouragement by pointing out that "the need for the more excessive types of political repression has proved to be rather temporary," as if enough or even some comfort could be found from the fact that within the last decade political dissent against a military dictatorship has been almost totally stifled or, mirabile dictu, that "elite groups have regained at least some of their civil and political freedoms."[37]

Those on the ideological left in Latin America who are still alive and continue to suffer under such authoritarian military regimes, have a quite different reading of what is going on in the name of "economic development." Brazilian economist Helio Jaguaribe, for example, argues that repression is used in his country for no other reason than to maintain and

extend the privileges of those who already own wealth
or exercise power. Repression is not employed to
revolutionize the status quo or to begin a process of
sharing the benefits of economic growth with those who
have not benefitted in any significant way in the
past. His term to describe Brazil's governmental policies and programs is, therefore, not "economic development" but rather "colonial fascism":

> . . . fascism because it was 'a model
> for promoting economic development
> without changing the existing social
> conditions'; colonial, because it
> depended on 'the West in general,
> and the United States in particular,
> due to its need for foreign assis-
> tance and foreign markets.'[38]

Brazilian theologian Hugo Assmann agrees that
"the excessive price paid for 'development' is the
growing alienation of large sectors of the community
and the repression of all forms of protest."[39] Such
repression is necessary, from the viewpoint of the
guardians of the status quo, to keep the present order
in place and to prevent those who suffer from economic
deprivations and inequities from organizing themselves
politically to alter their conditioning situation.
Penny Lernoux's summary statement of this dynamic is
straightforward:

> Without repression it is impossible
> for the rich to increase their income
> indefinitely at the expense of the
> mass of the people who, for all their
> ignorance and lack of political
> organization, have the advantage in
> numbers. These millions will not
> stay quietly on the farms or in the
> slums unless they are terribly afraid.
> As in Stroessner's Paraguay, the rich
> get richer only because they have the
> guns.[40]

Hewlett's own interest is not, intentionally, to
justify or defend the legitimacy of authoritarian governments, but she, too, moves toward the right by
failing to take into account, with sufficient clarity,
that within present power structures repressive measures are not now and cannot be expected to become
authentically "developmental" for the vast majority of

Brazil's poor. Rather, authoritarianism is serving only to extend the life of an unjust socio-economic order. Even if repression does, indeed, function to allow for "the extracting of a surplus," as Hewlett claims, the fact remains that any such increase of wealth is not and will not be distributed to the poor as long as political control remains concentrated within the military and civilian elite.

Because of her own awareness of these dynamics and her concern to remain sensitive to the political context of economic decision-making, Hewlett's steadfast refusal to entertain the possibility of moving toward a more radical, neo-Marxian analysis is all that more perplexing. Her own stated objection to a move leftward is predicated upon her rather simplistic reading that the left is somehow especially vulnerable to a "scapegoat syndrome" of blaming some kind of a "bad guy" for economic and political ills. The more telling objection at work, however, may well be that she cannot quite concede the need for being so "intensely pessimistic about the possibility for basic human rights within capitalist development."[41] To remain caught in the "development middle," however, may not be possible or even satisfactory much longer, especially if Hewlett and other liberal economists are finding authoritarian regimes necessary and unavoidable for economic development to occur in the first place. Miguez Bonino's depiction of the problem for the collapsing development center speaks accurately of Hewlett's own "cruel dilemma":

> . . . liberal ideologists sign the death warrant of their own dreams as they increasingly admit that military governments and an escalation of repression are the only means through which 'freedom and democracy' can be 'protected.' Thus, in the last stage of the process, freedom--the liberal freedom of the modernizers--becomes the ideological justification for a repressive police state. When a person shouts 'liberty' in Latin America today, one can immediately suspect him [sic] of being a reactionary; and one is seldom wrong.[42]

If progressive developmentalists within the ranks of social scientists are lending ideological support, willingly or not, to authoritarian military regimes in the Third World, they do so, in part, because their own economic theories and assumptions about social change lead them to speak, as Hewlett does, of a necessarily "cruel choice" or inescapable dilemma between the economic determinants which make capitalist development possible and the "temporary" perpetuation of suffering and human misery for the poor and marginalized. Hewlett's own summation of this dilemma is that "the fact of the matter is that industrial take-off in the mid-twentieth century has some supremely painful consequences," a rather understated opinion remarkably similar to Albert Hirschman's claim that economic and social inequalities are "to be expected" in the process of development and that they are, in fact, "requirements of economic change."[43]

Liberationists have countered such claims by pointing out that the fundamental issue is not whether costs are involved in economic development, but rather what costs are incurred and who is asked to pay them. Andre Gunder Frank's assessment of the "cruel dilemma" of development follows from the liberationist understanding that the most significant variable in economic transformation is not technological innovation, increased rates of growth, or forced savings and capital accumulation, but rather social and political change in power relationships in the direction of greater egalitarianism:

> The choice [Third World peoples] face
> is not . . . between the greater or
> lesser cost of development, but is
> between devoting the already existing
> sacrifice by the many for the perpet-
> ual benefit of the few or using the
> same sacrifice for an economic devel-
> opment which benefits the many and
> frees them from this sacrifice in the
> future.[44]

Because neo-Marxian dependency theorists, and liberationists in general, refuse to make wealth and poverty realities independent of each other, they are well aware that a primary limitation of liberal social scientific theory about economic development is precisely that it separates the process of generating power and wealth for the few from the process which

243

impoverishes and disempowers the many. Liberationists, therefore, reject the artificial distinction which divides economic from "non-economic" factors which condition development and seek, instead, to analyze economic activities within their political and cultural context. One consequence of this perceptual shift, as Samuel Parmar has noted, is that

> Once the relation between power and poverty is seen, the whole strategy of change from above falls apart. Pressure from below is the only way to galvanize decision-makers into responding to demands for justice. That means that education for radical change must motivate and mobilize people at the grass-roots for development action.[45]

The appearance within the last decade and a half of grass-roots social movements for social and economic justice, especially throughout Latin America but also in Africa and Asia, has been dramatic, and one of the most significant events in the contemporary history of Protestant and Roman Catholic churches has been the support of and participation in these movements. John Bennett has been moved to argue that

> The remarkable transformations in the church in Latin America are a miracle of the Spirit. Who would have guessed only a short time ago that in country after country today the church would be the greatest defender of human rights, not only of the rights of the church or of Christians but also the rights of all humanity?[46]

At the same time, however, that some liberal social scientists are shifting toward the right and making claims about the necessity of right-wing military dictatorships, powerful arguments are also being forwarded within the ecumenical church movement itself that the churches should back off from aggressive partnership in support of these grassroots movements for economic and social equality. C. I. Itty has observed, accurately it seems, that currently "the major differences of opinion arise around the issue of the churches' participation in the struggle for changes in the eco-

nomic and political structures . . . ."[47] It is to
this dynamic that we now turn our attention.

What Itty has also noted is that precisely
because some Christian communities have been actively
engaged in these grassroots movements for economic
justice, they have been able to arrive at insights and
convictions "based on actual experiences from different contexts" and to bring to the development debate a
"greater appreciation of the complexities of the development process."[48] One such insight among liberation
Christians is that the prevalent socio-economic values
of the present world order are inadequate because they
give priority to the pursuit of profit, economic
growth, and property over against the satisfaction of
human needs and the aspirations for social well-being
and community among equals. If the operative values
of the dominant world system are to be successfully
challenged, however, Parmar has correctly argued that
what that means in practical terms is

> . . . challenging structures of power
> which are custodians of these values.
> Can that happen without confrontation?[49]

Julio de Santa Ana has been no less clear that the most
controversial shift within the ecumenical movement and
the source of most conflicts has been the assertion of
the primacy of social justice over any economic growth
per se and the centrality given to the political
aspect of the struggle for socio-economic alternatives
to the present system. As he has explained,

> . . . the political aspect seems to be
> a main one to be taken into considera-
> tion when the problem of development
> is broached. It is at this level that
> one has to make a choice in the libera-
> tion process, which in turn poses
> demands for strategy and tactics which
> are not always clearly defined.[50]

Liberationists within the churches stand firm in
insisting that the development process is best understood as a political struggle against a system of economic exploitation and as a political struggle for new
institutional arrangements to maximize justice, especially for those least well-off.

245

The reactions within the churches against this liberation stance and the politicization of economic issues have not been slow in coming, but we shall cite only one example from the Roman Catholic context to indicate the present dynamics of the church-based development debates and to locate the shaky ground upon which those in the development center are attempting to stand.[51]

It was in preparation for the third General Conference of Latin American Bishops (CELAM III) held in Puebla, Mexico, in early 1979, that a Preliminary Document was circulated which had the strongest endorsement from Roman Catholics on the right. These conservatives wished to discredit liberation theologians and direct the churches' attention toward matters of internal security and order and away from even more explicit commitment to various grassroots struggles for economic justice.[52] This document, hereafter referred to as PD, can and should be read, therefore, as an intended refutation and a disclaimer of the theological and political positions arrived at a decade earlier at the Medellin General Conference. As discussed in Chapter II, it was at Medellin that the bishops stated their commitment to the struggles of the poor and determination to defend human rights throughout the continent. Two points will suffice to characterize this more recently attempted refutation on the occasion of the Puebla meeting.

First, in its interpretation of the Latin American socio-historical situation, the PD downplays or ignores altogether the realities of economic exploitation and class conflict and identifies widespread poverty as a problem rooted in cultural rather than in political and structural dynamics. It advances the argument that underdevelopment continues to exist and will persist until the church has been restored to a significant position of cultural influence and allowed to "infuse" the society and especially the political and economic orders with explicitly Christian values. As Clodovis Boff reads this ecclesial argument,

> The Preliminary Document places
> 'culture' in a central category.
> That is to say, the basic problem
> the Document sees in Latin America
> today is neither economic nor
> political. It does not treat of
> development, and even less of lib-

eration. It is not because there
is no diagnosis on these two
levels . . . , but rather that
it is not in function of this diagnosis that the action or mission of
the church in Latin America is
decided.

The main point of the document
is the question of 'culture,'
whether the 'new urban-industrial
society' emerging in Latin America
is going to create a 'new kind of
society' defined by religion, in
this case, the Christian religion.
And it is through culture--the document believes--that the problems on
the other two levels mentioned above
will also be solved.[53]

Because the Document places specifically religious
values at the foundation of society, what is considered
decisive in the Latin American situation is located "in
the will and conscience" of the people and especially
in the minds and hearts of their military and civilian
leaders. What the PD quite noticeably does not address
as important for socio-economic transformation are the
dominant economic interests and relationships of power
which maintain those interests within the national
security states.[54]

The second consideration to mention is that the
PD encourages the withdrawal of the churches from
political engagement in defense of the poor and in
struggles for social and economic equality. Instead,
the mission of the church is presented in terms of the
ideal of a New Christendom, the ascendency of the
church to a privileged position from which to inspire
a specifically Christian culture. As noted earlier,
this role for the church as the protector and dispen-
ser of cultural values is one conceded, most willingly,
by national security states which would welcome the
silence of the churches on social justice issues. As
Penny Lernoux has documented, Chile's General Augusto
Pinochet enthusiastically supported the themes of this
Preliminary Document and responded by saying of it,

. . . '[the Church] has a specific
mission in this world that has
nothing to do with politics . . . .

> The Church appears to have stopped
> in order to reexamine its situation
> and once again follow the course it
> is meant to take.'[55]

From the viewpoint of liberationists, the Preliminary Document offers a fundamental misreading of the social situation in Latin America and proposes a course of action for the church which would only lead to an entanglement once again with the political and economic powers that perpetuate an unjust status quo. It is silent about the major conflicts which have emerged over economic development concerns, and it does not provide positive resources for reflecting upon what Boff has called "the exact point at which the Christian conscience in our continent finds difficulty," precisely "in keeping these two functions united--the religious and the political, Christian identity and social liberation."[56]

In contradistinction to the analysis forwarded by the PD to Puebla, liberationists have come to insist that the problem of underdevelopment can be understood and responded to effectively only if the problem is located fundamentally in the structure of a capitalist world economy which produces inequalities and class divisions and only if the people who suffer from economic exploitation are empowered collectively to transform those power relationships which produce inequities in the direction of creating communities of well-being among equals. As we now turn to consider some implications of the development debate for engaging in Christian social ethics on economic justice issues, we need to take heed of the fact that the liberationists' concern for an adequate analysis of the socio-economic problem at hand is no less prominent than their concern for effective strategies. What we should also note as we move on is that liberation theologians recognize quite clearly that there are only two options available at this historical juncture. Either we can accept the parameters of the present world order and join with those who intend to keep it firmly in place, or we can deny the legitimacy and moral authority of the status quo and organize to resist its rigidification and to work toward a more just social order. Ironically, this is also an insight which they share with their most severe critics but one which those in the "center" seem to disregard. Those on the liberation left, however, are as well informed as those on the right who most wish

to discredit them that there is little if any space
remaining for those who still wish to straddle a
rapidly disappearing development center.

IV. Implications of the Development Debate
     for Christian Social Ethics

Among various learnings that we could appropriate
from an examination of this debate over socio-economic
development, there are several insights which deserve
special attention. They help us to account for and
evaluate our thesis regarding an irreconcilable conflict between developmentalist and liberationist parties to the debate. These insights follow from our
concluding remarks in the previous section. One
insight is that it is morally significant which social
scientific theory we depend on to figure out what is
going on--and what is going wrong--in our contemporary
socio-historical situation. The choice between social
theories is not arbitrary and never a matter of indifference. Reasons may be forwarded and judgments made
about the adequacy of each of the theoretical paradigms we have been examining, in terms of the problems
which are brought into view for analysis and in terms
of solutions proposed and actions considered.

Another insight is that it is not sufficient
methodologically to end socio-ethical inquiry with the
analysis of an issue. An adequate understanding of
social realities does not necessarily suggest or make
possible good strategies or appropriate actions to be
taken. Rather, we must also seek to clarify and
evaluate our options for moral agency and to assess
various strategies in terms of their capacities for
maximizing economic justice among persons and groups,
and especially for the least well-off.

Important as these two insights are, they take on
their particular significance for engaging in Christian socio-ethical reflection on issues of global economic justice only when coupled with a third and even
more fundamental insight. That insight has been most
steadily and persistently clarified and espoused by
liberation Christians. They insist that normative
ethical priority should be to embody solidarity with
the poor in their struggles to overcome oppression and
move toward more egalitarian forms of community life.
They also tell us that the most appropriate criterion
for judging whether or not a socio-economic order is
just is to consider how those most marginalized, those

249

who experience and view life "from below," are faring.
As described in the Introduction to this study, our
primary obligation as moral agents is to seek "concrete justice," to sustain the search for effective
ways to address the real needs and sufferings of persons most vulnerable to and victimized by social
inequities and to transcend the unjust institutional
arrangements which perpetuate human misery.

As we proceed to examine the significance of
these insights for Christian socio-ethical methodology,
we shall want to consider how the different "yields"
we encounter from the moral analyses of Denis Goulet
and the Latin American liberation theologians are
dependent upon their critical understanding and appropriation (or lack thereof) of precisely these insights.
In doing so, however, we need not minimize the fact
that Goulet and the Latin Americans share certain convictions which place them on more common terrain than
either has with the ideological right we have just
been discussing. They agree, for example, that
"allegiance systems [are] at the heart of ethics," as
Goulet proposes in his most recent book, The Uncertain
Promise.[57] How they explicate and embody those loyalties, however, are distinctively different, and these
differences are by no means inconsequential for those
concerned about economic justice throughout the globe.
To anticipate and encapsulate the substance of remarks
to follow, we can say that Goulet most readily speaks
of loyalties as a Christian idealist who is distanced
from any engagement in liberation struggles while the
Latin Americans have come to understand and concretely
experience loyalties won and sometimes lost in their
various attempts, both in social and ecclesial contexts, to overcome dynamics of exploitation and
oppression and to create more just communities
throughout their continent. Therefore, when Goulet
will speak of loyalty to a future world which elites
will be particularly instrumental in bringing about
for the common good, the liberationists declare the
primacy of the Christian virtue of solidarity with the
poor and oppressed and join with the organized poor in
their liberation struggles. Goulet's loyalty to
"ideals" and values, especially to "a new humanity in
gestation," is no less genuine than the Latin Americans' allegiance to the values of social justice and
human equality, but their loyalties have taken on a
particular, almost overwhelming concreteness arising
out of their political involvements which Goulet himself lacks. And their different, proximate "loyalties"

to quite distinct social scientific theories also generate perceptions and insights which are at certain
points discernibly discordant.

With these summary comments in mind, we do well
to repeat that even though Goulet and the liberation
theologians view the world and experience its conflicts from quite different social locations, they do
share much common ground within one moral universe and
have significant areas of agreement. For example, the
liberationists share his moral vision, namely, that

> Ultimately, there has to be some
> kind of deliberate policy to
> mobilize the total wealth of the
> whole planet according to priority
> human needs, with suitable mecha-
> nisms of production and redistribu-
> tion adjusted to these priorities.
> In order to be acceptable, actions
> on behalf of development must be
> taken in a spirit of world soli-
> darity, mutual ecological responsi-
> bility, serious respect for cultural
> diversity, and the subordination of
> the satisfaction of low priority
> needs [luxury goods] to meeting
> those of first necessity [food,
> shelter, health care, meaningful
> work, etc.]58

Goulet and the Latin Americans also agree that significant value transformations need to take place in
order to reorient economic activities toward justice
for the poorest, along with major structural changes
within the economies of both the advanced industrialized nations and the poor nations of the South.
Goulet's own statement of these changes echoes the
sentiments of Latin American liberationists within the
ranks of both social scientists and theologians:

> What I wish to see is a kind of
> reorganization which will abolish
> throughout the world the primacy
> of the economic motive; which will
> prevent the image of efficiency
> characteristic of the advanced
> countries from playing such a
> decisive role; and which will
> impede the realm of values from

251

> being subordinated to criteria
> which are peculiarly applicable
> only to a particular economic
> system operating within one par-
> ticular environment.[59]

There is also no quarrel between them that this broad-
ranging socio-economic change will come about only
through persistent efforts over a considerable length
of time.

Differences between Goulet and the Latin Americans
begin to surface, however, with their contrary judgments regarding the relative justice of the present
world economic order. Michael Harrington's claim
opens up this difference to us.

> To innocent Americans, the notion
> that their country is imperialist
> is a Communist myth. To the
> majority of the world's people
> with a minimal political conscious-
> ness, it is an overwhelming fact of
> life.[60]

Although Goulet himself does not regard North American
imperialism as a "Communist myth," he does not emphasize its reality in explicating the problem of underdevelopment, nor does he give significant weight to
"political consciousness." As detailed in Chapter
III, Goulet is much less skeptical than the liberationists about the difficulty of attaining economic
justice within the confines of present global arrangements and about overcoming the vulnerabilities of the
dependent nations in the South. Over against Goulet,
however, the Latin Americans show little or no interest in speaking about any current, supposedly beneficial operations or speculating about future possibilities of the present system, for they have long
reached the conclusion that the established patterns
of exploitation and oppression which dominate social
reality for the Third World are intrinsic to this system, such that they are produced and perpetuated by
the class structure of unequal relationships within
the capitalist world economy. In light of their perceptions and assumptions about the nature of present
global realities and their estimations about how to
move toward greater justice for those least well-off,
their loyalties to the present world order necessarily
differ from Goulet's. They show much less reluctance,

for example, to view the world through the grid of a neo-Marxian dependency theory of development and underdevelopment and not to depend on Goulet's developmentalist spectacles because from their social location the "world is conflict," as Assmann has noted.

In keeping with his declared sympathies with the Latin Americans, Goulet will, nonetheless, insist upon the need to examine the power dynamics within and among nations which either enhance or frustrate the movement toward authentic development for the majority of the world's poor. As already noted, Goulet's assessment of the task of the religious moral thinker is quite explicit on this score:

> . . . development ethics must cope
> with structures of differential
> wealth and power among societies.
> Were it otherwise, ethics would be
> reduced to mere preachments
> addressed to the 'good will' and
> generosity of the powerful, and to
> the escapist sentiments of the
> powerless.[61]

But because he leaves intact and relies almost exclusively upon the liberal developmentalist paradigm in order to figure out what is going on in the world, he proceeds to analyze development dynamics apart from any particular socio-political context and to concentrate rather narrowly on problems located on the cultural level, apart from political realities. Therefore, he speaks almost exclusively of a worldwide cultural crisis of values brought about by the passage to modernity and of the cultural resistance which Third World peoples gather against the First World's "modern" values and against any introduction of foreign technologies from the advanced industrialized countries.[62] As an unrepentant developmentalist, he also continues to locate the problem of underdevelopment within the dynamics of poor countries, as a problem internal to these specific cultures which he describes as traditional societies not yet versed in or adapted to "modern ways." It is in keeping with the analyses of Albert Hirschman and other liberal social scientists that Goulet also argues that the problems of underdevelopment may be overcome only through sufficient exercise of the will to reform and through the employment of better decision-making techniques by

elites. This argument has been reiterated in his
latest book, The Uncertain Promise:

> In order to create a decision-
> making system which could inte-
> grate and balance social, eco-
> nomic, and environmental pro-
> cesses, they [government plan-
> ners] devise a conceptual guid-
> ance system for making budgetary
> and programmatic decisions. What
> is germane here is simply the
> recognition by planning teams
> that only a 'highly technical
> discipline' can enable them to
> control and redirect growth
> toward humane ends.[63]

At those junctures at which liberationists speak
of the necessity and full moral legitimacy of living
out solidarity with the poor in their political struggles for emancipation, Goulet consistently appeals not
to the marginalized to organize themselves, but to
"enlightened" corporate managers in multinational
corporations to become an international vanguard of a
new, more just world order. He conjectures that this
moral vanguard will emerge steadily as loyalties are
shifted to a global "humanity in gestation." On the
infrequent occasions on which he has offered an explanation of the process by which this professional
"movement" for social change can come into place, he
has done so, characteristically, in distinctly a-polit-
ical terms:

> Most international meetings are so
> structured as to make participants
> unduly conscious of their nation-
> ality, their professional disci-
> pline, or the ideological system
> they are deemed to represent.
> Thus they are made accomplices of
> loyalties which may not be deeply
> felt. Deep within, however, pro-
> fessionals concerned with the future
> world order give their loyalty to a
> new humanity in gestation and to a
> future social compact only now begin-
> ning to delineate itself.[64]

This new global order and the "social compact" which Goulet envisions enthusiastically is one which liberationists actively protest against and seek to resist. They fear that governmental cooperation among the affluent nations, the extended reach of multinational corporations, and the entrenched powers of national security states will only hold the Third World nations more firmly in place as unequal partners in world economic production, distribution, and exchange. From their social location on "the underside of history" and in keeping with their reading of present global realities, they counter that Goulet's analysis is empirically inadequate because it fails to analyze the social system as a whole which is producing underdevelopment in the Third World. They are particularly critical of his claim that it is sufficient to propose changes only in particular values, institutional roles, or parts of the global economic system to make authentic development possible. Rather, they argue that the structure of the system itself must be transformed, and in keeping with the liberationist paradigm of development and underdevelopment, they conclude that global injustice is a political as well as a cultural problem which can be understood adequately only insofar as the network of relations which produce wealth for some and poverty for others is kept in view.

Goulet's own reluctance to move, for example, toward appropriating a non-developmentalist or even a neo-Marxian paradigm for his analysis of economic development issues is grounded, as discussed earlier, in his judgment that liberationists are ideologically "tainted" by their use of a Marxist social scientific perspective and, therefore, also especially vulnerable to moral scapegoating. His assumption that the developmentalist paradigm is ideologically "cleaner" or less suspect and more verifiable scientifically is questionable, however, for we have examined throughout this study the ideological nature of both paradigms and the particular support the developmentalist model gives to those who intend to maintain the global status quo, an order that is fundamentally unjust. What we have also observed is Goulet's interest as a liberal moral thinker in mediating between the two paradigms, to appropriate the best insights of both while maintaining his own neutrality and credibility as a critical observer "above the fray." In light of current structural shifts and the deepening crisis within the world economy, we have also offered counter examples

of how much more difficult it has become for those
liberals in the development center, both for social
scientists (e.g., Sylvia Ann Hewlett) and theologians-
ethicists (e.g., Puebla's Preliminary Document) to
stand upon firm ground. Brian Wren has suggested a
further reason to conclude that Goulet's centrist
position is untenable within the present dynamics of
the development debate:

> Liberal ideology also shies away
> from the realities of power and
> conflict. Its abiding value--a
> belief in reason and goodwill--
> is also its gravest weakness. It
> sees consensus when it ought to
> admit dissensus, is reluctant to
> face the fundamental clash between
> the beneficiaries of injustice and
> its victims, and clings to the
> belief that it can stay serenely
> above the conflict between them.[65]

Goulet's intended ideological and, therefore,
political neutrality also does not serve him well as
an advocate for global justice, for each of the two
prevailing theoretical paradigms of economic development has decidedly distinct moral and political implications. Those implications are noticeable in terms
of how loyalties are understood and exhibited, especially loyalties to the least well-positioned members
of society. Such allegiances are never politically or
morally "neutral." Therefore, Goulet might do well to
take into account with more seriousness than he has
exhibited so far, that "the correct decision is not to
try and cling to the illusion of neutrality but to
make a conscious political choice and remain critical
of it from within."[66]

The choice which Goulet has made is to remain
within the developmentalist paradigm, albeit as a
"friendly critic," especially of the ethnocentric
biases of some developmentalists. That choice has political but also distinct moral and strategic consequences.
Although Goulet explains that his own preference for
the dominant paradigm follows from his assessment that
this theoretical model best enables him to include
"non-economic" factors, such as normative value
choices, religion, and cultural dynamics, within his
analysis of development issues, what transpires at the
same time in his writings is a noticeable retreat from

any critical inspection of _economic_ factors which inhibit or enhance social change toward greater justice for the poor. He too readily assumes that the present capitalist economic order is open to significant modifications and readjustments to make authentic development for the Third World possible. Again, because he also focuses so extensively upon problems of value transformations within individuals, he does not sufficiently guard against reducing underdevelopment to a problem of acquiring proper values, to a problem of acculturation.

The socio-ethical consequence of this preoccupation on Goulet's part is that he offers us a truncated ethic of individual conversion and self-transformation, but one which may well leave the present unjust status quo unchanged. The reason for the lack of any serious or, better yet, transformative political impact of Goulet's ethic of individual change is that his heavy reliance upon the dominant liberal social theory and his abstract loyalty to some "future world" keep his expectations for social change bound within the limits of the present world order. No less serious is the fact that his moral vision remains unfortunately "directed by the ultimate norm of the existing, established social order to which the maladjusted individual or group has to become adapted."[67] His is a development strategy basically considered and implemented from the viewpoint of improving but not fundamentally altering the world economic order as it now functions.

Nowhere do liberationists differ more from Goulet than on their claim that underdevelopment and global injustice must be approached fundamentally as _social_ problems which arise out of the present world order and which require political responses by persons organized collectively to restructure those power relations which produce and maintain human suffering in the form of widespread poverty, illiteracy, and economic exploitation. Liberationists strongly resist, therefore, the tendency evidenced among developmentalists to be conditioned, as Paulo Freire has observed, "by their vision of liberation as an individual activity which should take place through a change of consciousness and not through the social and historical praxis of human beings."[68] Because of insights gathered from their own political engagements in social movements for economic justice, what the Latin Americans now insist upon is that all social ethical reflection must be investigated and judged "in relation to the praxis out of which it comes . . . asking what kind of praxis it supports, reflects, or legitimizes."[69] Their contention is that only social theory and ethical reflection which aims toward human emancipation and which functions effectively to make truly humanizing efforts toward communities of wholeness possible are to be considered anything other than (negative) ideological perspectives which mask human oppression and serve to bolster the status quo.

The political and moral choice Latin American liberationists have made is to join in practical solidarity with the poor to transcend economic and social oppression, and because of that choice, they have been able to come to the judgment that it is also imperative to abandon the dominant developmentalist paradigm. Their ability to work with a neo-Marxist dependency paradigm follows from their assessment that it is the best instrument presently available for describing what is going on in the world and for proposing strategies for social change. This choice is also validated by their judgment that only a liberation perspective starts from the point of view and concrete life experiences of the economically oppressed and supports their interests to overcome structures of injustice and to create human communities among equals. They also are cognizant that between the two social scientific paradigms, the neo-Marxist social theory of economic development alone offers a holistic and historical interpretation of the structural relationships between classes and nations which continue to produce such vast differentials of wealth and power as exist within the present world order. It is with this paradigm that they seek to understand more thoroughly and unmask more cogently social forms of human exploitation and also to locate alternative modes of organizing economic activities to minimize inequities within communities.

At this point let me say that for the very same reason Peter Berger finds liberation theologians in error, I find one, but not the exclusive reason that **they are most persuasive and right on target.** Berger complains that liberationists fail to understand contemporary social reality and the world "as it really is," and he states his critique as follows:

> A morality that is devoid of empirical referents will be an abstract business, finally with no bearing on the real concerns of human beings. This means,

however, that a political morality
such as this one must, first of
all, be examined on the basis of
its assertions about empirical
reality. And the most important
criticism to be made of the new
Christian leftism is not that it
promulgates false norms, nor that
it is theologically mistaken, but
that it is based on demonstrable
misperceptions of empirical reality.
Put differently: What is most wrong
about 'liberation theology' is neither its biblical exegesis nor its
ethics but its sociology.[70]

Contrary to Berger, I agree with the liberationists
that only social theory which begins with the class
structure of the global economy and seeks to propose
effective strategies to transcend those class divisions
does justice to our world socio-historical situation.
Along with Michael Harrington, I also concur that
social ethicists and moral thinkers, such as Denis
Goulet, will continue to mislocate the problem of
underdevelopment and will not, therefore, be able to
envision effective strategies for social change toward
maximizing economic justice unless they recognize that

The creation of the world with a
North Pole of affluence and a South
Pole of wretchedness is the outcome
of a systemic process. If that
theoretical point is not understood,
it is literally impossible to come up
with practical solutions for immediate
and outrageous problems.[71]

Although the problem-solving capacity of the liberation paradigm has yet to be tested fully, it is
rather clear from the historical evidence gathered
since the Second World War that the developmentalist
paradigm has not only failed to generate effective
strategies for overcoming poverty and underdevelopment
but has, in fact, supported policies and programs which
have been counterproductive. The testimony supplied by
liberal economists Irma Adelman and Cynthia Taft Morris,
cited in the Introduction, documents this failure most
emphatically. The expansion of capitalist economies in
the Third World has not produced self-sustaining econo-

mies of growth and autonomous development but rather an
increase of inequities and further disparities of
wealth and power.

To arrive at strategies of emancipation which
will be authentically developmental for those least
well-off in society is by no means a simple task.
Aaron Tolen has wisely pinpointed one very fundamental
reason for the difficulty of finding appropriate
strategies to enable progress toward just social
relations:

> . . . because this process [of
> political and economic libera-
> tion] is so complicated, because
> profit and the existing facili-
> ties for entering into the [glo-
> bal capitalist] system are so
> attractive and, most of all,
> because of the absence of any
> alternative to the system, it
> is easier to think along devel-
> opmentalist lines than to fight
> for self-reliance and liberation.[72]

To envision alternatives to present economic structures
is not an optional exercise but absolutely necessary,
however, for it is quite true that

> . . . if one accepts the current
> system as a given and simply pro-
> jects incremental changes in it,
> there is a profound tendency for
> the system to overwhelm--to co-opt
> --those changes. So, a radical
> transition to a new international
> economic order is all but inde-
> scribable . . . but reformist
> gains often merely rationalize
> the system of injustice.[73]

The bottom line for those who wish to join others in
the struggle to erect an authentically developmental
"economy of justice" on a planetary scale is that
"there is no alternative to seeking these difficult,
improbable changes."[74]

Liberation theologians offer impressive testimony
to those of us committed to social justice about the
indispensable resources which are available and offered

from within those social and ecclesial movements for economic justice which have emerged throughout Latin America. They, too, understand the importance of regaining our human capacity to exercise our moral imaginations, our capacity to "see" social problems as justice concerns and our ability to generate visions of new possibilities rather than those limited to the workings of the present social order. Theologian Beatriz Melano Couch speaks most eloquently about the social sources of this moral re-envisagement:

> From where does the vision come? For me it comes from the struggle . . . . The struggle gives power and strength and hope and concreteness to our vision, and the vision gives direction to our struggle.[75]

It is also from within their engagement in these social justice movements that liberation theologians have discovered the inadequacies of those strategies, which are economistic in nature and propose that development is a natural occurrence which will take place only if economic growth is accelerated. From their political experiences they have also come to acknowledge the inadequacies of those strategies which suggest that the problems of underdevelopment will "disappear" automatically if only external domination by foreign interests is brought to a close. They have also gained a more realistic assessment of the complexities of underdevelopment as a social and economic problem by their efforts--and by their failures--to devise strategies that will make humanizing transformations possible.

What liberationists have come to argue, quite persuasively, is that only those strategies are even conceivably adequate which do not ignore the reality of entrenched inequalities but rather aim to transform social relations and power dynamics within a society toward more just patterns of economic production and exercise of political control. They are no less adamant, as noted earlier, that the best and most important test, from a normative socio-ethical perspective, of the adequacy of any social action is to consider how such actions are affecting those most marginalized and what the least well-off say is valuable and "right action" on their behalf.

If social movements for liberation are keeping alive a vision of a different and better world, they are also providing the opportunity for self-criticism and constant reassessment of the effectiveness of various strategies in the pursuit of maximizing economic justice. No less important, however, is that these social and ecclesial movements are also the ground for and the context through which experiences of faith as liberating action for justice in the world are taking place and being articulated theologically. In our concluding section we shall give attention to the theological significance of the present paradigm shift from a liberal developmentalist theology to a radical liberation theology.

V. The Theological Task Ahead in Light of the Paradigm Shift from a Developmentalist to a Liberationist Theology

Our examination of the development debate has included consideration of a shift within theology from a developmentalist to a liberation paradigm. The learnings we may acquire from this inquiry are several, but foremost is the realization that contemporary theologians and ethicists must not reinforce the pessimism, abounding especially in the advanced industrialized nations, that no significant change toward greater justice is possible through human moral agency. Dorothee Soelle has spoken of apathy as a response to social suffering which arises out of a sense of powerlessness and hopelessness. To counteract such paralysis, she emphasizes the need for an authentically liberating faith which views the possibility of transcendence as an historical reality. As she explains,

> Modern capitalism offers the sensitized man [sic] a profusion of possibilities for escaping the consequences of his awareness [of social injustice] and settling down--though crippled and sold out--in the more comfortable world. Mere knowledge of causes and of their theoretical potential for transformation by no means provides an escape from powerlessness. Even that which becomes intellectually transparent releases no power for real change. What is missing is faith in the possibility of a new beginning . . . .[76]

The movement from despair to hope, liberation theologians tell us, is possible only by engaging one's whole self within the struggle for concrete justice along with others who no longer believe in the necesssity or the moral authority of this present global order but are empowered to "dream dreams" and organize diligently to establish alternative forms of living together in communities in which human exploitation is minimized.

What we are led to conclude is that the only kind of theology which is liberating in our contemporary situation, the only theology that is right for and fits well with our interests to maximize economic justice, is one which "breaks silences," as Jose Comblin has described:

> The wrong theology is a silent theology about the chief problems of the moment . . . . On the other hand, the right theology is the one that wants to face the primary problem of its time. Many of its particular statements may be wrong or inaccurate, but the whole is right if it serves God's word at a particular moment by dealing with the decisive problem of the time. Such a theology is a service for the people of God.[77]

The silences which contemporary Christian theology must help to break are the silences and denials which obscure and turn our attention away from the reality of the domination of the globe by a wealthy minority which perpetuates its privileges at the expense of the vast majority which is poor and victimized. And to begin to accomplish this task, theologians and ethicists do well, in my judgment, to notice and assimilate the significance of the emergence of the new liberation paradigm for theology, a paradigm which insists that the only truthful theology is one which

> . . . has a new understanding of itself and, therefore, a new subject. Its aim is no longer to discover a system of ideas, but to enlighten and judge the action of Christians.[78]

Our inquiry into the dynamics of the development debate further suggests to us that the "actions of Christians" which may have value and meaning in a world of injus-

tice such as ours are precisely those which can offer
resistance to the entrenchment of the status quo and
which open up possibilities for greater equality and
mutuality among persons and communities.

As a Christian social ethicist from an affluent
First World nation, I find myself with three observations, thoughts, or even moral claims to include at
this moment. First, we shall not be able to do the
work we need most to do and break the silences which
must be shattered if we continue to depend upon the
dominant developmentalist paradigm to interpret for us
what is going on in the world. To employ the neo-
Marxist paradigm has, therefore, become essential for
Christian ethicists to be able to speak accurately and
concretely about the real-world problems of the majority of humankind. We theologians can, therefore, no
longer afford our excessive fear of Marxism, and we do
well to advise our churches not to draw their primary
or even secondary battle lines against socialism or
even communism. Roger Garaudy has raised an unavoidable question for us and for any Christians considering the compatibility of Marxism and Christian faith.
He has asked, does the church reject communism primarily because it is atheistic or because it is revolutionary? Those engaged in the Christians for Socialism
movements in Latin America not only agree with Garaudy
that "no true dialogue can be established until being a
Christian does not necessarily mean being a defender of
the established order,"[79] but that the crucial point to
acknowledge is that "the chief contradiction is not
between Christians and Marxists but between exploiters
and exploited."[80]

In making our own political and moral choices
between the two paradigms concerning economic development in the world order, we also need to take seriously
Comblin's argument that there is enough historical evidence already accumulated to suspect that the churches'
fight against a Marxist alternative has most often been
motivated not by doctrinal or even pastoral considerations, but by geopolitical self-interests:

> The church exists in the West; the West
> seeks security in fighting the East
> (communism); so the church seeks its
> geopolitical security in doing the same.[81]

The churches' avoidance of Marxist alternatives may
well result, however, in not protecting their own

security, much less promoting the interests of the world's majority in attaining greater economic justice, but only in prolonging the vested interests and the political control of the minority who do not wish to see the churches involved in liberation movements.

My second moral claim is that the most significant question for us to ask these days is no longer, what difference does this paradigm shift make religiously or to the discipline of Christian theology or even to our professional status as ethicists and theologians. The answers to these questions will be decided only in the future by the course of actions we take. Rather, the question for us to ponder now is, what concrete difference does our being religious people--and even professional theologians--make in a world of such little justice and compassion? The reason I suggest the latter phrasing is to avoid any Christian triumphalism creeping in around the edges prematurely, as if to assume that we Christians somehow do know the answers and possess a powerful and liberating truth already. Let me only suggest that if being Christian makes any difference to the quality of human life on this planet, as I wager it does, then we citizens from the powerful North must go through the painful process of learning humility and patience enough to wait for others, especially those "from below," to tell us what that difference amounts to in concrete terms for their lives. Those whom we may seek to be just and compassionate toward, including ourselves, must be the ones to say whether our faithfulness has borne good or bad fruit. And we academic-based theologians and ethicists might pay special attention to the moral validity of Gustavo Gutierrez's claim, that

> The greatest refutation of a theology
> lies in its practical consequences and
> not in intellectual arguments.[82]

Finally, I wish to acknowledge the hope-filled observation which John Cort has made already, that "as everybody knows by now, socialism is once again on the agenda for Christians who are capable of thinking and feeling at approximately the same time."[83] My own sense is that the theological task ahead for us is to rediscover the grounds for our passion for justice in this world and to enable persons committed to the struggle for equality in their various communities to link together ever more powerfully their thinking and their feelings. As we begin to do this task more effectively, we might also gain greater clarity about the significance of the paradigm shift we have been examining, which signals an irreconcilable conflict between the old order seeking to maintain its privileges and the passion of the new for seeing that justice is done, even--or most especially--to the poorest of the poor.

As John Bennett has reminded us, the choices we make about which side of the shifting balance to align ourselves with have had and continue to have the greatest political and moral consequences, none less than "the survival of a large part of humanity, and the humanity of those who survive because they live in privileged and protected countries."[84] Along with Bennett, we have no other morally acceptable option at this historical juncture than to "return to economic ethics" and join with others in a more effective search for a truly emancipatory and global "economy of justice." As we do so, we might also do well to remember that when "things fall apart; the centre cannot hold."

NOTES

1. W. B. Yeats, "The Second Coming," in W. B. Yeats, The Collected Poems of W. B. Yeats (New York: The Macmillan Company, 1956), p. 184.

2. Sergio Torres, "Introduction," in The Emergent Gospel: Theology from the Underside of History, ed. Sergio Torres and Virginia Fabella (Maryknoll: Orbis Books, 1976), p. xiv.

3. Jose Miguez Bonino, Doing Theology in a Revolutionary Situation (Philadelphia: Fortress Press, 1975), p. 97.

4. See Chapter I, pp. 37ff.

5. Thomas S. Kuhn, The Structure of Scientific Revolutions (Chicago: The University of Chicago Press, 1962), p. 6. Kuhn recognizes that this shift in theoretical paradigm also signals a transformation of the "scientific imagination." In the remarks to follow, it is important to remember that Kuhn himself is speaking of paradigm shifts within the natural sciences. Any discussion in regard to the social sciences must attend, as well, to moral factors at play and to the centrality of value commitments which carry special power as shifts in paradigm transpire.

6. Miguez Bonino, Doing Theology in a Revolutionary Situation, p. 16.

7. Cf. Beverly Wildung Harrison, "Challenging the Western Paradigm: The 'Theology in the Americas' Conference," _Christianity and Crisis_, Vol. 35, no. 17 (October 27, 1975), pp. 251-254.

8. Kuhn, p. 91.

9. Robert L. Heilbroner, _An Inquiry into the Human Prospect_ (New York: W. W. Norton and Company, Inc., 1975), p. 17.

10. Michael Harrington, _The Vast Majority: A Journey to the World's Poor_ (New York: Simon and Schuster, 1977), p. 106.

11. Ibid., p. 218.

12. Alistair Kee, ed., _A Reader in Political Theology_ (Philadelphia: The Westminster Press, 1974), p. 92.

13. Ibid.

14. Kuhn, p. 93.

15. Gustavo Gutierrez, in Teofilo Cabestrero, ed., _Faith: Conversations with Contemporary Theologians_, trans. Donald D. Walsh (Maryknoll: Orbis Books, 1980), pp. 96-97.

16. Beverly Wildung Harrison, "Liberation Theology and Social Ethics: Some Theses for Discussion," unpubl. ms. (November 29, 1977), p. 4.

17. Kuhn, p. 93.

18. Lee Cormie, "Social Analysis and Theology: Detroit Working Paper," mimeographed (n.d.), p. 2.

19. _North-South: A Programme for Survival; Report of the Independent Commission on International Development Issues_, under chair of Willy Brandt (Cambridge: The MIT Press, 1980), pp. 22-23.

20. Ibid., p. 21.

21. Presidential Commission on World Hunger, _Preliminary Report of the Presidential Commission on World Hunger_ (December 1979), II.2.1 and III.6.

22. Frances Moore Lappe, Joseph Collins, and David Kinley, "Aid That Doesn't," _Christianity and Crisis_, Vol. 40, no. 5 (March 31, 1980), pp. 66, 80. My emphasis.

23. Richard Falk, "Geopolitics and Law: A Brief for New Rules," _Christianity and Crisis_, Vol. 40, no. 3 (March 3, 1980), pp. 47 and 48.

24. Ibid., p. 48.

25. Richard J. Barnet and Ronald E. Muller, _Global Reach: The Power of the Multinational Corporations_ (New York: Simon and Schuster, 1974), p. 65.

26. Ibid., p. 163.

27. Ibid., p. 379.

28. Jose Comblin, _The Church and the National Security State_ (Maryknoll: Orbis Books, 1979), p. 76.

29. Ibid., p. 73.

30. Ibid., p. 84.

31. See above, **pp. xxii-xxiii.**

32. Sylvia Ann Hewlett, _The Cruel Dilemmas of Development_: _Twentieth-Century Brazil_ (New York: Basic Books, Inc., 1980), p. 4.

33. Robert L. Heilbroner, _The Great Ascent_ (New York: Harper and Row, 1963), p. 28; _An Inquiry Into the Human Prospect_, p. 110.

34. Hewlett, p. 6.

35. Ibid.

36. Ibid., p. 78.

37. Ibid., p. 11. My emphasis.

38. Helio Jaguaribe, quoted in Penny Lernoux, _Cry of the People_: _The United States Involvement in the Rise of Fascism, Torture, and Murder and the Persecution of the Catholic Church in Latin America_ (Garden City, New York: Doubleday and Company, Inc., 1980), p. 172.

39. Hugo Assmann, _Theology for a Nomad Church_, trans. Paul Burns (Maryknoll: Orbis Books, 1976), p. 49.

40. Lernoux, pp. 35-36.

41. Hewlett, pp. 3 and 214.

42. Miguez Bonino, <u>Doing Theology in a Revolutionary Situation</u>, pp. 16-17.

43. Hewlett, p. 4; Albert O. Hirschman, <u>The Strategy of Economy Development</u> (New York: W. W. Norton and Company, 1978). p. 13.

44. Andre Gunder Frank, <u>Latin America: Under-Development or Revolution</u> (New York: Monthly Review Press, 1969), p. 129.

45. Samuel L. Parmar, "Issues in the Development Debate," in Richard D. N. Dickinson, <u>To Set at Liberty the Oppressed</u> (Geneva: The World Council of Churches, 1975), p. 177.

46. John C. Bennett, <u>The Radical Imperative</u> (Philadelphia: The Westminster Press, 1975), p. 199.

47. C. I. Itty, "Are We Yet Awake? The Development Debate Within the Ecumenical Movement," <u>The Ecumenical Review</u> (January 1974), pp. 14-15.

48. Ibid., p. 18.

49. Parmar, "Issues in the Development Debate," p. 170.

50. Julio de Santa Ana, "What Development Demands: A Latin American Position," in Dickinson, p. 140.

51. A similar illustration from the Protestant context is the recent attacks on the World Council of Churches from Edward Norman, <u>Christianity and the World Order</u> (New York: Oxford University Press, 1979), and Ernest W. Lefevre, <u>Amsterdam to Nairobi: The WCC and the Third World</u> (Washington, D.C.: Georgetown University, Ethics and Public Policy Center, 1979). These authors have accused the WCC of being much too sympathetic toward and giving too much support, including financial, to socialist movements in the Third World. Their critique is that the WCC has mixed religion (which <u>should</u> be conservative) with politics (which <u>should</u> <u>not</u> be radical). As John Bennett has put his finger on the sorest spot, however, the WCC is being attacked because of its recent history "of subordinating freedom to equality, of failing to understand the virtues of capitalism, . . . of being too open to Marxism . . . ." (John C. Bennett, "Neo-conservative 'Realism' vs. Third World Realities," <u>Christianity and Crisis</u>, Vol. 39, no. 17 [November 12, 1979], p. 276.) For additional responses to this reactionary backlash, see Dorothee Soelle and Roger L. Shinn's comments in "Continuing the Discussion: 'A Politicized Christ,'" <u>Christianity and Crisis</u>, Vol. 39, no. 4 (March 19, 1979), pp. 50-52 and 54-57.

52. For details about the reactionaries who sponsored this attack on liberation theology, see Penny Lernoux, Robert McAfee Brown, and Jon Sobrino's commentaries in John Eagleson and Philip Scharper, eds., _Puebla and Beyond: Documentation and Commentary_, trans. John Drury (Maryknoll: Orbis Books, 1979).

53. Clodovis Boff, "The Illusion of a New Christendom: A Critique of the PD of CELAM III," LADOC, Vol. IX, no. 1 (September-October 1978), p. 5.

54. Ibid., pp. 5-6.

55. General Augusto Pinochet, quoted in Lernoux, _Cry of the People_, p. 430.

56. Boff, p. 17.

57. Denis Goulet, _The Uncertain Promise: Value Conflicts in Technology Transfers_ (New York: IDOC/North America, 1977), p. 219.

58. Denis Goulet, "Discussion," in Neil H. Jacoby, _The Progress of Peoples_ (Santa Barbara, California: The Center for the Study of Democratic Institutions, June 1969), p. 27.

59. Ibid., p. 28.

60. Harrington, _The Vast Majority_, p. 201.

61. Denis Goulet, _The Cruel Choice: A New Concept in the Theory of Development_ (New York: Atheneum, 1975), p. 19.

62. For example, see Goulet's discussion of the cultural marginalization of Spanish gypsies in _The Cruel Choice_, pp. 195-208. His latest book, _The Uncertain Promise_, focuses on technology transfers and the cultural resistance introduction of "modern ways" generates within underdeveloped countries.

63. Goulet, _The Uncertain Promise_, pp. 40-41.

64. Ibid., p. 220. My emphasis.

65. Brian Wren, _Education for Justice: Pedagogical Principles_ (Maryknoll: Orbis Books, 1977), p. 110.

66. Ibid., p. 111.

67. Arend Theodoor van Leeuwen, _Development Through Revolution_ (New York: Charles Scribner's Sons, 1970), p. 78.

68. Paulo Freire, "Education, Liberation and the Church," Study Encounter 9:1 (WCC, 1973), in Kee, A Reader in Political Theology, p. 103.

69. Miguez Bonino, Doing Theology in a Revolutionary Situation, p. 91.

70. Peter L. Berger, "Continuing the Discussion: 'A Politicized Christ,'" Christianity and Crisis, Vol. 39, no. 4 (March 19, 1979), p. 53. Berger's emphasis.

71. Harrington, p. 103.

72. Aaron Tolen, "The End of All Pretenses: An African Perspective," in Dickinson, p. 160.

73. Harrington, pp. 31-32.

74. Ibid., p. 32.

75. Beatriz Melano Couch, "Statement by Beatriz Melano Couch," in Sergio Torres and John Eagleson, eds., Theology in the Americas (Maryknoll: Orbis Books, 1976), p. 376.

76. Dorothee Soelle, Political Theology, trans. John Shelley (Philadelphia: Fortress Press, 1974), p. 94.

77. Jose Comblin, The Church and the National Security State, p. 15.

78. Ibid., p. 48.

79. Roger Garaudy, Marxism in the Twentieth Century, trans. Rene Hague (New York: Charles Scribner's Sons, 1970), p. 152.

80. John Eagleson, ed., Christians and Socialism: Documentation of the Christians for Socialism Movement in Latin America (Maryknoll: Orbis Books, 1975), p. 245.

81. Comblin, p. 175.

82. Gustavo Gutierrez, "Freedom and Salvation: A Political Problem," trans. Alvin Gutierrez, in Liberation and Change, ed. Ronald H. Stone (Atlanta: John Knox Press, 1977), p. 67.

83. John C. Cort, "Toward Economic Recovery: A Review of Two Study/Action Guides," Christianity and Crisis, Vol. 40, no. 10 (June 9, 1980), p. 177. Cort himself is anti-Marxist, however.

84. Bennett, The Radical Imperative, p. 164.

SELECTED BIBLIOGRAPHY

Adelman, Irma, and Cynthia T. Morris. Economic Growth and Social
Equity in Developing Countries. Stanford: Stanford University Press, 1973.

Alexander, Robert J. A New Development Strategy. Maryknoll:
Orbis Books, 1980.

Alves, Rubem. "Christian Realism: Ideology of the Establishment,"
Christianity and Crisis, Vol. 33, No. 15 (September 17, 1973),
pp. 173-176.

Amin, Samir. Unequal Development, trans. Brian Pearce. New York:
Monthly Review Press, 1976.

Anderson, Gerald H., and Thomas F. Stransky, ed. Mission Trends
No. 3: Third World Theologies. New York: Paulist Press,
1976.

Arendt, Hannah. Crises of the Republic. New York: Harcourt Brace
Jovanovich, Inc., 1972.

Assmann, Hugo. Theology for A Nomad Church, trans. Paul Burns.
Maryknoll: Orbis Books, 1976.

Baran, Paul A. The Longer View: Essays Toward A Critique of Political Economy. New York: Monthly Review Press, 1970.

Baran, Paul A., and E. J. Hobsbawm, "The Stages of Economic
Growth," Kyklos, Vol. 14, pp. 234-242.

Barnet, Richard J. and Ronald E. Müller. Global Reach: The Power
of the Multinational Corporations. New York: Simon and
Schuster, 1974.

Barraclough, Geoffrey. "The Great World Crisis," New York Review
of Books, Vol. XXI-XXII, No. 1 (January 23, 1975), pp. 20,
29.

_____. "The Haves and Have Nots," New York Review of Books,
Vol. XXIII, No. 8 (May 13, 1976), pp. 31-41.

_____. "The Struggle for the Third World," New York Review of
Books, Vol. XXV, No. 17 (November 9, 1978), pp. 47-58.

_____. "Waiting for the New Order," New York Review of Books,
Vol. XXV, No. 16 (October 26, 1978), pp. 45-53.

_____. "Wealth and Power: The Politics of Food and Oil," New York Review of Books, Vol. XXII, No. 13 (August 7, 1975), pp. 23-30.

Bauer, P. T. "Western Guilt and Third World Poverty," Commentary, Vol. 61, No. 1 (January 1976), pp. 31-38.

Bauer, P. T., and B. G. Yamey. "Against the New Economic Order," Commentary, Vol. 62, No. 4 (April 1977), pp. 25-31.

Baum, Gregory, ed. Sociology and Human Destiny. New York: Seabury Press, 1980.

Bennett, John C. "Neo-Conservative 'Realism' vs. Third World Realities," Christianity and Crisis, Vol. 39, No. 17 (November 12, 1979), pp. 276-279.

_____. The Radical Imperative: From Theology to Social Ethics. Philadelphia: The Westminster Press, 1975.

Berger, Peter L. "Continuing the Discussion: 'A Politicized Christ,'" Christianity and Crisis, Vol. 39, No. 4 (March 19, 1979), pp. 52-54.

_____. Pyramids of Sacrifice: Political Ethics and Social Change. Garden City, NY: Anchor Books, 1976.

Bernstein, Henry. "Modernization Theory and the Sociological Study of Development," Journal of Development Studies, Vol. 7, No. 2 (January 1971), pp. 141-160.

_____. ed., Underdevelopment and Development: The Third World Today. Baltimore: Penguin Books, 1973.

Berryman, Phillip. "Popular Catholicism in Latin America," Cross Currents, Vol. 21, No. 3 (Summer 1971), pp. 284-301.

Bock, Paul. In Search of a Responsible World Society: The Social Teachings of the World Council of Churches. Philadelphia: The Westminster Press, 1974.

Boff, Clodovis. "The Illusion of a New Christendom: A Critique of the PD of CELAM III," LADOC, Vol. IX, No. 1 (September-October 1978), pp. 1-18.

Brown, Robert McAfee. Creative Dislocation--The Movement of Grace. Nashville: Abingdon Press, 1980.

_____. "from Detroit to Nairobi and Beyond: The Fifth Assembly of the World Council of Churches," _Radical Religion_, Vol. 2, No. 4 (1976), pp. 45-48.

_____. _Theology in a New Key: Responding to Liberation Themes_. Philadelphia: The Westminster Press, 1978.

Bucher, Glenn R., ed. _Straight/White/Male_. Philadelphia: Fortress Press, 1976.

Cabestrero, Teofilo, ed. _Faith: Conversations with Contemporary Theologians_, trans. Donald D. Walsh. Maryknoll: Orbis Books, 1980.

Casanova, Pablo Gonzalez. "The Economic Development of Mexico," _Scientific American_, Vol. 243, No. 3 (September 1980), pp. 192-204.

Christians for Socialism. _Option for Struggle: Three Documents of Christians for Socialism_. New York: Church Research and Information Project, 1974.

Cockburn, Alexander, and James Ridgeway, "Talking to Tony Benn: Can European Socialists Teach Americans Anything?" _The Village Voice_, Vol. XXV, No. 50 (December 10-16, 1980), pp. 28ff.

Cockcroft, James D., Andre Gunder Frank, and Dale L. Johnson. _Dependence and Underdevelopment: Latin America's Political Economy_. Garden City, NY: Anchor Books, 1972.

Colonnese, Louis M., ed. _Conscientization for Liberation_. Washington, DC: U.S. Catholic Conference, 1971.

Comblin, Jose. _The Church and the National Security State_. Maryknoll: Orbis Books, 1979.

_____. "Puebla: To Organize the Hopes," _LADOC_, Vol. IX, No. 4 (March-April, 1979), pp. 1-8.

Cormie, Lee. "Social Analysis and Theology: Detroit Working Paper," mimeographed (n.d.).

_____. "The Sociology of National Development and Salvation History." Unpubl. ms., January 1979.

Cort, John C. "Toward Economic Democracy: A Review of Two Study/Action Guides," _Christianity and Crisis_, Vol. 40, No. 10 (June 9, 1980), pp. 177-179.

Cosmao, Vincent. "Towards a Theology of Development," IDOC International, North American Edition, No. 5 (June 13, 1970), pp. 86-96.

Dadzie, K. K. S. "Economic Development," Scientific American, Vol. 243, No. 3 (September 1980), pp. 58-65.

deVries, Egbert, "A Review of Literature on Development Theory," International Development Review, Vol. X, No. 1 (March 1968), pp. 43-51.

Dickinson, Richard D. N. To Set at Liberty the Oppressed. Geneva: World Council of Churches, 1975.

Dickson, David. The Politics of Alternative Technology. New York: Universe Books, 1974.

DuBoff, Richard. "What Is Authentic Development?" Mimeographed, 1974.

Eagleson, John, ed. Christians and Socialism: Documentation of the Christians for Socialism Movement in Latin America, trans. John Drury. Maryknoll: Orbis Books, 1975.

_____, and Philip Scharper, eds. Puebla and Beyond: Documentation and Commentary, trans. John Drury. Maryknoll: Orbis Books, 1979.

Ellul, Jacques. The Technological Society, trans. John Wilkinson. New York: Alfred A. Knopf, 1965.

Emmanuel, Arghiri. Unequal Exchange: A Study of the Imperialism of Trade, trans. Brian Pearce. New York: Montly Review Press, 1972.

Erb, Guy F., and Valeriana Kallab, eds. Beyond Dependency: The Developing World Speaks Out. Washington: Overseas Development Council, 1975.

Evans, Joseph W., and Leo R. Ward, eds. The Social and Political Philosophy of Jacques Maritain: Selected Readings. New York: Image Books, 1968.

Fagen, Patricia Weiss. "Human Rights in Latin America: Learning from the Literature," Christianity and Crisis, Vol. 39, No. 20 (December 24, 1979), pp. 328-333.

Falk, Richard. "Geopolitics and Law: A Brief for New Rules," Christianity and Crisis, Vol. 40, No. 3 (March 3, 1980), pp. 44-48.

Fox, Matthew. A Spirituality Named Compassion and the Healing of
the Global Village, Humpty Dumpty and Us. Minneapolis: Winston Press, 1979.

Frank, Andre Gunder. Capitalism and Underdevelopment in Latin
America: Historical Studies of Chile and Brazil, revised
edition. New York: Monthly Review Press, 1969.

_____. Latin America: Underdevelopment or Revolution. New
York: Monthly Review Press, 1969.

_____. Lumpenbourgeoisie: Lumpendevelopment, trans. Marion
Davis Berdecio. New York: Monthly Review Press, 1972.

Freire, Paulo. Cultural Action for Freedom. Cambridge: Harvard
Educational Review and Center for the Study of Development
and Social Change, 1970.

_____. Pedagogy of the Oppressed, trans. Myra Bergman Ramos.
New York: Herder and Herder, 1970.

Furtado, Celso. Development and Underdevelopment, trans. Ricardo
W. de Aguiar and Eric Charles Drysdale. Berkeley: University
of California Press, 1971.

_____. Economic Development of Latin America, trans. Suzette
Macedo. Cambridge: The Cambridge University Press, 1970.

_____. Obstacles to Development in Latin America, trans.
Charles Ekker. Garden City, NY: Anchor Books, 1970.

Garaudy, Roger. Marxism in the Twentieth Century, trans. Rene
Hague. New York: Charles Scribner's Sons, 1970.

Gibellini, Rosino, ed. Frontiers of Theology in Latin America.
Maryknoll: Orbis Books, 1979.

Goodall, Norman, ed. The Uppsala Report 1968. Geneva: World
Council of Churches, 1968.

Goulet, Denis. "Beyond Moralism: Ethical Studies in Global Development," unpubl. ms. (June 1976).

_____. "Christian Ethics and Global Economics," Christianity
and Crisis, Vol. 38, No. 17 (November 12, 1978), pp. 273-278.

_____. "Christian Ethics and World Development: A Critical
Perspective," unpubl. ms. (January 1974).

_____. The Cruel Choice: A New Concept in the Theory of Development. New York: Atheneum, 1971.

_____. "Development for What?," Comparative Political Studies (July 1968), pp. 295-312.

_____. "Development . . . or Liberation?," International Development Review, Vol. XIII, No. 3 (September 1971), pp. 6-10.

_____. "The Disappointing Decade of Development," The Center Magazine, Vol. 2, No. 5 (September 1969), pp. 62-68.

_____. "An Ethical Model for the Study of Values," Harvard Educational Review, Vol. 41, No. 2 (May 1971), pp. 205-227.

_____. "Ethical Strategies in the Struggle for World Development," unpubl. ms. (June 1974).

_____. "Freedom Does Not Exist in a Vacuum," Worldview, Vol. 17, No. 11 (November 1974), pp. 39-42.

_____. "The High Price of Social Change: Peter Berger's Pyramids of Sacrifice," Christianity and Crisis, Vol. 35, No. 16 (October 13, 1975), pp. 231-237.

_____. "Is Gradualism Dead?," Ethics in Foreign Policy. New York: Council on Religion and International Affairs, 1970.

_____. "Lebret's Thought and the U.S. Presence in the Third World," Développement et Civilisations, No. 30 (June 1967), pp. 44-55.

_____. "A Missing Revolution," America, Vol. 114 (April 2, 1966), pp. 438-440.

_____. "Needed: Cultural Revolution in the U.S.," The Christian Century, Vol. 91, No. 30 (September 4, 1974), pp. 816-818.

_____. A New Moral Order: Development Ethics and Liberation Theology. Maryknoll: Orbis Books, 1974.

_____. "On the Ethics of Development Planning: General Principles and Special Application to Value Conflicts in Technology," unpubl. ms. (August 1975).

_____. "On the Goals of Development," Cross Currents, Vol. 18, No. 4 (Fall 1968), pp. 387-405.

_____. "Political Will: The Key to Guinea-Bissau's 'Alternative Development Strategy,'" _International Development Review_, Vol. 19, No. 4 (1977), pp. 2-8.

_____. "The Poorest of the Poor," _Center Report_, Vol. 8, No. 5 (December 1975), pp. 14-19.

_____. "Pour une éthique moderne du développement," _Développement et Civilisations_, No. 3 (September 1960), pp. 10-24.

_____. "A Pride of Prophets on Our Technological Future," _Worldview_, Vol. 21, No. 3 (March 1978), pp. 35-38.

_____. "Secular History and Technology," _World Justice_, Vol. 8, No. 1 (September 1966), pp. 5-19.

_____. "Sufficiency for All: The Basic Mandate of Development and Social Economics," _Review of Social Economy_, Vol. 36, No. 3 (December 1978), pp. 243-261.

_____. "Technology, Development and Values Defines," _The Center Magazine_, Vol. 5, No. 5 (September-October 1972), pp. 24-25.

_____. "That Third World," _The Center Magazine_, Vol. 1, No. 6 (September 1968), pp. 47-55.

_____. "Thinking About Human Rights," _Christianity and Crisis_, Vol. 37, No. 8 (May 16, 1977), pp. 100-104.

_____. "The Troubled Conscience of Revolutionaries," _The Center Magazine_, Vol. 2, No. 3 (May 1969), pp. 43-50.

_____. _The Uncertain Promise: Value Conflicts in Technology Transfers_. New York: IDOC/North America, 1977.

_____. "Voluntary Austerity: The Necessary Art," _The Christian Century_, Vol. 83, No. 23 (June 8, 1966), pp. 748-753.

_____. "World Hunger: Putting Development Ethics to the Test," _Christianity and Crisis_, Vol. 35, No. 9 (May 26, 1975), pp. 125-132.

_____. "World Interdependence: Verbal Smokescreen or New Ethic?," _Development Paper_. Washington, DC: Overseas Development Council, 1976.

_____. "The World of Underdevelopment: A Crisis in Values," _The Christian Century_, Vol. 91, No. 16 (April 24, 1974), pp. 452-455.

279

_____, and Michael Hudson. The Myth of Aid: The Hidden Agenda of the Development Reports. Maryknoll: Orbis Books, 1971.

Gremillion, Joseph, ed. The Gospel of Peace and Justice: Catholic Social Teaching Since Pope John. Maryknoll: Orbis Books, 1976.

Gruber, Pamela H., ed. Fetters of Injustice. Geneva: World Council of Churches, 1970.

Gudorf, Christine E. "Contested Issues in Twentieth-Century Papal Teaching: The Position of the Vatican in Light of Challenges from Liberation Theology." Ph.D. dissertation, Columbia University, 1979.

Gutierrez, Gustavo. "The Gospel According to the Poor," The Witness, Vol. 61, No. 8 (August 1978), pp. 15-17.

_____. "The Hope of Liberation," Worldview (June 1974), pp. 35-37.

_____. "The Power of the Poor in History," LADOC, Vol. 9, No. 6 (July-August 1979), pp. 15-32.

_____. Praxis of Liberation and Christian Faith, revised edition. San Antonio: The Mexican American Cultural Center, 1976.

_____. "Revelation and the Proclamation for God in History." Mimeograph for the Chicago Jesuit Project for Third World Awareness, 1975.

_____. "Theology and the Chinese Experience: Some Reflections," unpubl. ms., n.d.

_____. A Theology of Liberation, trans. Sr. Caridad Inda and John Eagleson. Maryknoll: Orbis Books, 1973.

Hageman, Alice L., ed., in collaboration with the Women's Caucus of the Harvard University Divinity School. Sexist Religion and Women in the Church: No More Silence! New York: The Association Press, 1974.

Hagen, Everett E. On The Theory of Social Change. Cambridge: MIT Center for International Studies, 1962.

Haq, Mahbub Ul. The Poverty Curtain: Choices for the Third World. New York: Columbia University Press, 1976.

Hardin, Garrett. "Lifeboat Ethics: The Case Against Helping the Poor," Psychology Today (September 1974), pp. 38-70.

Harrington, Michael. Socialism. New York: Bantam Books, 1973.

_____. The Vast Majority: A Journey to the World's Poor. New York: Simon and Schuster, 1977.

_____. "Why Poor Nations Stay Poor," Christianity and Crisis, Vol. 37, No. 15 (October 3, 1977), pp. 211-220.

Harrison, Beverly Wildung. "Challenging the Western Paradigm: The 'Theology in the Americas' Conference," Christianity and Crisis, Vol. 35, No. 17 (October 27, 1975), pp. 251-254.

_____. "Liberation Theology and Social Ethics: Some Theses for Discussion." Unpubl. ms. (November 1977).

Heilbroner, Robert (L.) The Great Ascent. New York: Harper and Row, 1963.

_____. An Inquiry Into the Human Prospect. New York: W. W. Norton and Company, 1975.

Hessel, Dieter T., ed. Beyond Survival: Bread and Justice in Christian Perspective. New York: Friendship Press, 1977.

Hewlett, Sylvia Ann. The Cruel Dilemmas of Development: Twentieth-Century Brazil. New York: Basic Books, Inc., 1980.

Heyward, Carter. "Speaking and Sparking, Building and Burning: Ruether and Daly, Theologians," Christianity and Crisis, Vol. 39, No. 5, pp. 66-72.

Higgins, Benjamin. Economic Development, revised edition. New York: W. W. Norton and Company, 1968.

Hirschman, Albert O. Journeys Toward Progress. New York: The Twentieth Century Fund, 1963.

_____, ed. Latin American Issues. New York: The Twentieth Century Fund, 1961.

_____. The Strategy of Economic Development. New York: W. W. Norton and Company, 1978.

Horowitz, Irving Louis, Josue de Castro, and John Gerassi, eds. Latin American Radicalism. New York: Random House, 1969.

Hoselitz, Bert F., and Wilbert E. Moore, eds. Industrialization and Society. Mouton: UNESCO, 1966.

ISAL (Commission on Church and Society in Latin America). "Christians, Churches and Development," Risk, Vol. 5, No. 2 (1969), pp. 33-46.

Itty, C. I. "Are We Yet Awake? The Development Debate Within the Ecumenical Movement," The Ecumenical Review, Vol. 26, No. 1 (January 1974), pp. 6-20.

Jacoby, Neil H. The Progress of Peoples. Santa Barbara: The Center for the Study of Democratic Institutions, 1969.

Jaguaribe, Helio. Economic and Political Development. Cambridge: Harvard University Press, 1968.

Jalee, Pierre. Imperialism in the Seventies, trans. Raymond and Margaret Sokolov. New York: The Third Press, 1972.

_____. "Third World? Which Third World?" Revolution, Vol. 1, No. 7 (1963), pp. 3-9.

Kahn, Herman, with the Hudson Institute. World Economic Development: 1979 and Beyond. New York: Morrow Quill Paperbacks, 1979.

Kahn, Herman, William Brown, and Leon Martel. The Next 200 Years: A Scenario for America and the World. New York: William Morrow and Company, 1976.

Kee, Alistair, ed. A Reader in Political Theology. Philadelphia: The Westminster Press, 1974.

Kuhn, Thomas S. The Structure of Scientific Revolutions. Chicago: The University of Chicago Press, 1962.

Lange, Ernst. And Yet It Moves: Dream and Reality of the Ecumenical Movement, trans. Edwin Robertson. Geneva: World Council of Churches, 1979.

Lappe, Frances Moore, and Joseph Collins. Food First: Beyond the Myth of Scarcity. Boston: Houghton Mifflin Company, 1977.

Lappe, Frances Moore, Joseph Collins, and David Kinley. "Aid That Doesn't," Christianity and Crisis, Vol. 40, No. 5 (March 31, 1980), pp. 66 and 80.

Laurentin, Rene. Liberation, Development and Salvation, trans. Charles Underhill. Maryknoll: Orbis Books, 1972.

Lebret, Louis Joseph. The Last Revolution: The Destiny of Over-
and Underdeveloped Nations, trans. John Horgan. New York:
Sheed and Ward, 1965.

Leeuwen, Arend Theodoor van. Development Through Revolution. New
York: Charles Scribner's Sons, 1970.

Lefevre, Ernest W. Amsterdam to Nairobi: The WCC and the Third
World. Washington, DC: Georgetown University, Ethics and
Public Policy Center, 1979.

Lerner, Daniel. The Passing of Traditional Society. Glencoe, IL:
The Free Press, 1958.

Lernoux, Penny. Cry of the People: United States Involvement in
the Rise of Fascism, Torture, and Murder in the Persecution
of the Catholic Church in Latin America. Garden City, NY:
Doubleday and Company, Inc., 1980.

MacEoin, Gary. Revolution Next Door: Latin America in the 1970's.
New York: Holt, Rinehart and Winston, 1971.

Magdoff, Harry. The Age of Imperialism. New York: Monthly Review
Press, 1969.

Maritain, Jacques. Integral Humanism: Temporal and Spiritual
Problems of a New Christendom, trans. Joseph W. Evans. New
York: Charles Scriber's Sons, 1968.

McFadden, Thomas J., ed. Liberation, Revolution, and Freedom:
Theological Perspectives. New York: The Seabury Press, 1975.

Meeks, M. Douglas. "Toward a Trinitarian View of Economics: The
Holy Spirit and Human Needs," Christianity and Crisis, Vol.
40, No. 18 (November 10, 1980), pp. 307-316.

Miguez Bonino, Jose. Christians and Marxists: The Mutual Challenge to Revolution. Grand Rapids: William B. Eerdmans Publishing Company, 1976.

_____. Doing Theology in a Revolutionary Situation. Philadel-
phis: Fortress Press, 1975.

Moore, Jr., Barrington. Injustice: The Social Bases of Obedience
and Revolt. White Plains, NY: M. E. Sharpe, Inc., 1978.

Mottesi, Osvaldo Luis. "Doing Theology in the Latin American Context," Church and Society, Vol. LXVIII, No. 3 (January-February 1978), pp. 8-14.

Mountjoy, Alan B., ed. Developing and Underdeveloped Countries.
    New York: John Wiley and Sons, 1971.

Munby, Denys, ed. World Development: Challenge to the Churches.
    Washington: Corpus Books, 1969.

Myrdal, Gunnar. The Challenge of World Poverty. New York: Pan-
    theon Books, 1970.

_____. Economic Theory and Under-developed Regions. London:
    Gerald Duckworth and Company, 1957.

Neal, Marie Augusta. A Socio-Theology of Letting Go: The Role of
    a First World Church Facing Third World Peoples. New York:
    Paulist Press, 1977.

Nisbet, Robert A. Social Change and History: Aspects of the West-
    ern Theory of Development. New York: Oxford University
    Press, 1968.

Norman, Edward. Christianity and the World Order. New York: Ox-
    ford University Press, 1979.

_____. "A Politicized Christ," Christianity and Crisis, Vol.
    39, No. 2 (February 19, 1979), pp. 18-25.

North-South: A Programme for Survival; Report of the Independent
    Commission on International Development Issues, under chair-
    manship [sic] of Willy Brandt. Cambridge: MIT Press, 1980.

Orbis Books. The Complete Orbis Catalog 1980. Maryknoll: Orbis
    Books, 1980.

Parmar, Samuel L. "Some Thoughts on Strategy," Risk, Vol. 3, No.
    1-2 (1967), pp. 111-117.

Paton, David M., ed. Breaking Barriers: Nairobi 1975. Grand
    Rapids: William B. Eerdmans, 1976.

Pellauer, Mary D. "The Religious Social Thought of Three U.S.
    Suffrage Leaders: Towards a Tradition of Feminist Theology."
    Ph.D. dissertation, The University of Chicago, 1980.

Perroux, Francois. "From the Avarice of Nations to an Economy for
    Mankind," Cross Currents, Vol. 3, No. 3 (Spring 1953), pp.
    193-207.

Peruvian Bishops' Commission for Social Action. Between Honesty
    and Hope, trans. John Drury. Maryknoll: Maryknoll Publica-
    tions, 1969.

Presidential Commission on World Hunger. <u>Preliminary Report of</u> <u>the Presidential Commission on World Hunger</u> (December 1979).

Quigley, Thomas E., ed. <u>Freedom and Unfreedom in the Americas:</u> <u>Towards a Theology of Liberation.</u> New York: IDOC, 1971.

Rhodes, Robert I., ed. <u>Imperialism and Underdevelopment: A Read-</u> <u>er.</u> New York: Monthly Review Press, 1970.

Rose, Stephen C., ed. <u>The Development Apocalypse</u>, <u>Risk</u>, Vol. III, No. 1-2 (1967).

Rostow, Walt W. <u>The Stages of Economic Growth: A Non-Communist</u> <u>Manifesto.</u> New York: Cambridge University Press, 1960.

Shinn, Roger L. "Continuing the Discussion: 'A Politicized Christ,'" <u>Christianity and Crisis</u>, Vol. 39, No. 4 (March 19, 1979), pp. 54-57.

Sills, David L., ed. <u>International Encyclopedia of the Social</u> <u>Sciences</u>, Vol. 10. New York, 1968.

Singer, Max, and Paul Bracken. "Don't Blame the U.S.," <u>New York</u> <u>Times Magazine</u> (November 7, 1976), pp. 34, 120-126.

SODEPAX. <u>In Search of a Theology of Development.</u> Geneva: Commis- sion on Society, Development, and Peace, 1969.

_____. <u>Partnership or Privilege? An Ecumenical Reaction to the</u> <u>Second Development Debate.</u> Geneva: Commission on Society, Development, and Peace, 1970.

Soelle, Dorothee. "Continuing the Discussion: 'A Politicized Christ,'" <u>Christianity and Crisis</u>, Vol. 39, No. 4 (March 19, 1979), pp. 50-52.

_____. <u>Political Theology</u>, trans. John Shelley. Philadelphia: Fortress Press, 1974.

_____. <u>Suffering</u>, trans. Everett R. Kalin. Philadelphia: For- tress Press, 1975.

Stivers, Robert L. <u>The Sustainable Society: Ethics and Economic</u> <u>Growth.</u> Philadelphia: The Westminster Press, 1976.

Stone, Ronald H., ed. <u>Liberation and Change.</u> Atlanta: John Knox Press, 1977.

Thomas, M. M., and Paul Abrecht, eds. <u>World Conference on Church and Society: Christians in the Technical and Social Revolutions of our Time</u>. Geneva: World Council of Churches, 1977.

Torres, Sergio, and John Eagleson, eds. <u>Theology in the Americas</u>. Maryknoll: Orbis Books, 1976.

Torres, Sergio, and Virginia Fabella, eds. <u>The Emergent Gospel: Theology from the Underside of History</u>. Maryknoll: Orbis Books, 1978.

Tracy, David. <u>Blessed Rage for Order: The New Pluralism in Theology</u>. New York: The Seabury Press, 1975.

Visser't Hooft, W. A., ed. <u>The New Delhi Report</u>. New York: Association Press, 1962.

Wilber, Charles K. <u>Political Economy of Development and Underdevelopment</u>. New York: Random House, 1973.

Wogaman, J. Philip. <u>The Great Economic Debate: An Ethical Analysis</u>. Philadelphia: The Westminster Press, 1977.

<u>World Development: The Challenge to the Churches</u>. Geneva: Exploratory Commission on Society, Development, and Peace, 1968.

Wren, Brian. <u>Education for Justice: Pedagogical Principles</u>. Maryknoll: Orbis Books, 1977.

Yeats, W. B. <u>The Collected Poems of W. B. Yeats</u>. New York: The Macmillan Company, 1956.